Beating Devils and Burning Their Books

Views of China, Japan, and the West

T0312566

Font cover image: from *Bixie jishi*, plate 10, 1861. Translations: (1) above title: "Beating Devils and Burning Their Books;" (2) right: "The Pig-Grunt religion is heterodox and is disseminated from afar. It is insulting to heaven and earth, and wipes away the cult of ancestor veneration. Even with a thousand arrows it would be difficult to clear them of their crimes;" (3) left: "Their bewitching, dog fart books reek of dung. They slander sages and worthies, and insult the immortals and Buddhas. All within the nine provinces and four seas equally hate them."

Back cover image by Thomas Allom (1804-72), who illustrated G. N. Wright's *China in a Series of Views* (1843). This image is Allom's rather romantic depiction of a Chinese "Rice seller."

Beating Devils and Burning Their Books

Views of China, Japan, and the West

Edited by Anthony E. Clark

ASIA PAST & PRESENT

Published by the Association for Asian Studies, Inc.

Asia Past & Present: New Research from AAS, Number 6

Asia Past & Present: New Research from AAS
Series Editor, Martha Ann Selby, University of Texas at Austin

"Asia Past & Present: New Research from AAS," published by the Association for Asian Studies, Inc. (AAS), features scholarly work from all areas of Asian studies. In addition to scholarly monographs, translations, essay collections, and other forms of scholarly research are welcome for consideration. AAS particularly aims to support work in emerging or under-represented fields.

Formed in 1941, the Association for Asian Studies (AAS)—the largest society of its kind, with more than 7,000 members worldwide—is a scholarly, non-political, non-profit professional association open to all persons interested in Asia.

For further information, please visit www.asian-studies.org.

© 2010 by the Association for Asian Studies, Inc.

All Rights Reserved. Written permission must be secured to use or reproduce any part of this book.

Published by:
Association for Asian Studies, Inc.
1021 East Huron Street
Ann Arbor, Michigan 48104 USA
www.asian-studies.org

Library of Congress Cataloging-in-Publication Data

Beating devils and burning their books : views of China, Japan and the West / edited by Anthony E. Clark.

p. cm. — (Asia past & present : new research from AAS ; no. 6)

Includes bibliographical references and index.

ISBN 978-0-924304-60-6 (pbk. : alk. paper) 1. China—Relations—Western countries. 2. Western countries—Relations—China. 3. Japan—Relations—Western countries. 4. Western countries—Relations—Japan. 5. China—Foreign public opinion, Western. 6. Japan—Foreign public opinion, Western. 7. Western countries—Foreign public opinion, Chinese. 8. Western countries—Foreign public opinion, Japanese. 9. East and West. I. Clark, Anthony E.

DS740.4.B43 2010

303.48'25101821—dc22

2010029998

Contents

Acknowledgments

As any honest scholar must admit, we could not have undertaken this collaborative work without the support of our respective institutions and other generous agencies. We would like to render our gratitude to the universities where we teach: University of Notre Dame, University of Oregon, Gonzaga University, Emory University, University of Kentucky, University of Alabama, and Whitworth University. We have also benefited in various ways from the support of the Williams Fund for Research; the J. William Fulbright Program; a David L. Boren National Security Education Program (NSEP) Research Grant; the National Central Library, Taipei; the National Diet Library, Japan; the Yunming Provincial Library, China; Academia Sinica, Taipei; the Archivio Segreto Vaticano/Vatican Secret Archives, Vatican City; the Biblioteca Apostolica Vaticana/Pope's Private Library, Vatican City; the Archives des Missions Étrangères de Paris, Paris; the Jesuit Archives and the Archive of Fujen University, Taipei; the Institut für Sinologie und Ostasienkunde, Münster University, Germany; and the Bibliothèques des Instituts d'Extrême-Orient at the Collège de France in Paris. The University of Alabama College of Arts and Sciences deserves particular mention for kindly bringing us all to Alabama for a colloquy to discuss our ideas in preparation for this volume. We render our appreciation for the thorough and helpful comments of our anonymous readers and to Amanda Clark for the many hours she devoted to refining this book and compiling its index.

In a special way we would like to honor the memory of Ronald Robel, Professor Emeritus of Chinese History at the University of Alabama, whose recent passing marks a sad loss to the field of Asian studies. And, finally, we thank our respective spouses, children, and friends, who have provided us with the most important support possible.

Contributors

Anthony E. Clark is Assistant Professor of Chinese History at Whitworth University. His research is in the areas of early Chinese historiography and late-imperial Christian missions. He is the author of *Ban Gu's History of Early China* (2008).

Eric P. Cunningham is Associate Professor of Asian History at Gonzaga University. He specializes in the area of modern Japanese intellectual history and Zen Buddhism. He is the author of *Hallucinating the End of History: Nishida, Zen, and the Psychedelic Eschaton* (2007).

Lionel M. Jensen is Associate Professor of East Asian Languages at the University of Notre Dame. His research revolves around Chinese religion, folklore, popular culture, Sino-Western relations, and Chinese nationalism. He is the author of *Manufacturing Confucianism: Chinese Traditions and Universal Civilization* (1997).

Catherine M. Pagani is Professor of Asian Art at the University of Alabama. Her research focuses on late-imperial Chinese art and material culture. She is the author of *Eastern Magnificence and European Ingenuity: Clocks of Late Imperial China* (2001).

Eric Reinders is Associate Professor of Chinese Religions at Emory University. His research considers Buddhist monasticism and the history of Christian missions in China. He is the author of *Borrowed Gods and Foreign Bodies: Christian Missionaries Imagine Chinese Religion* (2004).

Mark T. Unno is Associate Professor of East Asian Religions at the University of Oregon. His research centers on the intellectual and social practices of Medieval Japanese Buddhism. He is the author of *Shingon Refractions: Myoe and the Mantra of Light* (2004).

Matthew V. Wells is Assistant Professor of Chinese at the University of Kentucky. His research focuses on early China, especially the thought and work of Ge Hong. He is the author of *To Die and Not Decay: Autobiography and the Pursuit of Immortality in Early China* (2009).

Introduction

Contending Representations: East-West

Anthony E. Clark

Danger from the East!

William Shakespeare writes in *Henry IV*:

> If he fall in, good night! Or sink or swim:
> Send danger from the east unto the west,
> So honour cross it from the north to south,
> And let them grapple: O! the blood more stirs
> To rouse a lion than start a hare (*Henry IV, Part I*).

The East. It has been calumniated, and it has been juxtaposed with the "civilized West" for as long as "civilization" has been aware of it. Responding to the war in the Philippines, Rudyard Kipling (1865–1936) published his pro-imperialist poem, "The White Man's Burden," in the February 1899 edition of *McClure's* magazine. He urged the United States to take over the Philippines; it was the country's moral obligation to do so as a white nation. The Filipinos and their fellow Asians were, after all, "fluttered folk and wild—Your new caught sullen peoples, half devil and half child." And what must "civilization" do with this race of "half devils" from the East? "Take up the White man's burden—in patience abide / To veil the threat of terror / And check the show of pride." From Shakespeare to Kipling, the East has been represented as a menace to "civilized" white men; it is a "lion" or a place of "half devils" and "half children." But has the West been the only arbiter of true civilization? Have there been equivalent pejoratives directed westward?

Danger from the West!

Abundant counterexamples display similar sentiments coming from the East, inimically denigrating the "barbaric West." As early as Sima Qian (ca. 145–90 BCE) in the first century BCE, Chinese writers have imagined outsiders from the West as "barbarians." In his essay on the northwestern Xiongnu tribe, Sima writes that "in times of crisis they take up arms and go off on plundering and marauding expeditions. This seems to be their inborn nature. . . . Their only concern is self-advantage, and they know nothing of propriety or righteousness."[1] Sima Qian criticizes the "Mountain Barbarians" (*shan rong*) for being nomadic and pastoral rather than settled and agrarian and for having no writing system. They are "uncivilized" because they are different, because their culture is largely unknown.[2]

More recently, writers such as Chen Tianhua (1875–1905) have written of the dangers of the barbarian West. In his now enshrined *Jing shi zhong* (Alarm Bells), Chen trumpets his call to kill all westerners. He writes:

> Here they come, here they come! Here who comes? The westerners. The westerners! Young and old, men and women, rich and poor, officials, scholars, merchants and craftsmen—from this day on we're all just livestock in his pen, meat in his pot; not an inch of room to move, to kill as he chooses and stew to his taste. Alas, our day of death has come! . . . [A]ll will be seized by the westerner; our countrymen's cherished wives and children—he will tear every one from our sides; men and women, fathers, sons and brothers, husbands, wives, and children—none will be spared his sword or lust.[3]

What, then, is China to do with these "barbarians" from the West?

> Kill them, kill them all! . . . Let scholars put aside their pens, peasants their ploughs, merchants their business and craftsmen their tools; sharpen the steel, load the guns and drink the wine of blood; advance in your multitudes with warlike cry, to kill the foreign devils. . . . [K]ill them all, kill, kill, kill![4]

While westerners have depicted the East as posing an insidious "peril" to the civilized West, the East has manufactured images of a barbarian West lustily ravaging its lands and people. While an honest historian might feel a certain sympathy for both views, the violence and untruth that developed from these representations is unsettling. The works by Shakespeare, Kipling, Sima Qian, and Chen are only four of thousands of examples of such representational villainizing of the Other, an Other that must be demystified by demonization.

The present volume represents an attempt to analyze these attempts at demythologization through representation; it considers how distinctions between East and West have been, and are still, manufactured. The French writer and aviator, Antoine de Saint-Exupéry, (1900–1944) noted, "Only the unknown frightens men. But once a man has faced the unknown, that terror becomes known."[5] His final implication remains vague; does finally knowing what was previously unknown dispel terror or does it confirm it? Perhaps it is just this conundrum that compels the representations of the Other we discuss in this book; does the encounter with the unknown ameliorate the mysteries that cause contempt or does it aggravate it? History, and here I am inserting my own reading of history, appears to suggest both results in equal measure. As Eric Reinders suggests in his essay, contact with the Other is an analgesic to suspicions bred by mystery and distinction. My essay leaves this question somewhat unanswered, for, at least in late imperial China, contact between disparate cultures invoked conflicts and thousands of horrifying deaths.

As globalization brings the world closer together, ambiguating the cultural lines traditionally made in the clichéd stereotypes of literature and film, the average person is drawn more inescapably into a forced awareness of the Other. As a university professor I am constantly approached by students who wonder if China and Japan will "take over the world" with their recent economic growth. Students are both afraid of the "growing giant" in the East yet eager to tap into the potential profits to be made by doing business with it. We still seem to be afraid of the East, but this fear is now tempered by our growing familiarity; the East is familiar enough to excite our impulse to cooperate with our new "partners" in the global marketplace. But part of this new global market is the hackneyed practice of marketing impressions. There is still a market in the representation of the Other. As long as we are competing, whether for ideological space or profit, distinctions, it seems, must be drawn. Representation is as old as society and as new as discovery.

A Diversity of Views

The idea for this book emerged as a number of East Asia scholars from different academic disciplines and intellectual views began to exchange correspondences on the topic of cultural (mis)interpretation. Based on our initial exchanges, we conceived of a volume that would fit nicely into the curriculum of our various courses, a multidisciplinary study of the problem of cultural representation East-West. As disciplinary lines within academics grow less distinct—a trend we quite warmly welcome—we imagine that this book will provide a venue for lively interlocution on the subject of East-West representation from disparate approaches: historical, art-historical, literary, and religious. All of these respective disciplines are included here, and all center on a single theme: how do we (mis)represent other cultures and why. This work is a deliberately diverse consideration of a specific problem, a problem that is increasingly urgent in today's cultural milieu.

Eric Reinders opens this volume with an essay (chapter 1) that juxtaposes missionary accounts and horror fiction, highlighting representational parallels between these two presumably unlike genres. He demonstrates that both missionaries and novelists have similarly described late imperial China; it is a land of "heathen temples" wreathed in "sickening smoke" and the "presence of the devil" for missionaries and "sadomasochistic erotica" in the narratives of Sax Rohmer's (1883–1959, the pen name of Arthur Henry Sarsfield Ward) novels. His essay notes that metaphors in missionary accounts discursively depict the self (West) as "rational," and the other (East) as a "mindless body." The dichotomies manufactured in missionary accounts and horror fiction construct an impression, as Edward Said (1935–2003) has also noted, of a robust male West vis-à-vis a weak feminized East. Dr. Fu Manchu, Reinders recalls, "is never allowed to be manly." He concludes that how other cultures are imagined and represented is enmeshed in the justification to colonize: "Colonizing cultures constructed their images of the colonized in ways that confirmed their right to conquer and possess."

In my essay in chapter 2, I approach the issue of representation from another perspective, not necessarily in opposition to Reinders, in order to underscore the bidirectionality of pejorative and hostile cultural impressions. My chapter centers on how Chinese have conjured negative images of the West and how those impressions have motivated the actualization of violence. I describe how eighteenth- and nineteenth-century Chinese depicted the "Lord of Heaven religion" (*tianzhujiao*), or Catholicism, as the "pig grunt religion" (*zhujiao*) based on a convenient homophone. Chinese publishers were thus able to disseminate images of foreign missionaries worshipping a grunting pig with the characters for *Yesu*, or "Jesus," on its side. By dehumanizing the object of Western religious piety and printing accounts of Western missionaries who "rape" young converts and remove the body parts of hapless Chinese victims, a large popular movement against Christian foreigners was awakened. I also compare the medieval Western trope of *jus primae noctis* (the lord's right of first night) to Chinese attempts to attach similar crimes to foreign missionaries, suggesting that cultures often mirror one another in how they represent the Other.

In chapter 3, Catherine Pagani confronts the issue of representation from an art historical perspective, demonstrating how eighteenth-century British artists created a Western imagination of the East in the travel drawings and paintings they produced while in China. Looking at two such artists, William Alexander (1767–1816) and George Chinnery (1774–1852), Pagani reads their art within its imperialist context, suggesting that such "visual images document not absolute likeness—that is to say, the 'real'—but rather the representation, however subtle, of the differences between colonizer and colonized." Alexander and Chinnery's exoticization of China represented an imagined East that had little semblance to economic and political realities, but rather constructed an image of a land that Britain "hoped to dominate through trade." The wide audiences for their work, especially Alexander's, did indeed inform Western ambitions regarding the Far East, forming a conception of the East in the minds of eighteenth- and nineteenth-century British colonialists.

Lionel M. Jensen's essay (chapter 4) adds much to Edward Said's discussion of "Imaginative Geography and Its Representations" in his *Orientalism*. While Said questions the orientalizing distinctions of "Occident" and "Orient," Jensen challenges the long-held parallels of East and West, connecting such ready-made categories to the "politics of representation." He suggests that "Treating East and West as culturally definitive and different entities requires us to suspend our intellectual understanding of the globe and its constant revolutionary and rotational movement, accepting at the same time the imposition of a two-dimensional grid." It is precisely this "two-dimensional grid" that Jensen wishes to call into question. Borrowing from Tan Sitong's (1865–1898) concept of *tong* (communication/penetration), his essay reflects on Tan's rejection of "the West-enabling polarity for a universal vision of human fulfillment." Tan's vision, Jensen asserts, is one of a "world of immediate and enduring interconnection (*tong*)"; geographical distinctions become contingent rather than determinative. Looking carefully into another text, the seventeenth-century *Poxie ji* (The Compendium Exposing Heresy), a text known for its adamant sectarian diatribes against Christianity, Jensen notes the ways in which this work reveals an ironic convergence of Chinese and Western religious practice, even confirming "Jesuit Chineseness."

In line with our aim to include diverse disciplinary approaches to the problem of East-West representation, Matthew Wells's essay (chapter 5) addresses the problem of how Western categories of literary genre have conceived, if not created, modern understandings of classical Chinese works. Wells centers on the "autobiography" of an early intellectual, Ge Hong (283–343), in order to consider whether or not it is appropriate to impose such a literary category on an early Chinese text. In the wake of post-Enlightenment and postmodern notions of the inexorable role of the present moment while constructing the past, Wells's essay questions whether such presentism is useful or misrepresenting in the end. He suggests that the nineteenth- and early-twentieth-century works that "sifted through the traditional literary canon in search of an indigenous genre of autobiography" did little more than create a misrepresentation of early texts based on modern expectations. After demonstrating the spuriousness, at least by contemporary Western standards, of Ge Hong's "autobiography," his essay insists that "Chinese autobiographies bear little more than a superficial resemblance to early Western accounts of modern autobiographies." Ge's "autobiographical" sketch, quite unlike Western self-narratives, was not compelled to conform to a "standard of objective veracity." Chinese and Western visions of self-representation are not, it seems, the same, though expectations of the Other are.

Those who study Buddhism in China often identify three different types: Indian Buddhism, Indian Buddhism in China, and Chinese Buddhism. Each of these is quite unlike the others. Eric P. Cunningham's essay (chapter 6) adds to the consideration of these Buddhisms in his discussion of how Buddhism has been reinterpreted and represented in American pop culture, specifically "hardcore Zen," which "claims direct roots to the American punk scene." In this new manifestation of Zen expression, American punk anarchists such as Brad Warner deliberately employ odious and scatological syntax to disseminate the "Dharma" in quite a new fashion. Cunningham considers this new American Buddhist experience to be a historiographic problem, one in which modern expressions, vis-à-vis "orthodox" ones, bring about views of Eastern religion that perhaps reflect contemporary sensibilities more than the tradition on which these sensibilities purport to build. Cunningham, in agreement with scholars such as Robert Sharf, suggests that modern expressions such as "hardcore Zen" are twentieth-century constructs rather than an organic outgrowth of traditional Japanese Zen. This essay traces American arrogations of Zen imagery from Alan Watts's "Beat Zen" to Warner's "hardcore Zen" in order to question transcultural interpretation and representation, leading Cunningham to criticize a movement that in his view "masquerades as a spiritual path."

Chapter 7, the final essay in this volume, by the Buddhist scholar Mark T. Unno, centers on religious studies in the West in order to consider the problem of representation. He notes that "religions often tout ideologies that appose the process of commodification driving global economy." But religious institutions nonetheless "are also often beholden to the same process of commodification." The tension between inherent commodification and resistance to commodification in the context of an increasingly globalized economy has, Unno argues, informed religious (mis)interpretation in Western religious studies. While the discipline of religious studies has recognized the need to accommodate growing diversities, its "methodological sophistication" in dealing with these diversities has not kept pace. Traditional categories have been retained in the way the world's religions are represented in modern academic departments. The impact of scholarly interpretations and representations in both academe and outside it is demonstrated in Unno's discussion of Jeffrey Kripal's 1995 *Kali's Child*, a highly contested and lauded interpretation of the life and thought of Ramakrishna. Unno also highlights how Shinran (1172–1262) has been variously interpreted by different modern intellectuals "according to his [modern intellectuals] own needs and aspirations" within the turbulent changes precipitated by the "forces of globalization." This comparison contributes much to one objective of this volume, which is to explore the "increasingly context-sensitive nature of interpretation in the East-West study of religion." Unno's chapter concludes, in harmony with the others in this volume, with the assertion that where interpretation is concerned the interpreter and interpreted are inextricably enmeshed: representation and interpretation are "limited, incomplete, and humanly fallible."

Woven through each of the essays in this volume is the underlying question of how culture and religion are perceived and subsequently re-presented in text, image, and oral testimony. So far, the most active persons who have considered this question have done so on theoretical levels, employing constructivist and semiotic approaches. Theoretical considerations of representation have asked whether or not all perception is at some level mediated in the mind and psychologically reinterpreted in tidy categories. In other words, just as the words the reader now reads represent what I, the writer, am attempting to convey, so, too, is cultural representation a step removed from the culture itself once it is transcribed into a visual or written medium. Such considerations are indispensable when we attend to the way cultures have chosen to represent Others, especially when nationalism and religious intolerance color how Others are described. Thus, before reading the individual chapters of this book, a minimal grounding in the theory of cultural representation will be helpful.

Representation: A Theoretical Overview

Much of what we suggest in this volume is influenced by, or responds to, recent intellectual discussions of culture and cultural representation. In general there are two major historical strands of intellectual discourse regarding the issue of representation, both of which are decidedly configured as Western theoretical models. I should note at the outset that my abridgment of these two modes of discussion is unavoidably reductionist, the only solution to which I can imagine is to refer the reader to other, more exhaustive discussions of representation as a dialectic in contemporary scholarship.[6] The first strand is the postmodernist view, which suggests that, as Claire Colebrook summarizes, "there is nothing outside of representation."[7] Seminal thinkers such as Martin

Heidegger (1889–1976), Jacques Derrida (1930–2004), Michel Foucault (1926–1984), and Richard Rorty (1931–2007) interrogated assumed philosophical conclusions (truths), concluding generally that so-called truth, the real, and even philosophy itself are all linguistic constructions, the products of textuality.[8]

Heidegger rejected the dichotomy of "subjective" and "objective," Derrida questioned the linguistic infrastructure of Western metaphysics, Foucault viewed language as an instrument of discursive power, and Rorty was antiessentialist and antifoundationalist. These thinkers agreed that all truth claims are forms of representation, and this position is further nuanced by poststructuralist assumptions that there can ultimately be no reliable representation. One of the more knotty aspects of poststructuralism is that its seminal thinkers, either in later writings or conterminously, reject the postmodern acceptance of representation as a mode of depiction. Postmodern and poststrucuralist theorists both, for the most part, see representationalism as an intractable manifestation of Western Scholastic metaphysics; it is a dogged refusal to accept Friedrich Nietzsche's (1844–1900) conclusion that God is dead. God as *meta*physically real is replaced by *meta*narrative, which lies beyond its ostensible representation. Some argue that persistent postmodern and poststructuralist reference to a metanarrative is itself a replacement of the Thomistic metaphysical, revealing its own refusal to accept genuine presentism without any metareality. Foucault, Derrida, and Rorty are, then, also categorically poststructuralist, although they might themselves dismiss these categories.

One of the conundrums we faced as we considered the question of cultural representation East-West (at least one of us perceives these very terms as a form of subjective representation) was the old problem of whether we can agree if representation itself suggests the presence of something genuine that is re-presented. This problem is not just a postmodern one; the dilemma of signifier and signified, though in different terms, was already known and contested during the so-called nominalist medieval debates, which were later reconstituted in discourses regarding realism. Even though these medieval discussions over the question of whether universals only exist *post res* (after particulars) may appear to be only distantly connected to our project, such problems remain important since this issue relates to the question of whether any representation of another culture can ever truly depict it or if, as the poststructuralist position holds, there is even a particular on which we can fix.

French realists such as Honoré de Balzac (1799–1850) and Gustave Courbet (1819–77) dilated on the problem of whether truth could be represented, especially when the thing to be represented was not empirically identifiable or even imagined. The postromantic impulse to only represent the "real" is well stated in Courbet's assertion, "I cannot paint an angel because I have never seen one."[9] But what of things we *can* see? Reacting to the question of whether a "real" exists that can be represented, there are scholars, such as Clifford Geertz (1926–2006), who suggest that humans are essentially representational beings and it is pointless to consider a reality beyond representation.[10] The only "real" is "representation," and for our purposes this is helpful in that cultural representation configures the reality of whoever interprets (or creates) the representation. When ancient Chinese depict distant peoples as menacing headless beings in the *Shanhai jing* (Classic of Mountains and Seas) and medieval Europeans depict the "people of the Orient" as fabulous "single-footed sciapods" or men with "ears as large as winnowing fans," this was the "real" Other constructed and imagined through representation.[11] Several scholars, such as Jorge Arditi, Renato Rosaldo, and Charles Nissim-Sabat, have questioned Geertz's suspicions regarding the possibility of accurate representation.[12] There are those who remain uncomfortable with the notion that reality only exists secondhand as mere representation.

One of the most important contributors to intellectual discourse about representation is Edward Said, and whether we entirely agree with his assertions or not, the present volume is largely responsive to his claim that representation often fabricates cultural assumptions that do not actually exist. Said states of the orientalist, "His Orient is not the Orient as it is but the Orient as it has been Orientalised."[13] Otherwise stated, scholars often construct representations of another culture based on inaccurate or contrived views of the society represented. Said, unlike Geertz, insists that representation can indeed be accurate, though unfortunately depictions of the Orient, for example, have presented an imagined Orient quite unlike the one under study.

We share Said's moral outrage over the pejorative forms of representation employed by colonial powers to empower themselves and justify imperialist profiteering. Certainly fictive Others are created to juxtapose a morally superior self and a diminutive and unscrupulous Other, but there remain several underlying problems in Said's often contradictory and tautological discussion of, and use of, representation.[14] Before his introduction Said includes a quote from Karl Marx's (1818–83) *The Eighteenth Brumaire of Louis Napoleon*: "They cannot represent themselves; they must be represented."[15] This quotation is an interesting example of re-representation since Marx's notion of political representation is in Said's book used in a more Foucauldian sense, suggesting that things can only be *known* via representation. This is not what Marx had in mind.

Other points of Said's argument have been criticized. When he criticizes the West as representationalist, for example, Said is himself guilty of reductionistically representing the West. He is also guilty, as Philip Mellor demonstrates, of condemning Western modes of representation while being himself anchored in Western theoretical modes of interpreting the Orient. As Mellor suggests, Said, who equates orientalists with knowledge, which equals power and oppression, is self-empowered by his own power wielding; his own work is thus positioned within the group he critiques. He is by his own definition an orientalist.[16] The entire academic discussion of representation is itself a Western theoretical model, which tautologically participates in the representationalism it claims to stand above. Criticizing others is, in the end, Othering those we criticize. But scholars are increasingly aware of this and are becoming more truthful, admitting that universities themselves are manufacturers of representation, disseminating ideologically "acceptable," normative academic views of the Other. As Gregory Jay notes, "It follows that the current relationship of academic knowledge to political power can be understood, in some decisive ways, in terms of a *struggle for representation*."[17] This casts another light on the Marxist view that power belongs to those who own the means of *production*, for intellectual power in large (or total) measure belongs to those who own the means of *representation*.

We realize our own place within this intellectual history and within our own cultural contexts. And we also recognize that from both the postmodern and poststructuralist positions, the discursive power of representationalism (and orientalism) confines us and for some intellectuals renders all conscious intentions insignificant. But at least some of the contributors in this volume flatly deny this position as sophistic and do not wish to promulgate the notion that representation destroys the real. Some of us, however, myself included, wonder if the real is entirely accessible and representable, rendered as it is through imagistic and linguistic modes of representation. Without, I hope, appearing flippant, one of our objectives is to place our volume beyond such theoretical structures, to discuss representation metatheoretically (which is really, perhaps, a poststructuralist approach anyway). Another objective is to compile a volume of essays by scholars of varying theoretical opinions, ranging from theoretically critical of critical theory to explicit espousal of postmodern and poststructuralist approaches. But we share the view that views are commonly expressed to satisfy a will to dominance; representation is too often an act of violence.

Placing Representation into an Historical Context

We have deliberately avoided the general tendency to organize this book into a historical chronology. We have avoided placing our essays into such a chronology in order to highlight disciplinary and interpretive approaches; we are not so much concerned with historiographical aims to illustrate macrocausalities, as with how representation functions to manufacture impressions beyond national borders. This volume is not a "historical monograph," per se, by historians, but a collection of essays intended to incite discussion. Only two of the contributors received doctorates in departments of history. Most of us were trained in literary critical methods, religious studies, or art history, disciplines that typically supplement textual with interpretive methods of analysis. But this is not to say that historical context is given short shrift; we insistently support rigorous standards of scholarly accountability, for interpretation remains facile without veritable evidence. Much of what is included here seeks to look beyond the quotidian minutiae of historical antecedents toward the modes of representation that color history. We have, to quote Hayden White, "tried to show that, even if we cannot achieve a properly scientific knowledge of human nature, we can achieve another kind of knowledge about it, the kind of knowledge which literature and art in general give us in easily recognizable examples."[18]

While this book participates in and encourages the present move toward interdisciplinary scholarship, it nonetheless builds on previous noncollaborative works that have created space for such an enterprise as ours. Earlier scholars have already discovered the need for studies of how representation and interpretation influence our imaginations of the Other, East-West and West-East: Edward Said, John W. Dower, Jonathan Spence, Ros Ballaster, and Paul Cohen to name a small few. Our efforts are intended to continue intellectual discussions already in force concerning the topic of representation while adding novel insights into this discourse derived from our recent research in new territories. In the end it is our belief that, as Randolph Bourne (1886–1918) has said, "A good discussion increases the dimensions of everyone who takes part."

Notes

[1] Sima Qian, *Shiji* (Beijing: Zhonghua shuju, 1999), 110:2879. For a translation, see Sima Qian, *Records of the Grand Historian: Han Dynasty II,* rev. ed., trans. Burton Watson (New York: Columbia University Press, 1993), 129.

[2] See Sima Qian, *Shiji,* 110:2879.

[3] Chen Taihua, *Alarm Bells*, trans. Ian Chapman, *Renditions* 53–54 (spring–autumn 2000): 240.

[4] Ibid., 246.

[5] Antoine de Saint-Exupéry, *Airman's Odyssey* (Orlando: Harcourt Brace, [1939] 1984), 37.

[6] One history of philosophical discussions of representation is Harry Redner, "Representation and the Crisis of Post-Modernism," *PS: Political Science and Politics* 20, no. 3 (summer 1987): 673–79.

[7] Claire Colebrook, "Questioning Representation," *SubStance* 29, no. 2, issue 92 (2000): 47.

[8] Ibid., 47.

[9] Quoted in Nicholas Howe, *Visions of Community in the Pre-modern World* (South Bend: University of Notre Dame Press, 2002), 37.

[10] See Clifford Geertz, *The Interpretation of Cultures* (New York: Basic Books, 1973).

[11] See Peter Eberly and Andrew Morton, eds., *West Meets East: International Sinology and Sinologists* (Taipei: Sinorama, 1991), 43–44.

[12] See Jorge Arditi, "Geertz, Kuhn, and the Idea of a Cultural Paradigm," *British Journal of Sociology* 45, no. 4 (December 1994): 597–617; Renato Rosaldo, "Response to Geertz," *New Literary History* 21, no. 2 (winter 1990): 337–41; and Charles Nissim-Sabat, "On Clifford Geertz and His 'Anti Anti-Relativism'," *American Anthropologist*, n.s., 89, no. 4 (December 1987): 935–39.

[13] Edward Said, *Orientalism* (New York: Vintage, 1978), 104.

[14] For a protracted critique of Said's *Orientalism* and its exponents, see Phillip A. Mellor, "Orientalism, Representation, and Religion: The Reality behind the Myth," *Religion* 34, no. 2 (April 2004): 99–112.

[15] Karl Marx, *The Eighteenth Brumaire of Louis Bonaparte*, trans. Daniel de Leon (Chicago: Charles H. Kerr, 1913), 145.

[16] See Mellor, "Orientalism, Representation, and Religion," 100–112.

[17] Gregory J. Jay, "Knowledge, Power, and the Struggle for Representation," *College English* 56, no. 1 (January 1994): 10, emphasis in the original.

[18] Hayden White, *Tropics of Discourse: Essays in Cultural Criticism* (Baltimore: Johns Hopkins University Press, 1978), 23.

1

The Chinese Macabre in Missionary Publications and Horror Fiction

Eric Reinders

In the December 1907 issue of the Church of England magazine *Church Missionary Gleaner,* the missionary W. E. Hipwell wrote about his visit to a Chinese temple during a festival.

> I entered the temple for a few moments, but was compelled to withdraw quickly, on account of the horror by which I was overwhelmed as I watched those before the idol who with intense fervour besought the blessings which they desired. . . . The place was reeking with sickening smoke, and horrible because of the almost manifest presence of the devil, glorying over these multitudes thus enslaved by him.[1]

He was drawn into the temple by professional interest but also touristic curiosity, and a morbid fascination. But then, seeing a veritable orgy of abject bodies acting on their desires with such fervor and breathing into his lungs the sickening smoke offered on a heathen altar of Satan, he turns away, reeling, perhaps staggering backward in his need to escape the presence of evil.

The presence of evil and a sense of abomination triggered a visceral shudder of horror at the constricting space of an alien cult. This anecdote belongs to a genre of such stories, which typically include the leering faces of the idols, the strong but amorphous sense of danger, of delirium, of unreality and falseness, and of the alien; these are also the ingredients of classic horror, not of the present-day slasher variety, but the psychological, moral horror in the tradition of Edgar Allan Poe, H. P. Lovecraft, and Bram Stoker and of Sax Rohmer, who specialized in horrible images of Chinese. Rohmer wrote:

> In a chair piled high with dragon-covered cushions a man sat behind this table. . . . From a plain brass bowl upon the corner of the huge table smoke writhed aloft . . . smoke faintly penciled through the air—from the burning perfume on the table—grew in volume, thickened, and wafted towards me in a cloud of grey horror. It enveloped me, clammily. Dimly, through its oily wreaths, I saw the immobile yellow face of Fu-Manchu.[2]

Rohmer's visions of "the devil doctor" are very much like descriptions of temples by missionaries and of the idols, "with their hideous, grotesque expressions, staring fixedly in front of them."[3] This chapter focuses on certain images of the Chinese produced for public consumption (a) by the Church Missionary Society and (b) by horror fiction, specifically dealing with that most famously horrible of all fictional Chinese.

Missionaries did not write horror fiction as such, but their writing has a lot of horror at body practices (footbinding, taking opium, and idolatry) and places (the charnel house, battlefields, opium dens, and idol temples). That horror was not incidental, but rather it was an essential component of missionary public discourse. In an otherwise earnest and largely staid discourse, these stories are dramatic, sensational, and lurid. They are about the emotions of disgust, revulsion, shock, and pity. Missionaries certainly told other kinds of stories, such as conversion stories, which had happy endings (fig. 1.1). But these two form a pair; conversion stories are the yang side of the yin horror narratives. As Robert McClellan wrote, "One of the greatest needs for the mission worker as well as the minister at home with regard to the missionary effort was to justify the expense in life and money of an evangelism reaching halfway around the world. Since the first requirement for a conversion experience was the presence of a sufficiently depraved subject, missionaries frequently described the moral condition of the Chinese in the blackest possible terms."[4]

Fig. 1.1. Thomas M'Clatchie and a Chinese convert.
(Church Missionary Gleaner, January 1851, 113.)

This chapter seeks to isolate and question the reaction of horror in two very distinct discourses. Horror is visceral, a gut reaction, and signaled a strong sense of Othering, the process of emphasizing difference in terms of *us* and *them* and pushing away the different. Horror is also associated with a breakdown of rationality, concerned as it is with the line between fundamentally incompatible worlds or drawing the line between the rational *us* and the irrational *them*. The true object of horror is rationality's raw, unprocessed Other, discovered not so very far away but as close as the docks of London or as close as one's own soul. As the famous addict Thomas De Quincey (1785–1859) wrote of taking opium, "The dreamer finds housed within himself—occupying, as it were, some separate chamber of his brain—holding, perhaps, from that station a secret and detestable commerce with his own heart—some horrid alien nature."[5]

The Two Discourses

The Church Missionary Society of the Church of England and related organizations such as the Zenana Missionary Society published substantial reportage on China and Chinese religion during the nineteenth and twentieth centuries in publications such as the *Church Missionary Gleaner, India's Women and China's Daughters, The Round World, Homes of the East, Awake*, and *A Quarterly Token for Juvenile Subscribers*, as well as a large number of books and pamphlets. In 1916, Eugene Stock (1836–1928) gave circulation figures of seventy thousand copies per month for the *Church Missionary Gleaner*, sixty-five thousand for *The Round World*, and twenty thousand for *Awake*.[6] It is hard to estimate the actual readership of these journals because they were undoubtedly read by many churchgoers and their contents were probably used for sermons, but it is clear that they represent a major publicity machine with significant cultural authority.[7]

Our other case is the British fiction of Sax Rohmer. He wrote thirteen Fu Manchu novels between 1913 and 1959. The stories were initially published in weekly magazines such as *Collier's*, which in 1913 had a circulation of around one million. His first stories overlap most closely with substantial missionary reportage on China: *The Mystery of Dr. Fu-Manchu* (1913),[8] *The Devil Doctor* (1916),[9] *The Yellow Claw* (1915), and early short stories. Rohmer's literary style was rooted in popular scandal journalism and his plots in vaudeville, so his works are enjoyed today only with irony and a sense of camp.[10] In the first Fu Manchu story, an English doctor, Petrie, is suddenly led into adventure—a "race-drama" he calls it—by his old friend Denis Nayland Smith (later Sir Denis), just returned from colonial administration in Burma.[11] They seek to foil the evil machinations of Dr. Fu Manchu, who is in England to "pave the way" by killing off prominent old China hands who might pose a threat to his schemes.[12] As one would expect from a story written for serial publication, the plot is repetitive. Smith and Petrie dash around in the dark, revolvers in hand, or dress up as opium addicts. They sneak into lairs, fall into traps, and repeatedly find themselves powerless in the hands of a man they call "the greatest genius which the powers of evil have put on earth for centuries" (fig. 1.2).[13] "He has the brains of any three men of genius, . . . he is a mental giant."[14] And yet, this "mental giant" never quite manages to kill these two inept agents of the Crown. Repeatedly, Fu Manchu contrives a bizarre death for them but departs the scene shortly before their expected demise, and the heroes are saved by the exotic, alluring Bedouin slave girl Karemeneh, who is one of Fu Manchu's agents but has fallen in love with Dr. Petrie.

Fig. 1.2. Dr. Fu Manchu towers over his hapless captives, Petrie and Smith. (From the personal collection of Eric Reinders)

The literary effect of horror in these two discourses may be seen in at least two ways. The first is a kind of location known for its unhealthy fumes, its darkness, and the degradation of the people there through mind-deadening intoxication, empty illusions, false ritual, and sin. In other words, it is a *den of iniquity*. But the den of iniquity seems to come in two flavors: the opium den and the idol temple. Second, throughout the various discourses on opium and idolatry, one finds a pervasive fear of a threatened violation of English male identity, a crisis of masculinity often presented as a crisis of femininity.

Den of Iniquity: Opium

Missionary publications described the misery and death of opium smokers in ghastly detail. Addicts were usually depicted in lurid, pitiful terms. They were "known by their sunken cheeks, their glassy watery eyes, their idiotic look, and vacant laugh."[15] The opium sot's physical inertia, awful squalor, and mindless degradation became a frozen tableau in popular representations. The *Church*

Missionary Gleaner printed a picture captioned "Chinese Opium-smokers," for example, and the accompanying article explained that the picture showed four stages of influence: wild excitement, dreamy forgetfulness, unconsciousness, and finally removal to "a room behind the building, a kind of dead-house, where he is left to lie until morning" (fig. 1.3).[16]

Opium addiction invited missionaries to think theologically. It was like being in a fallen state. And, more specifically, opium addiction was analogous to heathenism, which, being false and vain, could only survive as a compulsive habit momentarily of sensual comfort but ultimately empty and self-destructive. So narratives of opium and heathenism shared a certain rhetorical style. In missionary discourses, the idolater and the addict shared an unsober irrationality, a belligerent refusal to accept a better way, and unhealthy

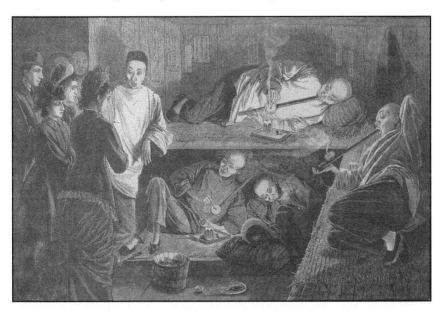

Fig. 1.3. Opium smokers on Kearney Street. (*Frank Leslie's Illustrated Newspaper*, August 24, 1874).

lifestyles. They also shared the fundamental image of an abject, passive body lounging in a drugged stupor or prostrated before a false god. Addicts and non-Christian worshippers were depicted in similarly depressing terms, an analogy made in this 1919 case by the proximity of poppies.

> A dark, grimy temple. . . . Just behind there is an opium field. Inside the temple is an altar covered with dust and candle grease; the large idols—dim, dusty, and shabby—fade away in the gloom of the shrine, their faces devoid of expression, huge in size and immense in their helplessness. . . . With a

wailing, sad, hopeless drone, with postures eloquent of laziness and unbelief, he [a priest] performs evensong, the onlookers apparently indifferent to the service.[17]

Images of opium addiction were resonant with the dominant image of Chinese religious life: dark, grimy, dim, dusty, and shabby, fading away in the gloom, faces devoid of expression, helpless, wailing, sad, hopeless, lazy, unbelieving, and indifferent. Far from providing aid to addicts, Chinese religion was seen as irrelevant, having no capacity to improve their morals or lifestyles. In contrast, a cure for this addiction was associated with Christianity either directly, through medical missions, or associatively through the assertion that conversion would cure all ills, spiritual and behavioral. Concern about backsliding into opium use was one reason to delay baptism. The treatment of addicts by medical missionaries was also an opportunity for evangelism.[18]

As Keith McMahon notes, opium became a "signifier of an uncanny otherness. Opium euphoria exposes a new form of insatiability—a monstrous type of enjoyment that appears profoundly narcissistic to the sober subject."[19] While earlier descriptions of opium dens in London were not necessarily hostile, by the 1870s fear of the spread of opium in England became associated with immigrant Chinese communities (fig. 1.4).[20] By the time *The Yellow Claw* (1915) was published, a daring investigation of the Chinese provision of opium to England was a stock plot. The genre of visits to dens in Limehouse—the heart of "darkest England"—was already well established as part ethnography, part sermon, and part confession.[21] Smith and Petrie visit Shen-Yan's opium den.

> The next moment I found myself in an atmosphere which was literally poisonous. It was all but unbreathable, being loaded with opium fumes. Never before had I experienced anything like it. Every breath was an effort. A tin oil-lamp on a box in the middle of the floor dimly illuminated the horrible place, about the walls of which ten or twelve bunks were ranged and all of them occupied. Most of the occupants were lying motionless, but one or two were squatting in their bunks noisily sucking at the little metal pipes. These had not yet attained to the opium-smoker's Nirvana.[22]

Complete with its analogy of Buddhist salvation as a sensual stupor, this description could have been taken from a missionary magazine.

In fact, opium addiction had long been associated with the Chinese macabre. As Anne Witchard remarks, "Opium was becoming a poetic cipher for Chineseness that encompassed the allure of the illicit, the mysterious and demonic East of De Quincey and the erotic languor of the chinoiserie dream of Cathay."[23] Thomas De

Fig. 1.4. Chinese opium smokers. (*Church Missionary Gleaner*, October 1850, 73.)

Quincey's *Confessions of an English Opium-Eater* (1821) is one of the first literary accounts of opium addiction written from the point of view of an addict, and he had a few specific things to say about a land he'd never seen.

> I have often thought that if I were compelled to forego England, and to live in China, and among Chinese manners and modes of life and scenery, I should go mad. The causes of my horror lie deep. . . . In China, over and above what it has in common with the rest of Southern Asia, I am terrified by the modes of life, by the manners, and the barrier of utter abhorrence, and want of sympathy, placed between us by feelings deeper than I can analyze. I could sooner live with lunatics, or brute animals."[24]

In this widely read account of tragic addiction, the Chinese were abhorrently incomprehensible, and too close an association could only result in madness.

Opium and the Sins of England

In Rohmer's fiction, it is easy to see fear about opium dens in London; indeed, the fear fuels the plots. But in missionary writing it is a guilty fear. The specter of the colonized turning the tables on the colonizer was more painful for many missionaries and church activists because of the sense that England deserved it. Rohmer's point was primarily about the tragedy of British addiction, and the blame fell on the Chinese; but when missionaries wrote about opium, and England's complicity, their language expressed anguish and guilt—their own sin—a "national sin."[25] "Wherever we go the women pour into our ears the sad, sad story of the opium, and the misery it brings to their husbands and sons, and almost invariably they turn to us and ask, 'Does it not come from your country?'"[26] "England has been—not a smuggler indeed, but a poisoner."[27] "England forced opium into China at the point of a bayonet."[28]

A poem by the moralist Martin Tupper, published in the *Church Missionary Gleaner* in 1856, is at its most lurid in describing the greed of England poisoning the miserable Chinese.

> Yonder vast industrious realm
> > We, at lucre's bated breath,
> Like a torrent overwhelm
> > With the very juice of death;
> China, poisoned to the core,
> > Pleads to God against our spell
> English commerce dares to pour
> > O'er her people drugged by hell!
> Oh, the sorrow and the shame,
> > That for millions slaughtered so
> England, England bears the blame—
> > Yea, their everlasting woe!
> England pours her opium in,
> > Though sad China pleads to spare,
> And the mis'ry and the sin
> > Riot infamously there![29]

Although these verses express the predominant tone of missionary comments on opium in China, some missionaries tried to mitigate England's sin and edge toward some kind of self-justification or lessening of the sense of sin. The General Conference of the Protestant Missionaries of China, held at Shanghai in 1877, presents a sample of such arguments. There were arguments that the Chinese had always used opium, and there was a preexisting market shown by the demand for it. Others placed "the opium trade simply on a par with the spirit trade as to morality," which demoted opium to the level of whiskey.[30] Chinese officials were blamed for failing to stop the smuggling. Some said attack the trade but don't attack the trader for "there are many good men engaged in it."[31] Others said, "[T]he evil had now become so great,—humanly speaking—so *irreparable*, that the remedy was out of our hands. God alone could save China from this awful curse."[32] Thus, "[O]ur chief duty in the matter was the duty of prayer. Our only hope was in the power of the Holy Ghost acting on the minds of men."[33] Or, at an extreme, opium was in some way God's doing. H. C. DuBose (of the very conservative American Southern Presbyterian Mission) spoke on Suzhou's many opium dens and asserted, "It is a terrible thought;—one that makes me tremble; but it does seem that God is pouring out his vials of wrath upon that guilty city."[34]

Despite such evasion of blame, on the whole, missionaries felt more culpable, whereas Rohmer blamed the Chinese for getting Britons addicted. Also, Rohmer was not explicitly theological. But stylistically, in terms of the imagery and their emotional reactions to the dens, the two discourses were quite consonant.

In both missionary stories and horror fiction, the opium den and the idol temple shared *atmosphere*, in a literary sense but also literally: the air and its smell. Rohmer's locations often have swamps, gloom, the smell of rotting vegetation, fog, poison gasses, and generally evil atmospheres. Around a villain's house there was "a palpable atmosphere of gloom . . . a veritable miasma of death."[35] In an opium den, "The air of the room was disgusting, unbreathable; it caught Soames by the throat and sickened him."[36] "It was a breath of the East—that stretched out a yellow hand to the West."[37] Health reformers took "miasmas" very seriously as bad-smelling air was associated with diseases such as cholera. But especially in missionary discourse a lack of fresh air assumed meaning as a metaphor for a dire spiritual condition: "In visiting one of the largest temples in our district, which is not only the seat of 300 idols, but also contains sixty bedrooms for the accommodation of worshippers, we felt the very power of Satan in the atmosphere, making it quite a relief to be outside in God's free air once more."[38]

Opium smoke, as well as sex, which will be discussed below, was perceived as a medium of corruption. Barry Milligan writes:

> The specific means by which opium supposedly transmits this infection are varied. Sometimes the seductiveness and will-usurping quality of the drugs are implicitly portrayed as enabling Oriental men to gain sexual power over Englishwomen, thus setting the stage for anxieties about racial purity, fears that were exacerbated by growing apprehensions that the increased mixing of cultures and races in the British Empire would dissipate British identity and undermine Britain's control of the empire. But the contagion is more often portrayed as being communicated by inhalation of the opium smoke itself, without any other physical contact between English and Oriental. Orientalness is thus portrayed as a transmittable disease, and opium smoke as the means of transmission.[39]

Certainly, missionaries visiting temples singled out the thick incense smoke as a key repellant, as if heathenism itself was an airborne infection.

The image of the addicted Englishman is not only deathly but prostrate, passive, and lost in illusions. Another interesting intersection of opium and idolatry was the depiction of opium as a goddess in Rohmer's stories (though not as far as I can tell in missionary publications). There are many references to opium as a deity, as "Our Lady of the Poppies" or "the goddess." Taking opium is "worship" at her "shrine," or "temple." Those who work there are "priests," the presiding evil genius of the den "might be the Spirit of Opium," and "true communicants must retreat to the temple of the goddess if they would partake of Paradise with her."[40] In *The Yellow Claw*, the evil Chinese mastermind has even built an actual shrine to opium.

> In niches of the wall were a number of grotesque Chinese idols. The floor was jet black and polished like ebony. Several tiger-skin rugs were strewn about it. But dominating the strange place, in the center of the floor stood an ivory pedestal, supporting a golden dragon of exquisite workmanship; and before it, as before a shrine, an enormous Chinese vase was placed, ... It contained a mass of exotic poppies of every shade conceivable.[41]

Note that opium deified is female, which underscores the sense that it absorbed masculinity. As McMahon writes, "In terms of culturally defined entities, the effeminate 'Asiatic' acquires a strange fullness that in turn threatens to envelope and consume the sober, masculine 'European.' In gendered terms, opium phallicizes the inferior while emasculating the superior."[42]

Den of Iniquity: Idol Temple

A distinct but closely related species of den of iniquity is the idol temple. Although missionary rhetoric about idols was often materialistic (it's not a god, it's a lump of wood), just as often one finds a demonic interpretation (there is a presence in the idol, but it is evil). The materialistic interpretation lends itself to intellectual scandal or even humor, whereas the demonic view leads to the macabre. The distinction was there every time a missionary evaluated whether a spirit possession was real or fake, as, for example, when Frances Johnson wrote in 1917, "Some are false, only pretend to communication with demons; others really seem to have uncanny dealings!"[43] F. Boreham similarly described a medium possessed: "It did not seem to us that he was by any means unconscious, or acting involuntarily, but on the contrary he seemed to be acting a vigorous part."[44]

Missionary reportage is particularly Gothic when it describes Buddhist and Daoist temples, as, for example, Boreham's descriptions of "devil worship": "The whole place was filled with the aroma of incense and the smoke of burning paper, while the gloom, lighted only by the flickering candles in front of the idol, increased the weirdness of the scene."[45] Or here is another account, published in 1921.

> There on the steps before they enter, they see the big image of the god, ugly, and worn by wind and weather. . . . The temple is dark and very dirty. Cobwebs hang from the walls. The place is never washed, and but rarely swept. . . . The group of idols stands before them. The images with fierce or grinning faces, streaked with red paint and blackened by smoke from candles and incense sticks, look at the worshippers with staring immovable eyes. Sometimes long rows of these images glare and stare in hideous fashion.[46]

The emphasis on the filth is matched by the sense of being watched intently by the unblinking eyes of the idols: "The scenery surrounding the monastery is exquisite, but as one enters the place and sees the priests at their senseless worship, enslaved by the devil in the awful darkness and wickedness of their heathen rites, one is struck by the almost diabolical expression on many of their faces."[47] Numerous articles attested to spirit possession in China.[48]

The icons were sometimes bloody. In a truly gruesome anecdote worthy of Poe or Lovecraft, Mary Darley wrote, "[W]e heard of a horrible discovery in the north of the Prefecture. A huge procession following a brand new brass idol; bloodstained, it attracted notice, and suspicion was aroused. Inside the idol a hollow place was found full of eyes and mutilated parts of the human body!"[49]

Certainly there were real dangers for missionaries in China in those turbulent times, but I have read no account of any direct danger in temples. The horror was expressed in physical terms as a visceral reaction, but the danger seems to have been all in their heads or in their souls. Even when horror is the climax of the story, it is followed by anticlimax. In the materialistic interpretation, idolatry is declared to be merely degrading nonsense. In the demonic interpretation, the idol is declared to be powerless before the incontestable might of God. And, of course, a happy ending was always held out. Horror fiction, by contrast, tirelessly rehearsed the "almost palpable" terror, the consciousness of the eerie, and the always looming, always growing threat that can strike at any time from any direction, even in the heart of England. The mood of paranoia, this formless dread, was best expressed in horror by Lovecraft, or perhaps Poe, who referred to "intolerable yet objectless horror."[50] Both seem reserved by modern standards of horror fiction; there is a gradual buildup of nervous tension, pent up but rarely released (except in madness) or released only in the last blood-curdling paragraph. Lovecraft's "The Shadow over Innsmouth" (1931) repeatedly asserts a mood of evil menace, as, for instance, when the protagonist peers into the cellar of the Esoteric Order of Dagon (an inhuman cult that had originated in "the South Seas") and feels a "momentary conception of nightmare which was all the more maddening because analysis could not show a single nightmarish quality about it."[51] In classic horror, it is all about anticipation, as when Petrie and Smith are captured but not killed: "Do you think he is saving us for—" "Don't, Petrie! If you had been in China, if you had seen what I have seen—"[52] The sentences are never finished. It is all about implied horror: "My very soul *recoiled from bare consideration* of the fate that would be ours if ever we fell into his hands."[53] While there were a few—a very few—real opium dens in London, there were no "idol temples" there except in fiction, and we must look for a British correlate in more diffuse imagery associated with countercultural dabblers in oriental religion with buddhas on their mantelpieces or in association with opium. Berridge notes the impulse to associate opium with the occult, exotic religions, homosexuality, and bohemian lifestyles.[54] Fu Manchu seems to want to poison the West, but he cannot be a mere drug dealer. His ultimate goal remains too horrible for words, and here Rohmer relied more on the fear of idolatry than fear of addiction.

Fu Manchu is not only the most titanic genius ever known; he is also a demigod or god or demon. As they travel over England's green and pleasant lands, Petrie wonders "how an evil demigod had his sacrificial altars amid our sweetest groves."[55] Fu Manchu cackles: "I am the god of destruction!"[56] Clive Bloom notes "Fu Manchu's power to fascinate."

> The Sinophobic message of Rohmer's books is underpinned by three theories: the notion of a conspiracy which is based upon a corporate, international secret society acting out of Limehouse, the notion of a parallel supernatural plane of existence and the notion of eternal recurrence. The modern world, represented by Nayland Smith, is a world essentially haunted by an international mafia with supernatural power; powers which at once uphold and destabilize reality and whose presence is material yet invisible. Rohmer, who was a lapsed Catholic and whose fanatical Catholic mother died an insane alcoholic, wrote thrillers at whose core is a repressed noumenal immanence. It is an immanence that is profoundly disturbing and distressing; it is satanic and fascinating—the commodification of desire; the supernaturalization of the capitalist enterprise."[57]

Smith and Petrie have to do some nasty things—they get filthy in swamps and dungeons, have to choke on opium fumes, stumble over corpses, and shoot men—but the greatest moment of disgust occurs when Petrie has to *touch* Fu Manchu's body to search for hidden weapons: "And never have I experienced a similar sense of revulsion from any human being. I shuddered, as though I had touched a venomous reptile."[58] The body of Fu Manchu is quintessentially the inhuman body of the Other. He is "the evil of the East incarnate."[59] Note the word *incarnate*: "We are dealing with a Chinaman, with the incarnate essence of Eastern subtlety."[60]

Aside from some vague references to Fu "paving the way," there is little indication of what he intends to achieve. His gravest threat seems to be to make Britons into idolaters. Although Rohmer does not take us into an actual Chinese temple, his meetings with Fu are set pieces that resemble missionary descriptions of idol temples. And there is a consistent postural logic of forced idolatry: "Together, chained to the wall, two medieval captives, living mockeries of our boasted modern security, we crouched before Dr. Fu-Manchu."[61] The characters are always crouched or lying down or looking up from the bottom of stairs: "[H]e looked down upon us."[62] Another passage describes "the Satanic Chinaman towering over us where we lay" (fig. 1.5).[63] As a goal in life, as a grand plan, to stand above England seems simultaneously absurd and powerful. But beyond that ritual posture, Fu's plans are always left unsaid. To speak the end of these unconsummated sentences, or to reveal the grand plan, would be to expose them as banal or preposterous. The exoticism was essential to the horror; the reader is invited to feel the terror of Fu's evil plans without ever knowing what they are.

Fig. 1.5. Dr. Fu Manchu towering over his chained captives. (From the personal collection of Eric Reinders)

Feminized Body of the Other

We have seen repeatedly that concern over opium dens was implicated with gender anxieties, that the drug feminized men and left English women receptive to the sexual advances of foreigners. Similarly, women were thought to have a congenital weakness for idolatry and its domestic variation, ritualism, which was also thought to feminize men. For all of Rohmer's failings as a writer, his early novels express a kind of gender panic with great clarity.

One way of thinking about patriarchy as a cognitive process is that the less powerful element in any distinction is gendered female. The feminized Other is not just the best example and model for Othering but in fact the überexample, treating women as weak and the weak as women. The always implicit assumption, the default position, is that women are weaker and more passive than men, and thus to be weak and passive is to be like a woman. In a culture that was busy using its physical (industrial, material, military) strength to subdue "weaker" peoples, fetishization of the robust (male) was also a spiritual justification of conquest. The strengths attributed to women were largely the consolation prizes of patriarchy: beauty, babies, and virtue. Opium threatened the supposed purity of English women. From 1860 on, "Popular magazines portray Englishwomen assimilated—by both opium addiction and sexual unions with Chinese opium masters—to opium dens and Oriental identities. This assimilation of women destabilizes the totemized center of English domestic life by darkly mirroring 'the angel in the house' in what should be the antithesis of the sacred English hearthside, and Oriental den of vice."[64]

As the basis of a religious metaphor, gender had wide application in the mission field. According to an 1874 report, the (Daoist or Buddhist) priest's mind is "a strange compound of fanaticism and imposture, and it is his policy to keep his followers in a gross and credulous state, the women especially, who, in all countries, are easy captives to superstition."[65] Missionaries frequently regarded women (in China and in fact everywhere) as more inclined to piety but also to idolatry. The logic of *male is to female as rational is to emotional* meant that women were supposed to be less inclined to doubt the true or the false. Most reports of temple activities mentioned or even stressed that the majority of devotees were women. They visited the temples most conscientiously, often bowing to female deities. The symbolic feminization of the idolater has a long history in anti-Catholic polemics, as well as in descriptions of worshipping Chinese, and always in connection with obeisance. During the 1860s and 1870s, at the height of the English movement against ritualists—who were seen as cryptopapists—the association of Catholicism with femininity was explicit. Ritualists were viewed by critics as silly, effeminate, babyish, and sensual; as "effeminate fanatics . . . sentimental ladies and womanish men"; or, as Sabine Baring-Gould (1834–1924) put it, "not conspicuously virile men who delight in tinsel and paper flowers."[66] The perceived crisis of masculinity evinced by Victorian machismo was not the existence of femininity but confusion of the boundaries between them.

Women were often represented as inherently more interested in the display of beauty and as happier with subordinate roles, hence their attraction to ritualism, which was called a "female movement." This kind of gender distinction assumed male and female spheres that should not be confused. Victorian reports often focused with disapproval on the blurring of gender distinctions in China. J. R. Wolfe disapproved of the Chinese custom of giving a boy a girl's name, and even dressing the boy in girl's clothing, to avoid premature death.[67] The queue also feminized the Chinese. The Presbyterian Samuel Woodbridge wrote, "Long hair . . . was never intended for men. When the tartars forced the queue upon the Chinese, there must have been the ulterior purpose, born of Satan himself, to deaden the sensibilities of the conquered race."[68] Satan himself inspired the hairstyle. Foreigners ridiculed the queue or regarded it as an abomination. Along with bound feet, long hair on men was regarded as a deformity and an outrage against nature. Victorians were undoubtedly aware of Saint Paul's opinion of gendered coiffure: "Doth not even nature itself teach you, that, if a man have long hair, it is a shame unto him? But if a woman have long hair, it is a glory to her: for her hair is given her for a covering" (1 Cor. 11:14–15).

Petrie and Karemeneh

Fu Manchu is never allowed to be manly. But to feminize him explicitly would have undermined the sense of a threat, so he tends to be more animalized or inhumanized than feminized. Rohmer probed the tension between English men and the sexual/racial Other most dramatically in the figure of Karemeneh, the exotic Bedouin slave girl. She falls instantly and inexplicably in love with Petrie, who in turn struggles in a manly way with his attraction to her. Her exotic beauty threatens Petrie's proverbial stiff upper lip, and he admits, "I never was quite master of myself in her presence."[69]

In the early stories, it is quite clear that their mutual attraction will never be consummated, for, as Petrie remarks, "East and West may not intermingle. As a student of world-policies, as a physician, I admitted, could not deny, that truth."[70] As in so much fiction of empire, there is a fear of racial pollution, of racial boundary violations brought on by sexual desire. In Rohmer's early stories, a recurrent motif is the danger of racial mixing. As Witchard writes, "The association of white women and Chinese men symbolised ethical abandonment and heralded the degeneration of society."[71] Rohmer demonized the fruits of racial mixing but differentiated them according to their sex. Eurasian women are all hypnotically beautiful, and often tragic, whereas Eurasian men are all effeminate, cruel, dangerous, and alluring to white women.[72] Even Fu Manchu is only part Chinese. Rohmer's villains tend to be Chinese and Malay or Chinese and Arab; Karemeneh is *pure* Bedouin. Hybridity is demonized even more than any particular race.

Although exoticism was the basis of the risqué appeal of this pulp writing, even the racial Otherness was hedged: "With a skin of a perfect blonde, she had eyes and lashes as black as a Creole's, which, together with her full red lips, told me that this beautiful stranger whose touch had so startled me was not a child of our northern shores."[73] Though her hair was black, her skin, her flesh, was "perfect blonde."

The risqué, or racy, aspects of Petrie and Karameneh's relationship were revved up in another episode. Karameneh rescues Petrie from captivity and, to give her an alibi, he binds her: "I seized the flimsy muslin and tore off half a yard or so from the hem of the skirt. . . . I fastened the strip of fabric over the girl's mouth and tied it behind, experiencing a pang half pleasurable and half fearful as I found my hands in contact with the foamy luxuriance of her hair."[74] Surely the nadir of Rohmer's work, this kind of sadomasochist, misogynist smut certainly eroticizes the exotic (makes the foreign something to be desired sexually), but does it thus exoticize the erotic (make sexual desire something foreign)? Maybe. We see a kind of hostility toward sexuality, or, more accurately, hostility toward women, insofar as the women are sexually attractive. Certainly, Nayland Smith is never tempted by foreign women. Desire for exotic women was linked to the loss of empire. Rohmer's work was part of what Victor Sage has called "Empire gothic," a burst of popular literature in the early twentieth century obsessed with fears that the British Empire was threatened by the aliens it claimed to control.[75] As Keith McMahon writes, "The late Victorian specter (c. 1890s) was the revenge of the colonial world on the colonizer. The Asiatic and his opium were already speeding toward England and America and threatening to cross and confuse boundary lines of race and gender."[76]

In a particularly interesting passage, the more experienced Smith explains to Petrie why Karameneh does not give him her full cooperation.

> You don't know the Oriental mind as I do: If you would only seize her by
> the hair, drag her to some cellar, hurl her down and stand over her with
> a whip, she would tell you everything she knows, and salve her strange

Eastern conscience with the reflection that speech was forced from her. I am
not joking; it is so, I assure you. And she would adore you for your savagery,
deeming you forceful and strong![77]

She won't just *accept* being forced, she'll *admire* it. And in fact Karemeneh
agrees with Smith on this point. This is colonialism as rape mentality.

In missionary discourses, the sense of rape mentality is not there, but
there is on occasion a sense of the necessity of violence for the good of the
Chinese. Since China is so stagnant, and the ruling dynasty so isolationist,
anything that stirs it up, breaks its barriers, and disabuses the Chinese of
their notions of superiority or self-sufficiency can be good.[78] Even the Taiping
Rebellion was looked on as a great opportunity until its heretical theology
became clear.

A number of commentators have noted opium as a threat to racial, sexual,
and gender boundaries, and one sees this sense of danger, this horror, in the
language of addiction, which emphasized the unmanly passivity, emotional
sentimentalism, and wallowing in aesthetic pleasure that were the negative
side of a widespread Victorian construction of femininity. Phrased more
positively, these vices were the virtues of peacefulness, patience, modesty,
compassion, and sensitivity. For men, however, such virtues constituted a
dangerous passivity.[79] So much is clear in discourses on opium. Certainly idol
worship (the worship of Buddha, say) was not perceived as anything like that
kind of threat to the English or the empire, but, under the rubric of Christian
manliness, attacks on ritualism carried the same charge. And, in the mission
field, idolatry was perceived as a threat, a greater threat than opium in fact.
Idolatry was a threat to religious or spiritual boundaries between truth and
delusion, Christianity and heathenism, and salvation and damnation. But the
horror of idolatry was also pervaded with racial and gender tensions. When a
missionary staggered out of a temple for fear of breathing "the very power of
Satan," when the demonic rather than materialistic interpretation of idolatry
held sway, it is clear that this particular kind of experience (or at least this
genre of narrative) was a matter of "repressed noumenal immanence" in
Bloom's words.

Humanizing Visions of the Chinese

Out of a consciousness of the missionary role in colonialism, today the
missionary is on occasion demonized as well. But there is another story to
tell. One response to the dehumanizing of a remote people is direct person-
to-person contact. According to what is known as the contact hypothesis,
seeing people face-to-face increases and improves communication and dispels

misconceptions, so that conflict tends to be less likely, because any violence would involve killing real human beings. Violence on the other side of the world, against people whose faces are never seen, is more easily accepted. One of the necessary components of violence on the scale of warfare is the erasure of the victims either through silence or a subhumanizing representation (fig. 1.6). Furthermore, seeing an image of a face is in some ways close to seeing a real face, because of the similar perceptual and cognitive processes. Recent works on icons in the fields of art history and the anthropology of art have attempted to consider the agency and power of artificial persona created by representation.[80]

Louseous Japonicas

The first serious outbreak of this lice epidemic was officially noted on December 7, 1941, at Honolulu, T. H. To the Marine Corps, especially trained in combating this type of pestilence, was assigned the gigantic task of extermination. Extensive experiments on Guadalcanal, Tarawa, and Saipan have shown that this louse inhabits coral atolls in the South Pacific, particularly pill boxes, palm trees, caves, swamps and jungles.

Flame throwers, mortars, grenades and bayonets have proven to be an effective remedy. But before a complete cure may be effected the origin of the plague, the breeding grounds around the Tokyo area, must be completely annihilated.

Fig. 1.6. "Louseous Japonicas." (*Leatherneck*, March 1945.)

Missionaries were certainly major agents in the patronizing or hostile objectification of Chinese culture. And yet, missionary media humanized the Chinese in ways that other media did not. True, they were humanized as victims of heathenism and related ills, but many accounts are more or less folksy or human-interest stories such as the missionary wife who has tea with the local mandarin's wife, children at play, or the bravery of Chinese Christians under pressure.

For example, in the first twenty-five years of the Anglican magazine *Awake* (1891–1915) the total number of written items related to China was 449. We read about: Chinese converts, preaching, women and girls, conversions, unrest, hospitals, rickshaws, schools, funerals, the ancestor cult, Chinese religion, trades, industry, crafts, processions, festivals, cities, streets, Buddhism, opium, marriage, weddings, lepers, children, food, and so on. There were 362 illustrations of China, about 40 percent of which were of people (converts, local officials, farmers, artisans, lepers, and children).

In 1900, three Anglican monthly journals, *Awake, Church Missionary Gleaner*, and *India's Women and China's Daughters*, ran forty-four photographs of Chinese individuals and small groups plus another fourteen larger group shots. That is, every month there were an average of four or five fairly straightforward pictures of Chinese people at a time when England was at war, not officially with China but in any case with Chinese people. The benevolent representations of the Chinese were in contrast to the dominant tone of public discourse. Witchard sees the Boxer Rebellion as a turning point, a time when "newspaper articles about 'Oriental London' and 'John Chinaman' took on a decidedly different and lurid tone. The reportage of 'horrible' events in which a Chinese 'secret society,' with the suspected collusion of the 'wicked' Manchu Empress, employed sorcery in its attempts to annihilate all Westerners living in China underscored the tenuous nature of imperial authority."[81] In striking contrast to popular journalism, these missionary representations should be treated as meaningful efforts to show the Chinese as people, neither inscrutable nor nefarious but (despite their clothing and facial features) "like us." This kind of humanization actively resists the construction of what De Quincey called "the barrier of utter abhorrence" so essential to horror fiction.

As often as missionaries portrayed the Chinese as a people mired in sin, drugged or asleep, and enslaved by the devil, there were also images to which readers in England could relate, could feel as though those far-off people were understandable, the same "on the inside," the same in the ways that counted most. It is certainly true that inclusion rather than exclusion—of "us-ing" rather than Othering, of emphasizing resemblance to the self—may be just as inaccurate as Othering discursive practices. The positive representations of Chinese by missionaries are no more authentic than the negative ones, but at least they are positive.

For example, another white man's fantasy of a Chinese was Charlie Chan. His creator, Earl Derr Biggers (1884–1933), trucked in various broad stereotypes, so Fu Manchu and Charlie Chan are not to be contrasted as an inaccurate image and an authentic one but rather a hostile image and a friendly one. Biggers did not demonize or mock the Chinese. In books, Charlie spoke strangely—mysteriously—but no more so than Hercule Poirot or Sherlock Holmes. And he did not speak in pidgin. There are moments in the books and films where Charlie Chan turns his sarcasm on fools who ignorantly display patronizing attitudes. And the books include numerous racial compliments. The books have a rather better record than the films, in which Charlie's speech is barely above the level of pidgin. Sheng-mei Ma's *The Deathly Embrace* and James Moy's *Marginal Sights* primarily criticize the Charlie Chan films.[82]

Charlie Chan, one might say, is the more insidious orientalist stereotype precisely because he is a good guy. Patronization is often more objectionable than demonization. Fu Manchu was always such a ludicrous villain, and one can read Rohmer now as either a document for the relatively detached historian's eye or as camp. Today Fu Manchu is better known than Charlie Chan primarily because of the power of kitsch. "Fu Manchu" has become a 1960s dance, a candy (Fu Man-chews), a rock band, and a mustache (even though, "canonically" speaking, Fu Manchu never had a "Fu Manchu").

Critiques of the American representation of Asians often express indignation, which presumably stems from the association of such colonizing discourses with the violence they seemed to justify. While all cultures form stereotypes of Others, the capacity for violence has never been evenly distributed. Some stereotypes seem offensive while others seem merely sour grapes, or therapeutic, but this difference has little to do with accuracy. Critiques of orientalism have been marked at times by an anger that borders on simple demonization of "the West." Ziauddin Sardar's book *Orientalism* (2000, which followed Edward Said's better-known 1978 book of the same title), for example, presents orientalism as a Western sin against Islam but finally notes a series of stereotypes about Britons in two episodes of *Friends*—Big Ben, funny accent, envy of American wealth, silly social pretensions—and concludes that even England has been orientalized.[83] If England can be orientalized, it is clear that we must separate the specific history of power imbalance under colonialism from the universal tendency toward stereotyping.

Conclusion

Many missionaries' eyewitness accounts of opium addiction do not have a Gothic tone. There is pity, certainly, but not always horror or fear. Horror, on the other hand, is the principle intended response of sensational fiction. I have isolated one essential but relatively minor element in missionary discourse and compared it to a similar but now central element in horror fiction. Some of the imagery is similar, but the plots are very different. The lurid sense of in-your-face degradation was primarily written to shock and, in the case of Rohmer's readers, also to titillate. The "human degradation" subgenre of missionary literature was first and foremost about pity. The missionary horror story came with a call to action based on a sense of common humanity. It was a call to action tinged with frustration about the indifference of those at home who fail to recognize the horror, as when A. M. D. Dinneen lamented, "Oh, if only you knew how we out here rely on you at home, if only we could make you understand the horror of all this wickedness and fear, you would not fail us, you would not fail those lost children of our Father, you would not fail our Lord."[84] This frustration has some rhetorical similarity to Nayland Smith's repeated assertion that the danger is far greater than the complacent English public imagines, but Rohmer's fiction was about violence and fear and came with a call to consume (to buy the next issue of the magazine at least); what call to action there is in Rohmer is primarily xenophobic. In contrast, missionaries most frequently worked against hysteria about the "yellow peril."[85]

Missionary discourse could not fixate exclusively on the negative. Missions were driven by optimistic ideals of service and compassion, and mere condemnation would not have spoken to these ideals. Damnation required salvation. Taking missionary stories from the field as a whole, the strong sense of menace and degradation is dispelled, triumphantly and joyously, in what Tolkien called a eucatastrophe, the climactic deliverance from doom resolved in an unexpected happy ending.[86] The blissful emotion we feel reading such fairy stories was in Tolkien's view a glimpse of the real, true, happy ending eternally written by God. Horror, as an evil-fixated quasi theology fixated on what some call superstition,[87] cannot exist without the intrusion of the Other and cannot deliver any eucatastrophe; missionaries saw a happy ending.

People often have simplified, generalized, and negative ideas about other groups. Physical distance has something to do with it; the Other is far-fetched because it has been fetched from afar. Even with some means of (relatively) immediate verification or falsification, even with well-intentioned instruction, the faraway may be a place of our fears and lusts. Whether in search of what is called "escapism" or (as Tolkien would have it) a glimpse of divine joy, the faraway invites us to fantasize. While fantasy is normally *falseness* or *lies* or *insanity*, or simply *irrelevance* in most of our lives, it is a supreme pleasure in our play. In our stories we need villains and monsters and victims as much as heroes. While stereotypes have been interpreted as stemming from fear of the Other, they also derive from pleasure, not just from fear of the unknown but from desire for it.

Notes

[1] W. E. Hipwell, "Union in Face of the Foe; or, Co-operation in Evangelistic Effort in China," *Church Missionary Gleaner,* December 1907, 185.

[2] Sax Rohmer, *The Insidious Dr. Fu-Manchu* (New York: Dover), 81–82.

[3] Church Missionary Society, "The Idol's Protection," *Homes of the East,* (London: Church Missionary Society, 1910) 4.

[4] Robert F. McClellan, "Missionary Influence on American Attitudes toward China at the Turn of This Century," *Church History* 38, no. 4 (December 1969): 476.

[5] Quoted in Barry Milligan, *Pleasures and Pains: Opium and the Orient in Nineteenth-Century British Culture,* (Charlottesville: University Press of Virginia, 1995), 47.

[6] Eugene Stock, *The History of the Church Missionary Society* (London: Church Missionary Society, 1916), 4:533.

[7] McClellan, "Missionary Influence on American Attitudes toward China at the Turn of This Century," 475–76.

[8] The American title of this British work was *The Insidious Dr. Fu-Manchu.*

[9] The American title was *Return of Dr. Fu Man-chu.*

[10] For comments on Rohmer's influences, see Clive Bloom, *Cult Fiction: Popular Reading and Pulp Theory* (New York: Macmillan, 1996), 179–80, 187–88; and Anne Witchard, "Aspects of Literary Limehouse: Thomas Burke and the 'Glamorous Shame of Chinatown,'" *Literary London: Interdisciplinary Studies in the Representation of London* 2, no. 2 (September 2004): n.p.

[11] Sax Rohmer, *The Mystery of Dr. Fu-Manchu* (London: Methuen, 1913), 168.

[12] Ibid., 50.

[13] Ibid.

[14] Ibid., 22.

[15] "Opium and Its Victims," *Church Missionary Gleaner,* October 1850, 78.

[16] "Ibid. The picture is on page 73.

[17] A. E. Hamilton, quoted in "A Contrast," *Church Missionary Gleaner*, January 1919, 13.

[18] W. C. White described the 1906 visit of a Dr. Wilkinson and others to a village in Fuzhou where they treated a large number of opium addicts with the support of the village elders. As Wilkinson dispensed pharmaceuticals, White held services and preached. Hence, curing opium was an opportunity for preaching and conversion.

They set up in the midst of the patients in the big ancestral hall and "took turns at the preaching. . . . Of the seventy-nine, as far as we could make out, forty-three had definitely decided to become Christians." W. C. White, "Three Weeks with 'Opium Fiends,'" *Church Missionary Gleaner,* January 1907, 7. For more on Christian antiopium activities, see Ryan Dunch, *Fuzhou Protestants and the Making of a Modern China, 1857–1927,* (New Haven: Yale University Press, 2001), 49–55. Interestingly, public rituals for burning opium paraphernalia, such as that shown in a photograph on page 53 of Dunch's book, resemble the rituals for burning the idols of converts.

[19] Keith McMahon, *The Fall of the God of Money* (New York: Rowman and Littlefield, 2002), 3.

[20] Milligan, *Pleasures and Pains,* 19; Virginia Berridge, *Opium and the People: Opiate Use and Drug Control Policy in Nineteenth and Early Twentieth Century England* (London: Free Association, 1999), 195–97.

[21] Milligan, *Pleasures and Pains,* 85; Berridge, *Opium and the People,* 196–97.

[22] Rohmer, *The Insidious Dr. Fu-Manchu,* 33.

[23] Witchard, "Aspects of Literary Limehouse." Charles Dickens was influential in developing the imagery of opium dens. Witchard writes, "With his portrayal of John Jasper's secret life in *The Mystery of Edwin Drood* (1870) 'the filthy but harmless opium den described by Victorian reporters was superseded by the depiction of the opium den as a palace of evil,' its occupants invariably iniquitous" See also McMahon, *The Fall of the God of Money,* 40.

[24] Thomas De Quincey, *Confessions of an Opium Eater,* in *English Prose and Poetry (1137–1892),* selected and annotated by John Matthews Manly (Boston: Ginn, 1916), 441. On De Quincey and the evolving image of opium, see McMahon, *The Fall of the God of Money,* 69–70; and Milligan, *Pleasures and Pains,* 46–68.

[25] Eugene Stock, "The Opium Question," *Church Missionary Gleaner,* July 1906, 97. Elsewhere Stock notes "that morality and religion and the happiness of mankind were very fine things in their way, but that we could not afford to buy them at the cost of the Indian revenue." Eugene Stock, *The History of the Church Missionary Society* (London: Church Missionary Society, 1899), 470.

[26] Miss Rodd and Miss Bryer, "In Chinese Villages," in *India's Women: The Magazine of the Church of England Zenana Missionary Society* (London, 1893), 558.

[27] Arthur E. Moule, "The Use of Opium and Its Bearing on the Spread of Christianity in China," *Church Missionary Society* (London, 1877), 358.

[28] Eugene Stock, "The Opium Question," *Church Missionary Gleaner,* July 1906, 97.

[29] "The Opium Traffic," *Church Missionary Gleaner,* August 1856, 90. A 1906 *Church Missionary Gleaner* editorial noted past discussions in the House of Commons with the common view "that morality and religion and the happiness of mankind were very fine things in their way, but that we could not afford to buy them at the cost of the Indian revenue." Stock, "The Opium Question," 97.

[30] Moule, "The Use of Opium," 354. See also McMahon, *The Fall of the God of Money,* 76.

[31] Records of the General Conference of the Protestant Missionaries of China, held at Shanghai, May 10–24, (London, London School of Economics Selected Pamphlets, 1877), 364.

[32] Ibid., 363.

[33] Ibid.

[34] Ibid., 366.

[35] Rohmer, *The Yellow Claw,* 56.

[36] Ibid., 164.

[37] Rohmer, *The Insidious Dr. Fu-Manchu,* 69.

[38] Rodd and Bryer, "In Chinese Villages," 556. Similarly, another evangelist feels relief to breathe fresh air again outside a temple he visits. F. Boreham, "Devil Worship among the Chinese Hills," *Church Missionary Gleaner,* September 1919, 119.

[39] Milligan, *Pleasures and Pains,* 85–86.

[40] The cult of "Our Lady of the Poppies" is referred to in *The Yellow Claw,* 174, 175, 251, and elsewhere. Ho-Pin calls opium "the goddess" in *The Yellow Claw,* 175. "In common with the lesser deities," he continues, "our Lady of the Poppies is exacting. After a protracted sojourn at her shrine, so keen are the delights which she opens up to her worshipers, that a period of lassitude, of exhaustion, inevitably ensues. This precludes the proper worship of the goddess in the home, and necessitates—I say *necessitates*—the presence, in such a capital as London, of a suitable temple. You have the honor, Soames, to be a minor priest of that Temple!" (175–76). And "as the worshipers of old came by the gate of Fear into the invisible presence of Moloch, so he—of equally untutored mind—had entered the presence of Mr. King!" (184). Moloch is a pagan god in the Old Testament. Mr. Gianapolis, a slimy Greek character, calls Mr. King "a high priest of the cult" (278) and suggests that he "might be the Spirit of Opium" (312).

[41] "It was a cavern! –but a cavern the like of which he had never seen, never imagined. The walls had the appearance of being rough-hewn from virgin rock—from black rock—from rock black as the rocks of Shellal—black as the gates of Erebus [Hades]" (ibid., 145). There are pillars and arched latticework above.

[42] McMahon, *The Fall of the God of Money*, 3. Berridge quotes a Society for the Suppression of the Opium Trade tract that describes the opium smoker as "weak and unmanly" (*Opium and the People*, 198).

[43] Frances Johnson, "Powers of Darkness," *Fukien Diocesan Magazine*, July 1917, 30.

[44] Boreham, "Devil Worship among the Chinese Hills," 118. Boreham concludes that the people are "possessed," but only metaphorically, by "the great spirit of evil, who delights in falsity, superstition, and any lie" (119).

[45] Ibid., 117.

[46] "Kwan-Yin," in "Working Girls of China," *Homes of the East*, January 1921, 2.

[47] "Kushan and Kuliang: A Contrast," *Church Missionary Gleaner*, August 1906, 121.

[48] For three examples among many, see "Demoniacal Possession," *Church Missionary Gleaner*, January 1907, 14–15; Boreham, "Devil Worship among the Chinese Hills," 117–119; and Johnson, "Powers of Darkness," 27–30.

[49] Mary Darley, "Kien-Ning Prefecture and Its Needs," *India's Women and China's Daughters*, (London: Church Missionary Society, 1905), 84.

[50] Quoted in Victor Sage, "Empire Gothic: Explanation and Epiphany in Conan Doyle, Kipling, and Chesterton," in *Creepers: British Horror and Fantasy in the Twentieth Century*, ed. Clive Bloom (London: Pluto, 1993), 7.

[51] H. P. Lovecraft, *Tales of H. P. Lovecraft Selected by Joyce Carol Oates* (Hopewell, NJ: Ecco, 1997), 234.

[52] Rohmer, *The Insidious Dr. Fu-Manchu*, 83.

[53] Ibid., 19, emphasis added.

[54] Berridge, *Opium and the People*, 204.

[55] Rohmer, *The Mystery of Dr. Fu-Manchu*, 161. Blood sacrifice was tainting England because of "that enemy of the white race who was writing his name over England in characters of blood" (161).

[56] Ibid., 265.

[57] Bloom, *Cult Fiction*, 191.

[58] Rohmer, *The Insidious Dr. Fu-Manchu*, 114.

[59] Rohmer, *The Mystery of Dr. Fu-Manchu*, 285.

[60] Ibid., 46.

[61] Rohmer, *The Insidious Dr. Fu-Manchu*, 84.

[62] Ibid., 85.

[63] Rohmer, *Return of Dr. Fu Man-chu*, 131. The film *The Mask of Fu Manchu* (1932) is quite emphatic about this. Boris Karloff, as Fu Man-chu, insists that Nayland Smith approach him from below and remain below him.

[64] Milligan, *Pleasures and Pains*, 13. See also page 93.

[65] "Sketches of Idol-Worship IV: The Strength of Idolatry as an Agency of Priestcraft," *Church Missionary Gleaner*, October 1874, 117.

[66] John Shelton Reed, *Glorious Battle: The Cultural Politics of Victorian Anglo-Catholicism* (Nashville: Vanderbilt University Press, 1996), 211.

[67] "I have seen boys grow up almost to the age of manhood in females' dress, and treated in every way by their parents as if they were girls, and all this in order to outwit the devil, and save the boy from his fangs." "A Week at Lo-nguong," *Church Missionary Gleaner*, March 1874, 33. For a similar reason it is customary to admire an infant by saying how ugly it is. In fact, dressing little boys in girls' clothing was also a common practice in Victorian England, and it had more to do with hygiene than the devil. See Sally Mitchell, *Daily Life in Victorian England* (Westport, CT: Greenwood, 1996), 136.

[68] Samuel Woodbridge, *Fifty Years in China* (Richmond: Presbyterian Committee of Publication, 1919), 112. Sarah Conger described the long hair of her "house boys" (adult male servants), who seemed "more like well-bred girls than men." Sarah Conger, *Letters from China* (Chicago: McClurg, 1909), 36.

[69] Rohmer, *The Mystery of Dr. Fu-Manchu*, 223–24. As Hevia remarks, "The ability to cause this confusion, to destabilize white male rationality was, in turn, a function of Fu-Manchu's unusual mental capacities." James L. Hevia, *English Lessons: The Pedagogy of Imperialism in Nineteenth-Century China* (Durham: Duke University Press, 2003), 252.

[70] Rohmer, *The Mystery of Dr. Fu-Manchu*, 188.

[71] Witchard, "Aspects of Literary Limehouse." See also Milligan, *Pleasures and Pains*, 92–93; and Richard Austin Thompson, "The Yellow Peril, 1890–1924," PhD diss., University of Wisconsin, 1957, 31–32.

[72] In Rohmer's "The Daughter of Huang Chow," Huang Chow has a Eurasian daughter, beautiful and available yet ambiguous, called Lalá Huang. Her appeal is "insidious and therefore dangerous." Sax Rohmer, "The Daughter of Huang Chow," in *Tales of Chinatown* (New York: Doubleday, 1922), 25. Our hero vacillates over his attraction to her and feels guilty about using her: "The morality of the case was complicated and obscure, and more and more he was falling under the spell of Lalá's dark eyes" (45). In another passage Rohmer wrote, "She was perhaps a vampire of the most dangerous sort, one who lured men to strange deaths for some sinister object beyond reach of a Western imagination" (33). She inevitably dies. In "Kerry's Kid," a fashionable

Eurasian man (a "child of a mixed union") dallies with a white, blonde, married Lady, who is drugged and abducted. Sax Rohmer, "Kerry's Kid," in *Tales of Chinatown* (New York: Doubleday, 1922), 80. In "The White Hat," the villain is a Eurasian man. Sax Rohmer, "The White Hat," in *Tales of Chinatown* (New York: Doubleday, 1922).

[73] Rohmer, *The Mystery of Dr. Fu-Manchu*, 17.

[74] Sax Rohmer, *The Book of Fu-Manchu* (New York: R. M. McBride, 1929),198.

[75] Sage notes the prevalence in this literature of "a dynamic of foregrounded testimony, a reported witnessing of the uncanny and the marvelous" ("Empire Gothic," 3).

[76] McMahon, *The Fall of the God of Money*, 6. See also Berridge, *Opium and the People*, 198–200. Even when built on preposterous premises, invasion narratives (although most of them commonly involved France, Germany, or Russia) were a popular genre in the late nineteenth and early twentieth centuries. Cecil Degrotte Eby, *The Road to Armageddon: The Martial Spirit in English Popular Literature, 1870–1914* (Durham: Duke University Press, 1987), 10–60.

[77] Romher, *The Mystery of Dr. Fu-Manchu*, 125.

[78] See Eric Reinders, *Borrowed Gods and Foreign Bodies: Christian Missionaries Imagine Chinese Religion* (Berkeley: University of California Press, 2004), 42–43.

[79] "Observers saw something menacing in the very passivity which smoking the drug induced." Berridge, *Opium and the People*, 199.

[80] Alfred Gell, *Art and Agency: An Anthropological Theory* (Oxford: Clarendon, 1998); David Freedberg, *The Power of Images: Studies in the History and Theory of Response* (Chicago: University of Chicago Press, 1989).

[81] See Witchard, "Aspects of Literary Limehouse."

[82] Sheng-mei Ma, *The Deathly Embrace: Orientalism and Asian American Identity* (Minneapolis: University of Minnesota Press, 2000); James Moy, *Marginal Sights: Staging the Chinese in America* (Iowa City: University of Iowa Press, 1994).

[83] Ziauddin Sardar, *Orientalism* (Buckingham: Open University Press, 1999), 115.

[84] Alice Maud Dalton Dinneen, "The Worship of Gang Niang," *Newsletter of the CMS Central China Mission*, April 1917, 140.

[85] For example, see John L. Bacon, "The Yellow Peril," *Newsletter of the CMS Central China Mission,* April 1917, 90–92.

[86] J. R. R. Tolkien, "On Fairy-Stories," in *Poems and Stories* (Boston: Houghton Mifflin, 1994), 175–76, 178.

[87] Sage, "Empire Gothic," 22–23.

2

Rape, Baptism, and the "Pig" Religion: Chinese Images of Foreign Missionaries during the Late Nineteenth Century

Anthony E. Clark

Mary Ann Evans (1819–80) said much about representation. She was a woman who represented, or misrepresented, herself as George Eliot, a man. In one of Mary's, or George's, letters, she writes, "Life is too precious to be spent in this weaving and unweaving of false impressions, and it is better to live quietly under some degree of misrepresentation than to attempt to remove it."[1] She wrote in another letter that preserving her nom de plume secured "all the advantages without the disagreeables of reputation."[2] But is misrepresentation and anonymity really the best course for nations and their cultures? Even more, why do nations and their cultures misrepresent other nations and cultures, remaining themselves veiled in the apparent safety of anonymity? I am not convinced that representation should be anything but honest, and honest representation, I suggest, requires the casting off of the safety net of anonymity. So, my modus operandi here shall follow the advice of the French painter, Georges Braque (1882–1963), who wrote, "Truth exists; only lies are invented."[3] I will, however, focus more on misrepresentation than accurate portrayal and lies more than truth.

My discussion of misrepresentation is centered on perhaps the most violent event in the history of Chinese-Western interaction, the Boxer Uprising (1898–1900), and I shall focus somewhat myopically on Chinese representations of the West.[4] In chapter 1, Eric Reinders has already provided a more exhaustive account of Western modes of misrepresenting the East. I will not be so myopic, however, as to promulgate the false impression that Western nations did not render pejorative representations of China in order to legitimize their imperialist impulses. We must not forget Bret Harte's (1836–1902) condescending 1870 American poem "Plain Language from Truthful James," wherein he writes:

Which I wish to remark,
And my language is plain,
That for ways that are dark,

> And for tricks that are vain,
> The heathen Chinee is peculiar,
> Which the same I would rise to explain.[5]

In the July 17, 1900 issue of the London *Times*, written during the fifty-five-day Boxer siege of the Beijing legations that started on June 20, it was heralded that "a universal uprising of the yellow race" was endangering Western society.[6] And an Iowa woman wrote a poem that illustrates well the yellow peril demonology of the time.

> Day after day, while screaming shells are flying
> And throb barbaric drums,
> Our own folk wait, amid the dead and dying,
> For help that never comes.
> Millions of yellow, pitiless, alien faces,
> Circle them round with hate;
> While desperate valor guards the broken places,
> Outside torturers wait.

Here the Chinese are described as "yellow," "pitiless," and "alien"; never mind the fact that the Western militaries were the real aliens, and the native Chinese viewed their resistance as an attempt to protect their homeland and indigenous culture.[7]

A cartoon published in the July 14, 1900 issue of *Brooklyn Eagle* is typical of the anti-Chinese literature disseminated in the West during the late nineteenth century. Entitled "The Open Door That China Needs," it depicts a large portal identified as the entrance to China with a towering pagoda in the background (fig. 2.1). From inside China is seen the broom of "civilization" and the "allied powers" sweeping out China's cultural claptrap: the Boxers, incense sticks, bigotry, intolerance, antiprogressivism, antiforeignism, false gods, and superstition. Resonating with such caricatures is the sustained belief that the West represents the world's "great white hope" and that China is merely an enclave of backwardness, superstition, and false religions.[8] And while the West was peddling its array of pejorative depictions of China, China was busily producing a similar mythos about its counterpart. It is unfair and historically inaccurate to insist that either the West or China *alone* was distorting representations of the "Other." We may nuance Edward Said's (1935–2003) comment that every European who discussed the Orient was a "racist, an imperialist, and almost totally ethnocentric" by adding that residents of the East did the same in their depictions of the West.[9] Said's "orientalism" has its analogue: "occidentalism."

Fig. 2.1. "The Open Door That China Needs." (Brooklyn Eagle, July 14, 1900).

One of the pioneering attempts to elucidate the bidirectional nature of misrepresentation—orientalism and occidentalism—was John Dower's exposition of hate propaganda produced by Japan and America during the Second World War (1939–45), a war that killed more than fifty million people. Dower demonstrates that besides the armed conflicts between the American and Japanese militaries, racist and derisive misrepresentations were produced and disseminated by both sides. He notes that while the Western Allies "consistently emphasized the 'subhuman' nature of the Japanese, routinely turning to images of apes and vermin to convey" the "primitivism, childishness, and collective mental and emotional deficiency" of the Japanese, Japan construed equally pejorative depictions of the United States.[10] Dower asserts that Japanese leaders "affirmed their unique 'purity' as a race and culture" vis-à-vis the American West.[11] The array of examples he cites to intimate the harmfulness of misrepresentation is quite exhaustive.

Imagination and Response: Foreign Religion in the Middle Kingdom

It is appropriate here to set our eyes on China during the late nineteenth century and consider native representations of the West, most specifically the religious West. Few persons were more misrepresented or violently vilified and assaulted as the foreign missionaries, derived in large numbers from America, France, Germany, Spain, and Italy. I shall focus particularly on Catholic priests and religious, about whom I have acquired most of my data.[12] During the second half of the nineteenth century a battery of anti-Catholic propaganda spread through northern China: poems, placards, ditties, and books. One popular ditty often sung in Hunan province was a tune called, "Mie gui ge" (Exterminating the Demons Song), and it conjures most of the popular contra-Catholic themes, which include accusations of rape, injustice, kidnapping, and the removal of human organs to produce pharmaceuticals and precious metals.[13] Before I outline its lyrics, however, I should first address the title attached to Catholics in popular anti-Christian propaganda.

During the sixteenth century, Jesuit missionaries such as Matteo Ricci (1552–1610) and Adam Schall von Bell (1591–1666) deliberated painfully on how to translate the words *God* and *Catholic* into Chinese.[14] The term finally settled on for *God* was *Tianzhu* 天主, which means roughly "The Lord of Heaven," and the term for *Catholic* was *Tianzhujiao* 天主教, the "Lord of Heaven Religion." The last two characters for *Catholic*, *zhujiao*, sound homophonically similar to another set of graphs, *zhujiao*, 豬叫, which means "pig grunt." Thus, in popular Chinese parlance Catholics were said to be worshippers of a grunting pig.

In the ditty "Exterminating the Demons Song," the major topoi of misinterpretation are sketched in vivid imagery, often in quite vulgar language. The Hunan song reads:

> The pig grunt of heaven [religion]
> Bewitches its followers;
> Their wanton deeds
> Are all unspeakable.
> Men of every family must be aware,
> Or the hat of a cuckold you will wear.
>
> The pig grunt of heaven [religion]
> Cuts open your wombs,
> Drags out your fetuses,
> Slices off your nipples:

All goes into the potions they prepare.
Women of every family must beware.

The pig grunt of heaven [religion]
Goes for kidneys;
Who knows how many kids
Their knives have killed?
Children of every family must beware,
Or else your lives they will not spare.[15]

The pig grunt of heaven [religion]
Easy to tell:
They worship Jesus the only pig;
Emperor and parents they heed not.
In their temples there's no incense at all;
In their homes there's no ancestral hall.

Anyone in your district behaving like this
Has turned himself into a grandson of the demons.
Have him tightly bound,
Force some shit down his throat,[16]
And search his house all around:
Any demon-book should go in the fire.
Then draw a cross on the ground
With a devil hanging down,
And tell him to piss on this thing
If he wants to be unbound.
Should he dare to disobey,
Throw him into the waterway,
And see how he'll scream in dismay!

Fathers and brothers who teach this song
Will reap blessings and virtue aplenty;
Boys and girls who learn this song
Will be free from menace their whole life long.
Though the demons may come in a horde
We're sure to put them all to the sword.[17]

The song contains two distinct elements, a description of the improprieties of
the "Pig Grunt of Heaven" religion (Catholics) and advice regarding how to
extricate someone from the "bewitchment" of conversion post facto. Catholics

are here described as, first, worshippers of a grunting pig; second, lascivious cuckolds; third, apothecaries who concoct pharmaceuticals out of women's fetuses and nipples; and, fourth, irreligious and unfilial demons who do not burn incense in temples or establish ancestral halls in their homes. How is a Chinese convert to Catholicism to be dealt with? He is to be bound, fed excrement, and made to urinate on an image of a crucifix traced on the ground. Refusing these directives, he must be pitched into a waterway and left to scream.

Popular songs and antiforeign edicts proliferated in several Chinese provinces: Sichuan, Guizhou, Hunan, and Hubei.[18] And in the wake of the Opium Wars (1840–42), an increasing anti-Christianism began to flourish after 1860. Paul A. Cohen notes that during this turbulent era "the empire was deluged with a growing torrent of violently anti-Christian pamphlets and tracts."[19] In 1842, a Hunan literatus named Wei Yuan (1794–1857) visited the recently condemned commissioner Lin Zexu (1785–1850), who instructed Wei to produce an illustrated world geography. That same year Wei published his *Haiguo tuzhi* (Illustrated Treatise on Oceans and Countries), which included, among geographical illustrations, discussions of foreign histories, customs, and religions.[20] In a footnote appended to his "Examination of the Catholic Religion," Wei describes the conversion process, and the Virgin Mary figures prominently in the account. Standard tropes are conjured early in the passage.

> New converts are made to swallow a pill and are . . . required to rid their homes of ancestral tablets. Male and female followers are known to spend the night together in the church. And followers, once deceased, have their eyes gouged out by their mentors.[21]

As in the Hunan ditty, converts are said to repudiate the traditional veneration rendered to one's ancestors, to engage in sexual improprieties, and to use body parts to produce medicines and precious metals. The "pill" mentioned here perhaps bears the most interesting relevance to the issue of misrepresentation.

In light of the popular notion that Catholic priests provided new converts with monetary rewards for conversion, a doctor from Beijing who had suffered financial loss decided to become Catholic. Wei recounts that since the doctor knew in advance that he would be required to take a pill, the physician prepared a laxative and instructed his wife to give it to him if he appeared bewitched after returning from the church. Wei recalls, "[H]e went to a Catholic church, where a foreigner made him swallow a small flaky pastry [pill], and gave him the sum of over a hundred taels [of silver]."[22] The doctor returned home and began removing the ancestral tablets while murmuring incoherently. His wife administered the laxative, he evacuated his bowels, and he was forthwith returned to his senses.

> Then he spotted something wriggling on the wall. When he washed it and took a closer look, it turned out to be a female human form about an inch long, with perfectly life-like features. He put it in a medicine bottle. At the crack of dawn his mentor came, a sharp knife in hand, to reclaim the female human form.[23]

Of course the doctor, being somewhat confounded by the experience, asked what the human figure was. The priest informed him, "This is the Virgin Mary. Those who have converted long enough will have their hearts embraced by the Virgin Mary, and their faith will remain firm for the rest of their lives."[24]

So in Wei's note concerning initiation into the Catholic faith he describes a process wherein one is given a pill, or rather a "small flaky pastry," which consists of a small Virgin Mary, who in time embraces his heart, rendering him irreversibly converted. Defecation, as in the Hunan ditty, appears to be the best course of remedy. The misinterpretations here are clear: the Holy Communion wafer is interpreted as a magical concoction that contains a latent Virgin Mary, normally viewed as an intercessory advocate but in Wei's narrative as a malignant creature that bewitches its bearer. In the conclusion, his footnote contains an equally inventive representation of Extreme Unction. While a dying convert is in his final agony, Wei writes, the family is made to kneel outside the room of the dying person while the priest surreptitiously gouges out the eyes of the deceased.[25] Even more astonishing, Wei notes that the eyes of Chinese people were valued by foreign priests precisely because they could be mixed with lead to produce silver, thus accounting for the perceived wealth of the Catholic missionaries.

Mythologizing Heterodoxy: Popularizing Misrepresentation and Disdain

Other works broadcast similar themes. Perhaps the most acrid anti-Catholic text to emerge during the late nineteenth century was the *Bixie jishi* (A Record of Facts to Ward Off Heterodoxy), authored under the nom de plume *Tianxia diyi shangxin ren*, "the world's most heartbroken man."[26] It was first published in 1861 and contains several inventive misrepresentations, among them illustrations of Catholics worshipping a grunting pig, removing the fetus from a pregnant woman, gouging out the eyes of a convert, and behaving lecherously with native Chinese women. One passage describes Sunday Mass in rather lurid language.

> On this day work ceases entirely and old and young, male and female, all assemble at the Christian church. The pastor takes his seat at the front and extols the virtue of Jesus. . . . The whole group mumbles through the liturgies, after which they copulate together in order to consummate their joy.[27]

The charge of sexual impropriety is perhaps the most commonly expressed protest against missionaries in the *Bixie jishi*, a theme I shall return to shortly. Such works unfortunately precipitated several years of violence against foreign priests and religious. In an 1870 letter, an American Protestant missionary, Henry Blodget, described an anti-Christian booklet he had located, recounting, "It is filled with the most loathsome obscenity and the grossest misinterpretations and falsehoods. Nothing could be more calculated to foment disturbances in the minds of the ignorant people."[28]

Perhaps the most detailed study of the *Bixie jishi* is Paul A. Cohen's monograph on Chinese antiforeignism, *China and Christianity*. Cohen translated several passages of the *Bixie jishi* text, some of which detail imaginative accounts of supposed Catholic sexual habits. One such description recounts that Christian infants are given a special treatment during their first three months in order to dilate their anuses to facilitate sodomy, a practice said to be common among all foreign Christians. The passage also notes that:

> Fathers and sons, elder and younger brothers, behave licentiously with one another, calling it the "joining of vital forces." They say, moreover, that if such things are not done, fathers and sons, as well as brothers, will become mutually estranged. . . . Are they not really worse than beasts?[29]

The illustrations contained in the *Bixie jishi* are no less eccentric than the prose. In one image two foreign priests kneel in front of a large pig with the characters *Yesu* on its side, identifying it as "Jesus" (fig. 2.2). The caption reads, "The Demons Worship the Pig Spirit." The accompanying explanation briefly outlines a biography of Jesus of Judea.

> He was a very licentious man. Of all the wives and daughters of the high officials of the country of Judea there was not one who did not fall prey to his lust. Subsequently his licentiousness extended to the king's concubines and he schemed to usurp the throne. Therefore a high official memorialized, making known his crimes. He was bound upon a cross and fastened to it with red-hot nails. He emitted several loud cries, assumed the form of a pig, and died.[30]

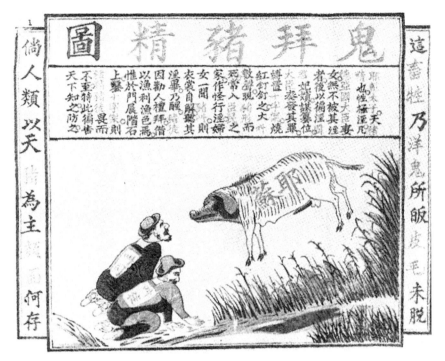

Fig. 2.2. "The Demons Worship the Pig Spirit." (Bixie jishi, 1861, fig. 1.)

Here, the foreign god, "Jesus," is said to have turned into a grunting pig while being crucified for sexual improprieties and plotting to usurp the throne to gain access to the king's concubines. This account resonates with a popular Ming dynasty (1368–1644) Chinese novel, *Xiyou ji* (Journey to the West), wherein a pig-monk, Zhu Bajie, is a representative of sexual misbehavior (fig. 2.3).[31] It appears that in the *Bixie jishi*, "Yesu" and Zhu Bajie have been conflated into a single motif, lust.

Two other images in the text highlight an additional theme, procuring Chinese body parts to produce pharmaceuticals. In one illustration, entitled "The Pig Grunt Religion Removes a Fetus," what appear to be several Jesuit priests, identifiable by their hats, are depicted cutting open a woman's womb to extract the placenta and fetus (fig. 2.4). The text below the image states, "Everyone hates conscienceless [unfilial] cuckolds. Hasten therefore to sweep away heterodoxy and exterminate the [foreign] devils."[32] Besides the exhortation to "exterminate" foreign demons, the text adds that the removal of fetuses is among the most deplorable of acts. According to Chinese sensibilities, not to have offspring is the greatest of unfilial behaviors. In an early Confucian work, the *Mengzi*, it is asserted, "Of unfilial acts, there are three, and not having an heir is the greatest."[33] It is in fact common for cultures to contrive pejorative representations of foreign people by employing elements distasteful to their own cultural traditions.

Fig. 2.3. Zhu Bajie. (woodblock print from Wu Cheng'en, Journey to the West, trans. W. J. F. Jenner [Beijing: Beijing Languages Press, 1990], fig. 6.)

Fig. 2.4. "The Pig Grunt Religion Removes a Fetus." (Bixie jishi, 1861, fig. 4.)

Fig. 2.5. "The Pig Grunt Religion Carves Out Eyes." (Bixie jishi, 1861, fig. 6.)

Another image portrays foreign missionaries cutting out the eyes of a Chinese convert for alchemical purposes (fig. 2.5). The caption reads, "The Pig Grunt Religion Carves Out Eyes," and the appended commentary warns native Chinese not to convert to Christianity, for, "while those with sight may seek to become blind, only in vain can the blind seek [to recover] their sight."[34] In the foreground of the illustration there are two kneeling Chinese converts who appear to have just had their eyes carved out. Such antiforeign works as the *Bixie jishi* mark the beginning of a gathering tempest that culminated in a sweeping slaughter of foreign Christians and Chinese converts. By 1898, ditties, pamphlets, and placards had already molded Chinese images of foreign missionaries, and bands of disenchanted peasants formed Boxer societies to, as Joseph Esherick has noted, "rid China of the foreigners and their religion."[35]

Colonialism, Rape, and the Charge of Jus Primae Noctis

I would like to consider one final trope often conjured against Catholic priests before discussing the proposed means of excising Christian missionaries from China, *jus primae noctis*, or the "Lord's right of first night." This theme, first developed during the late-nineteenth-century anti-Christian fever in northern China, matured into a widespread popular trope during the twentieth century, and its most virulent manifestations appeared after the Catholic Church honored foreign and Chinese Christians for martyrdom. On October 1, 2000, Pope John Paul II (1920–2005) canonized 120 Chinese martyrs, and while the prelates of Taiwan and Hong Kong celebrated the new saints, the mainland Chinese media reacted with heated invectives against the Vatican. October first is National Day, the celebration of the founding of the People's Republic of China and its "liberation" from "feudal" tradition and foreign imperialism. October first, however, is also the feast of Saint Thérèse of Lisieux (1873–97), the patron saint of foreign missions, a day that seemed eminently appropriate for such a ceremony. Chinese officials nonetheless viewed this event as a deliberate insult to national pride.

Priests and bishops in the "official Church" were directed not to celebrate, or even mention, the canonizations.[36] Responding to the Vatican's March 2000 announcement that the canonizations would take place on October 1, the *People's Daily*, on September 26, groused, "The proposed canonization falls on October 1, which is China's National Day, a day that marks the Chinese people getting rid of imperialist and colonialist aggression and pillage . . . and the timing is an insult and defiance to the Chinese people and the Chinese Catholic Church."[37] Sun Yuxi, of China's Ministry of Foreign Affairs, issued a statement on the day of the canonizations, asserting that "some Catholic missionaries were the very perpetrators and accomplices in the colonialist and imperialist invasion of China" and further that "Some of those canonized by the Vatican perpetrated outrages such as raping and looting . . . and committed unforgivable crimes against the Chinese people."[38]

On October 2, the newspaper *Xinhua News Agency* released a report excoriating the Vatican's canonization of three European missionaries, Auguste Chapdelaine (1814–56), Francis Capillas (1607–48), and Alberico Crescitelli (1863–1900), asserting that they were all lecherous and that, in the case of Crescitelli, baptism had been merely a euphemism for rape.[39]

> [Crescitelli] went to this area [Shaanxi] to preach in 1898 and ordered all the daughters of his church followers to be "baptized" by him on the eve of marriage. No one could escape being raped by this "saint." The wives of local Catholics, Pan Changfu, Zheng Ganren, and Yang Hai, had all been raped by the missionary before marriage.[40]

The article concludes its account of Crescitelli with the statement that the local people "could no longer put up with his sinning, so they killed him."[41]

Finally, on October 6, the *People's Daily* published an additional criticism of the canonizations, this time noting, "Over twenty experts on history and religions held a symposium . . . exposing the crimes committed by recently 'canonized' foreign missionaries and their followers."[42] The article condemned "the Vatican's vicious intention to intervene in China's internal affairs through religious activities . . . [trampling] on the sovereignty of the Chinese Catholic Church and severely provoking the 1.2 billion Chinese people."[43] Several other articles published around that time presented similar critiques, one quoting the head of the Chinese Patriotic Catholic Association, Bishop Fu Tieshan (1931–2007). In several ways, the Chinese media accusations of rape directed toward Chapdelaine, Capillas, and Crescitelli resonate in tenor with the medieval legend of *jus primae noctis*, the purported jurisdictional right of a landed lord to deflower virgins under his auspices.[44] This is a common theme the world over, as it recalls and highlights obvious power disparities.

By the fifteenth century, medieval Europe had become accustomed to the popular belief that the lord of a manor had first right to the new brides of peasants under his authority, an idea that swept across temporal and cultural boundaries. In the *Epic of Gilgamesh*, Gilgamesh, the Mesopotamian king of Uruk, is said to have had intercourse with new brides before their husbands, noting, "His lust leaves no virgin to her lover, neither the warrior's daughter nor the wife of the noble."[45]

Herodotus's (ca. 490–425 BCE) *Histories* inform us that one of the tribes of Libya had the particular custom of allowing its king first sexual rights to virgins who would soon be wed. He writes, "They are the only Libyan tribe to follow this practice . . . of taking girls who are about to be married to see the king. And the girl who catches his fancy, leaves him a maid no longer."[46] Irish monks recorded in the eighth century that Vikings required first-night privileges from Christian newlyweds, writing that "the chief governor of them should have the bestowing of any woman in the kingdom the first night after marriage, so before her own husband should have carnal knowledge of her."[47] And Marco Polo's (1254–1324) *Travels* mentions sexual customs wherein men must deflower women before they are married.[48]

Some texts recall ritual deflorations of virgins by socially dominant men. In the narratives of the putative fourteenth-century traveler John of Mandeville, there is an account of an island where poor peasants are required to deflower virgins prior to their husbands because female sexual organs are believed to be cursed and poisonous.[49] The peasants thus protect the new husbands from contamination, an idea typical of early hymeneal blood fears common among some cultures. It is noteworthy that in all appearances of these topoi, the narratives describe either foreign people who are enemies, as in the account of the Vikings; foreign people as curiosities, as in Polo's Tibetan women; or people who are empowered above others such as landowners and rulers. *Jus primae noctis* and the ritual defloration of virgins are reserved as pejorative distinctions for the Other.

In one peculiar passage in the *Bixie jishi*, the author notes that women are esteemed above men in the West because it is believed that their menstrual flow is the most valued gift God bestows upon humanity. The text accordingly recounts that, as Cohen paraphrases it, "[W]hen a woman's period arrives, the barbarians vie with each other to obtain some of her menses and drink it—thus accounting for the unbearable stench which many of them have."[50] Indeed, the contrivances intended to disparage Christian "improprieties" become increasingly inventive. I think Cohen is correct in his statement that "charges of sexual license and perversion have always, in the most varied cultural milieus, been the favorite devices by which indignant upholders of orthodox order have sought to incriminate their real or maligned foes."[51] While I am not suggesting here an exclusively Foucauldian interpretation of *jus primae noctis* and its use in Chinese sources, there can be little dispute that these legends are enmeshed in a discourse of power. They function to highlight the apparent misuse of power and underpin the incivility and cultural invasiveness of an unfamiliar culture, one that has perhaps inserted itself into one's native rhythms without invitation.[52]

Let me turn now to the case of Alberico Crescitelli (fig. 2.6). His biographical information is mostly recounted in hagiographical works, but brief mentions are also made in secular Chinese texts. Principal documents on Catholic missionaries such as Crescitelli include the *Positio* kept in the Vatican's Secret Archives; two Chinese hagiographies, the *Zhonghua xundao shengren zhuan* (Biographies of the Chinese Martyr-Saints) and an abridged recension of the same text, the *Zhonghua xundao shengren zhuan lüe* (Abridged Biographies of the Chinese Martyr-Saints); and three short works published by the congregation to which Crescitelli belonged.[53] The most important Chinese works dealing with the Crescitelli account, however, are the *Ningqiang xianzhi* (Local Gazetteer of Ningqiang Province) and *Zhongguo jiao an shi* (History of Chinese Missionary Cases) by Zhang Li and Liu Jiantang. The primary value of these documents rests in their extra-ecclesiastical provenance.

Alberico Crescitelli was born in Altavilla Irpina, Italy, on June 30, 1863, and entered the Pontifical Seminary of Saints Peter and Paul in 1880. He was ordained in Rome on June 4, 1887 and arrived in Shaanxi, China in August of 1888, taking the Chinese name Guo Xide. He lived in China for twelve years before his martyrdom on July 21, 1900, during the height of Boxer Uprising violence. Much of what we know of his activities in China is recorded in several hundred letters he sent to his family while in Shaanxi, although modern Chinese documents rely almost exclusively on charges of sexual misconduct that are largely taken a priori as historical truth.[54]

Vatican documents report that Guo fled his village after hearing of his intended assassination and shortly afterward entrusted

Fig. 2.6. Alberico Crescitelli, PIME, 1888. (Courtesy of the Archives des Missions Étrangères de Paris, Paris.)

himself to the care of a nearby tax official.[55] That evening, a crowd surrounded the customs office calling for his capture, after which he was seized, tortured, and killed the following day. The narrative notes:

> As he spoke one of the most bloody and infuriated among them, hit him on his left arm, almost cutting it off. At first signal of the massacre, all the others, like hyenas, wounded him with their knives and sticks while one of those most angry lifted a large sword and dropped the blade on his head to open it totally.[56]

Despite the hagiographical tenor of the Vatican account, the local Chinese gazetteer renders an almost identical history. The *Ningqiang xianzhi* states:

> At nine o'clock that evening a crowd of people rushed to the front of the tax office, shouting angrily, "Capture the foreigner!" The tax official, Yao, said to Guo Xide, "You can see how many people there are; I have no way of holding them back. Your only recourse is to flee." Guo exited the rear door and knelt, looking up to God in prayer. The angry peasants seized him. Guo Xide said to them, "What have I done? Take me to the local authorities." The crowd took no account of his words, but used their great swords and long spears to hack and pierce him indiscriminately, injuring his left arm, nose, and mouth.[57]

The skeletal details of the story are the same: Guo sought sanctuary at the office of a tax official, a crowd gathered there calling for his capture, and once he was seized he was indiscriminately struck with weapons, injuring his left arm and face. Except for their tenors, both narratives retain similar details throughout. Guo Xide was finally taken to the Jialing River, where two inebriated men slowly sawed off his head, dismembered his body, and threw it into the water.[58] Significantly, nowhere in the local gazetteer is Guo's alleged molestation of women mentioned; such details are conspicuously absent from the local record. We first encounter these accusations in a Chinese text published in the late twentieth century.

The *Xinhua News Agency* reported on October 2, 2000, that "The wives of local Catholics Pan Changfu, Zheng Ganren, and Yang Hai had all been raped by the missionary before marriage." The account appears to have relied completely on Zhang Li and Liu Jiantang's 1989 *Zhongguo jiao an shi*. Indeed, the newspaper's syntax is an almost verbatim retelling. The original 1989 text reads:

Guo Xide obliged Christian girls who were to be wed to go to the church to be "baptized," as in the Western European Middle Ages practice of "right of first night" (*jus primae noctis*). Everyone who went encountered his lecherous seduction and rape. The wives of such Yanghai men as Pan Changfu and Zheng Gan were all raped before marriage by Guo Xide. The church required Christian believers to send their daughters to be "nuns" in order to satisfy the Father's sexual needs. . . . Since the church cooperated with the feudal regime, pressuring and exploiting the people, they hated the Christians more and more, and continually thought about when they could start an uprising.[59]

Here we have a typical example of the *jus primae noctis* trope commonly conjured against Western missionaries. Guo is first accused of practicing the medieval "right of first night," and then two women are identified, the wives of Pan Changfu and Zheng Gan. The passage also notes that the church required women to become nuns to satisfy the sexual appetites of the priest and finally suggests that the people rose up against Guo because Christians cooperated with the Qing (1644–1911) "feudal regime" and exploited them. But we note that neither the 1989 book nor any of the recent newspaper articles appear to have relied on the local gazetteer written immediately after the event for evidence of rape, for the text says nothing to validate any accusations of sexual impropriety.

Gianni Criveller has written a small English and Chinese pamphlet attempting to exonerate Guo Xide, wherein he briefly mentions the *jus primae noctis* trope. In his work he also notes that the wives of Pan Changfu and Zheng Ganren were never Christians. They would thus never have been "baptized" or married by Guo Xide; he perhaps did not even know the two women. Indeed, Criveller writes, "Pan Changfu . . . [was] among Crescitelli's assassins, and later (1901) condemned to death for this crime."[60] It is therefore quite unlikely that Zhang and Liu's 1989 account is credible. And if the *Zhongguo jiao an shi* was indeed the source for the recent articles accusing Crescitelli of sexual improprieties, then these later reports, too, are suspect.

It is true, however, that once an accusation of sexual impropriety such as *jus primae noctis* is made, there remains, perhaps, a bit of suspicion, and an objective scholar must not dismiss documentary evidence because of personal bias. Historians must weigh evidence impartially, and in light of the literary history of making such accusations based on otherness, unfamiliarity, and fear the Chinese newspaper charges appear to be little more than an *argumentum ad ignorantiam*, an argument based on ignorance of the facts. Accusations of sexual misconduct were commonly ascribed in China to missionaries and foreigners in general, to Matteo Ricci and Johann Adam von Schall, for example.[61] Robert Entenmann writes, "Christians were often suspected of sexual license, a charge often made against the White Lotus sectarians."[62] A Chinese official from Xintu, among those who conflated Christians and the White Lotus Sect, wrote to local Christians, "[T]hey say that every day, morning, and night, you pray to God, and men and women gather together; that at night, you keep in good order as long as the prayer lasts, then as soon as it is over, you extinguish all lights and engage in shameful and abominable crimes. Is that true?"[63]

In one woodblock print in the *Bixie jishi*, we see a crucified pig surrounded by worshippers, and below them are foreign priests and a Chinese Christian with women on their laps (fig. 2.7). The captions read:

> The stench of [Christianity] has flowed through two thousand years of time.
> . . . From all quarters people who hardly know each other freely mate and
> pair, human beings [Chinese] and devils [foreigners], women and men,
> sleeping upon the same pillows. . . . Let all join with their relatives, their
> neighbors, and the members of their parents' and wives' clans in taking
> stringent precautions against the entry of cuckolds—the brothers of the pig
> of heaven—into their homes.[64]

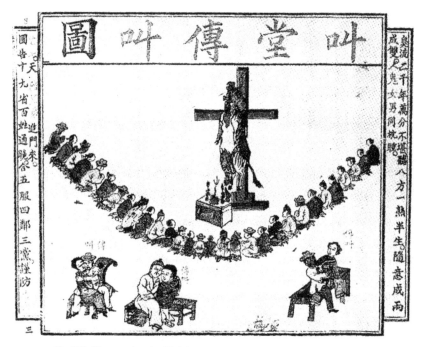

Fig. 2.7. "Propagating the [Pig] Grunt Religion." (Bixie jishi, 1861, fig. 3.)

The men in the print wear green hats, the traditional Chinese sign of a cuckold. With such images and rumors disseminated during the late nineteenth century, it is no wonder that the *jus primae noctis* trope was so readily attached to foreigners such as Guo Xide.

In light of the evidence, most of the nineteenth- and twentieth-century Chinese accusations of *jus primae noctis* may be consigned to the same status given to the medieval belief in the "right of first night," namely, legend.[65] Chinese sources demonstrate that histories of Guo Xide have evolved from that of an innocent victim of local hostilities in the early-twentieth-century *Ningqiang xianzhi* to a lascivious rapist in the 1989 *Zhongguo jiao an shi* and recent Chinese newspapers. The *People's Daily*, *Xinhua News Agency*, and other Chinese sources published at the time of the canonizations share a common theme, historical misprision inspired by reactions to what seems to be colonialist invasion, itself an apparent form of rape.[66]

Razing, Looting, and the Reclamation of Culture

What, then, was the late-nineteenth-century response to the popular representations of Catholic priests, religious, and converts? As we have seen, rumors proliferated that the worshippers of the grunting pig, "Yesu," administered pills to initiates, which grew into small "Virgin Marys" that enchanted the newly converted; indulged in orgiastic gatherings after Mass; removed fetuses from women to produce medicines; gouged out eyes to make silver; and perpetuated the medieval practice of *jus primae noctis*. The solution was a violent one. As one illustration in the *Bixie jishi* suggests, native Chinese must "Beat the Devils and Burn Their Books" (fig. 2.8). As the image caption explains:

> Their nonsensical [lit. "dog fart"] magical books stink like dung. They slander the sages and worthy ones and revile the Daoist immortals and Buddhas. All within the nine provinces and four seas [the empire] hate them intensely. . . . Even if they are [punished] with ten thousand arrows and a thousand swords, it will be difficult for their crimes to be expiated.[67]

The general opinion in late-nineteenth-century anti-Christian propaganda was that foreign missionaries could only be excised from China via violent confrontation. In the 1903 Shanghai publication *Quanfei jiliie* (A Short Chronicle of Boxer Bandits), there is an illustration of Boxers razing a Christian church (fig. 2.9).[68] As Cohen notes, the most typical response to anti-Christian propaganda in 1900 was, "the destruction (usually by fire) of churches and chapels and the looting of convert homes and other properties,

Fig. 2.8. "Beating Devils and Burning Their Books." (Bixie jishi, 1861, fig. 10.)

usually in rural areas."[69] Razing and looting were not the only forms of violence, however; people, too, were assailed.

I should note here that, contrary to most accounts, the Boxers did not kill the largest number of foreign missionaries and Chinese converts; imperial Qing troops did. And there remains a large amount of historical research to be done on the slaughters of Christians that occurred from 1898 to 1900 in northern China. While it is important to objectively critique the imperialist Western superciliousness that afflicted China during its late imperial era, it is irresponsible to villainize the West at the expense of historical veracity. Several thousands of Christian missionaries and converts were killed in China during the late nineteenth century, with passions fueled by such misrepresentations as the popular ditty "Mie gui ge" and the book *Bixie jishi*. The slaughter of over three thousand Catholics in a small Hebei village, Zhujiahe, is not discussed in the standard texts on the Boxer Uprising.[70] This massacre illustrates well the violence precipitated by the anti-Christian literature and songs of the time. The research done so far on the accounts of such events as the Zhujiahe slaughter has been undertaken only by Protestant, Eastern Orthodox, and Catholic scholars.[71]

Fig. 2.9. Boxers razing a Catholic church.
(Quanfei jilüe, 1903.)

A ceremony was held in the diocese of Xianxian, Hebei on April 22, 1928, officially opening the case for beatification and canonization of the Catholic martyrs of China, and there a French Jesuit, Fr. Pierre-Xavier Mertens, was assigned the task of acquiring data on the Zhujiahe massacre. The monograph he finally produced based on the documents and testimonies he had gathered, *Du sang chrétien sur the fleuve jaune* (Christian Blood on the Yellow River), remains uncited in any text on the Boxer Uprising. His narrative of the Zhujiahe massacre is quite exhaustive.

In May of 1900, Christian communities began to hear accounts of fierce attacks against foreign missionaries and Chinese converts. The villagers of Zhujiahe thus began to provision themselves with food and weapons, hoping to be able to resist Boxer incursions. The French Jesuit in charge of the community, Fr. Leon Ignace Mangin (1857–1900), wrote a final letter to his superior on July 7, 1900, eight days before the village was besieged (fig. 2.10). He wrote, "At Gucheng the mandarin has urged the Christians to sign their *tuijiao*, 'apostasy'."[72] One could avoid personal calamity by apostatizing, typically done by stomping on a crucifix or exclaiming "*Beijiao*," "I denounce my religion." It is clear in light of documentary evidence that the imperial militia and Boxer attacks on Chinese Christian villages were motivated more by religious issues than political ones.[73] Mertens recounts, for example, that during the killings at Zhujiahe those who "called out the two words *beijiao* . . . were spared."[74] That apostates were spared once they denounced non-Chinese beliefs, I suggest, was primarily due to the wide proliferation of pejorative representations of foreign religion.

Fig. 2.10. Leon Ignace Manjin, S.J.
(Courtesy of the Archives des Missions Étrangères de Paris, Paris.)

Mertens records that Boxer societies attacked the village on the morning of Sunday, July 16, and that the villagers were able to resist their sieges until July 20. By then, however, the Boxers had obtained the assistance of two thousand imperial troops under Empress Dowager Ci Xi's (1835–1908) orders to march from Nanjing to protect the capital from approaching Japanese and European armies.[75] The July 20 attack began at 4:00 a.m., and by 10:00 Boxers and imperial troops had breached the walls and made their way to the village church, which harbored a thousand children, women, and elderly (fig.2.11). They were shot at and finally burned to death in the church;

only around fifty Chinese Christians were kept alive. The Boxers intended to sell the women, and the men were tortured to find out where the foreigners' "treasure" was hidden, that is, the alleged "wealth" they believed priests possessed, the silver presumably produced from the eyes of Chinese converts. Merton recounts that the next day, July 21, the imperial soldiers "continued their march to Beijing. The fathers and Christians besieged in the central residence near Xianxian were on the ramparts, and saw . . . [that the] soldiers were wearing medals and scapulars which they had taken from the martyrs of Zhujiahe."[76] The medallions and scapulars were believed to have magical properties, something the troops and Boxers had heard of in popular stories. The church structure was later reconstructed, monuments were erected, and the remains of the several thousand martyrs were placed beneath the main altar of the new church and in a special sepulcher built nearby.[77] All of these were destroyed again, in 1966, during the Cultural Revolution (1966–76).[78]

This massacre was by no means an isolated event; several similar attacks occurred in northern China during the height of the antagonism between foreign missionaries and dignitaries and native Chinese forces in 1900. Equally curious tales were disseminated about the foreigners besieged in other locations. Some of the most outlandish rumors contrived by Boxers about Catholics were spread during the siege of Beijing's Northern Catholic Cathedral (Beitang) in June of 1900. From around June 20, until the arrival of the Allied

Fig. 2.11. Mortal remains of the Christians of Zhujiahe village.
(Courtesy of the Archives des Missions Étrangères de Paris, Paris.)

Fig. 2.12. Bishop Pierre-Marie-Alphonse Favier, C.M.
(Courtesy of the Archives des Missions
Étrangères de Paris, Paris.)

forces in Beijing on August 14, the cathedral was assaulted by some 10,000 Boxers under the direction of Prince Duan (Duan Qinwang).[79] The Boxers were unable to bring down the cathedral, despite the large number of men and two months of steady attacks. In their frustration, several fictions were added to the a priori mythologies already believed. The large-girthed and grizzly-bearded French bishop of the Northern Cathedral, Bishop Pierre-Marie-Alphonse Favier, C.M. (1837–1905), was called a "demon king" (*guiwang*) and said to be, as Cohen puts it, "two hundred years of age . . . skilled as a strategist," and a sorcerer who was an "expert at divination" and "had the power to render himself invulnerable by daubing his forehead with menstrual blood" (fig. 2.12).[80] The purported reason why the cathedral walls could not be breached was because the 3,400 Catholic defenders had practiced various forms of magic, which included attaching women's skins to the inside walls, removing fetuses to nail to the walls, and a special "ten-thousand woman hair flag" (*wan nü mao*) woven from female pubic hair.[81] While many such misrepresentations faded into the rational realm of curious memory, the impulse to construct binarisms between the cultural and religious "East" and "West" have persisted in China.

(Mis)Interpretation and National Pride

In the final chapters of *History in Three Keys,* Paul A. Cohen demonstrates how contemporary Chinese have arrogated the image of the Boxers as a sign of anti-imperialist patriotism. Again, representation is employed as a means of bolstering national pride vis-à-vis the foreign Other. His comment on

historians in general aptly applies to all who represent another, namely, that
"the historian's outsideness, precisely because it is outside, has the potential
to misconstrue and distort, to introduce meanings alien to the material under
examination."[82] And when interpretation and representation are brought
into the realm of nations, so often clouded by the myopia of nationalism,
interpretation and representation are easily reconfigured as misinterpretation
and misrepresentation. John Dower notes that when nations are in conflict,
"At a conspicuous public level, each side . . . engages in the ritual reenactment
of patriotic anger."[83] Certainly, as Jacques Gernet successfully attests in *China
and the Christian Impact*, there were legitimate cultural and religious conflicts
between the Christian West and China; however, the proliferation of contrived
misrepresentations by both sides resulted in unnecessary violence such as the
massacre at Zhujiahe.[84]

While I am not always in agreement with Jacques Derrida (1930–2004),
I remain intrigued by his assertion, "We need to interpret interpretations
more than to interpret things."[85] But then Derrida's statement was derived
from Montaigne (1553–92), who said, "It is more of a business to interpret
the interpretations than to interpret the texts, and there are more books on
books than on any other subject: all we do is gloss each other. All is a-swarm
with commentaries: of authors there is a dearth."[86] Montaigne's lament that
there are fewer original authors than interpretations of interpreters was
reinterpreted by Derrida and perhaps even misrepresented. What interests
me about Derrida's statement is that, while it is itself a misrepresentation of
Montaigne's assertion, it does recommend a long-needed investigation into
how people, cultures, and religions are interpreted and represented. Billy
Wilder's (1906–2002) now hackneyed comment "Hindsight is always twenty-
twenty" remains true. In hindsight it is known that Catholic missionaries did
not administer pills that transmogrified into small "Virgin Marys," they did
not worship a lascivious criminal who magically turned into a grunting pig,
they did not remove fetuses to produce medicines, they did not gouge out
eyes to make silver that they hid in their churches, and they did not force their
female converts to sleep with them on the eve of their weddings.

In the end, there are salutary lessons to be gleaned from the mutual
misrepresentations from both the East and West contrived during the late
nineteenth century. The tension between truth and fiction is antagonized
by the intersection of two distinct and proud nationalisms. Indeed, the
binary of East and West disintegrates in light of such unsettling memories
as Zhujiahe and the thousands who died in large part because of religious
misrepresentation. As the long-held binarism East and West is losing hold in
the global view, and as the lexicon of "they" and "we" slowly diminishes, so

does the impulse to misrepresent the Other dishonestly. Perhaps by looking critically at cultural and religious misrepresentation, we can disassociate ourselves from the rhetoric of the "great white hope," the "yellow peril," and such fictions as foreigners who gouge out eyes, remove fetuses, and enchant religious converts with magical pills.

Notes

[1] Letter to Mrs. Peter Taylor, June 8, 1856, reproduced in Ziauddin Sardar, *Orientalism* (Buckingham: Open University Press, 1999), 254.

[2] Letter to William Blackwood, February 4, 1857, in *The George Eliot Letters*, ed. G. S. Haight (New Haven: Yale University Press, 1954), 2:292.

[3] Georges Braque, *Le Jour et la nuit: Cahiers, 1917–52* (Paris: Gallimard, 1988).

[4] In what is probably a conservative estimate, Yan Kejia states that "five bishops, 31 priests and nuns were killed. More [than] 30,000 Chinese Catholics were killed and about three-quarters of the Catholic churches were destroyed. In some places, the church organizations were nearly wiped out." Yan Kejia, *Catholic Church in China*, trans. Chen Shujie (Beijing: China Intercontinental, 2004), 70–71. The original title of the book is *Zhongguo tianzhujiao*. Of course, this estimate does not include Protestant missionaries and converts who died during the Boxer Uprising violence. For a general account of Protestant deaths, see Luella Miner, *China's Book of Martyrs: A Record of Heroic Martyrdoms and Marvelous Deliverances of Chinese Christians during the Summer of 1900* (Cincinnati: Jennings and Pye, 1903); and *Martyred Missionaries of the China Inland Mission with a Record of the Perils and Sufferings of Some Who Escaped*, ed. Marshall Broomhall (London: Morgan and Scott, 1901).

[5] Bret Harte, *The Best of Bret Harte* (Boston: Houghton Mifflin, 1947), 431. There were several popular book series in American homes near the beginning of the twentieth century that perpetuated such representations of the Chinese as Harte's, generally emphasizing the "conniving," "odd," or "un-Christian" idiosyncrasies of their culture. In the first volume of *Our Wonder World*, the Chinese are described in terms typical of the period: "The Chinese are members of the Mongol race. They are well built but rather short, with yellowish, dark complexion, coarse black hair, narrow slanting eyes, short, flat noses, and rather thick lips." *Our Wonder World: A Library of Knowledge in Ten Volumes* (Chicago: Shuman, 1918), 1:331. Before the "Odd Customs" portion of the work's essay, the text describes the Chinese in somewhat commendable, if not condescending, language: "The yellow man has a firmer hold on life than the white. He is wonderfully tough, and able to endure hardship and exposure and to withstand bad conditions more successfully than the Caucasian peoples" (ibid.). However, a later passage describes the Chinese as quick tempered, which "leads to many family quarrels, which they take no pains to hide" (ibid.). Other late-nineteenth- and early-twentieth-century Western histories of China commonly rendered entirely Westcentric accounts of the East, couching their ostensibly charitable descriptions in pejorative terms. See, for example, the 1906 *The Story of the Greatest Nations: From the Dawn of History to the Twentieth Century*. The chapters devoted to China—which comprise volume 8—provide extensive narratives of the Opium Wars and Boxer Uprising, emphasizing the heroism

of Western society and the backwardness of China. *The Story of the Greatest Nations: From the Dawn of History to the Twentieth Century* (New York: Niglutsch, 1906), 8:1345–1424. The most openly unfriendly description of China is found in the multivolume *Outline of Knowledge*, edited by James A. Richards in 1924. In a chapter entitled "The Peculiar Heathen Chinee," by C. Whitney Carpenter Jr., the author suggests that until it emulates the successful Westernization of the Japanese, China will remain backward. Carpenter laments that the Chinese mind-set is sadly anchored in a stagnating reverence for the past, although he praises the "few live men of the present generation who have awakened from their Rip Van Winkle sleep and are trying to pull their brothers out of the past by their pigtails." James A. Richards, ed., *Outline of Knowledge* (New York: J. A. Richards, 1924), 15:119. Among the several unpalatably choice turns of phrase in the short chapter is a note that "The most general bad habit which renders the maximum discomfort to the Occidental is the oriental expectoration" (120).

[6] *Times* (London), July 17, 1900.

[7] I should note here that European incursions into China have been interpreted and disparaged in disparate ways. While the preponderance of Chinese discussions emphasize European religious insinuation, economic and ideological reasons have also precipitated criticism. The propagandist booklet published by Beijing's Foreign Languages Press, *The Yi Ho Tuan Movement of 1900*, quotes a statement by Vladimir Ilyich Lenin (1870–1934), who said, "Yes! It is true the Chinese hate the Europeans, but which Europeans do they hate? The Chinese do not hate the European people, they have never had any quarrel with them—they hate European capitalists and the European governments obedient to them." Vladimir Lenin, "The War in China," in Vladimir Lenin, *Collected Works*, (Moscow: Progress Publishers, [1960], 1972), 4:373. The Chinese booklet that contains this quote ends in rather emotive revolutionary terms, lauding the Boxers for their political resistance and noting, "In the annals of the Chinese nation, the anti-imperialist and anti-feudal exploits of the Yihetuan will always be a lustrous chapter. Long live the anti-revolutionary spirit of the Yihetuan!" *The Yi Ho Tuan Movement of 1900* (Beijing: Foreign Languages Press, 1976), 127–28. Here we see that the Boxer movement, steeped as it originally was in antireligious rhetoric in 1900, has been reinterpreted and re-represented as an anti-imperialist Marxist revolution.

[8] The term *great white hope* commonly refers to the white boxer James J. Jeffries (1875–1953). In 1910 Jeffries came out of retirement to try and defeat the first black world boxing heavyweight champion, Jack Johnson (1878–1946). When Jeffries announced his emergence from retirement, he said, "I am going into this fight for the sole purpose of proving that a white man is better than a negro." See David Remnick, "Struggle for His Soul," *Observer*, November 2, 2003. While the crowd in Reno, Nevada, yelled "Kill the nigger," Jeffries was knocked out by Johnson in the fifteenth round.

[9] Edward Said, *Orientalism* (New York: Vintage, 1979), 204.

[10] John Dower, *War without Mercy: Race and Power in the Pacific War* (New York: Pantheon, 1986), 9.

[11] Ibid.

[12] I should, however, note here that there are several good works relevant to Protestant missions in China, including Archie Crouch, *Rising through the Dust: The Story of the Christian Church in China* (New York: Friendship, 1948); Nat Brandt, *Massacre in Shansi* (Syracuse: Syracuse University Press, 1994); Luo Weihong, *Christianity in China*, trans. Zhu Chengming (Beijing: China Intercontinental Press, 2004); R. A. Bosshardt, *The Restraining Hand: Captivity for Christ in China* (London: Hodder and Stoughton, 1936); Arthur Smith, *The Uplift of China* (New York: Educational Department of the Board of Foreign Missions of the Presbyterian Church in the U.S.A., 1907); and Jane Hunter, *The Gospel of Gentility: American Women Missionaries in Turn-of-the-Century China* (New Haven: Yale University Press, 1984).

[13] The song appears in Wang Minglun, ed., *Fan yangjiao shuwen jietie xuan* (Selections of Anti-foreign Religion Books and Placards) (Jinan: Qi lu shushe, 1984), and is translated in *Renditions* 53–54 (spring–autumn 2000): 251–52.

[14] There are several good studies regarding the thorny problem of translating Christian terms and ideas into Chinese characters. See, for example, Walter Medhurst, *A Dissertation on the Theology of the Chinese with a View to the Elucidation of the Most Appropriate Term for Expressing the Deity, in the Chinese Language* (Shanghai: Mission Press, 1847). Also see Walter Medhurst, *An Inquiry into the Proper Mode of Rendering the Word God in Translating the Sacred Scriptures into the Chinese Language* (Shanghai: Mission Press, 1848); Walter Medhurst, *Of the Word Shin, as Exhibited in the Quotations Adduced under That Word, in the Chinese Imperial Thesaurus, Called the Pei-Wan-Yun-Foo* (Shanghai: Mission Press, 1849); and Douglas G. Spelman, "Christianity in Chinese: The Protestant Term Question," Papers on China, no. 22A (Cambridge: Harvard University Press, 1969). The question of which Chinese character best matches Christian terms and ideas was in the end less a Jesuit dilemma than a Protestant one. For this issue, see Norman J. Girardot, *The Victorian Translation of China: James Legge's Oriental Pilgrimage* (Berkeley: University of California Press, 2002). Also, for a somewhat polemical discussion of the "term question," see Bertram Wolferstan, *The Catholic Church in China from 1860 to 1907* (London: Sands, 1909), especially chapter 2. In addition to these texts, there are other useful general works on Jesuits in China, including Andrew C. Ross, *A Vision Betrayed: The Jesuits in Japan and China, 1542–1742* (Edinburgh: Edinburgh University Press, 1994); David E. Mungello, *Curious Land: Jesuit Accommodation and the Origins of Sinology* (Honolulu: University of Hawai'i Press, 1989); M. Howard Rienstra, ed., *Jesuit Letters from China, 1583–84,*

(Minneapolis: University of Minnesota Press, 1986); George H. Dunne, *Generation of Giants: The Story of the Jesuits in China in the Last Decades of the Ming Dynasty* (London: Burns and Oats, 1962); and Thomas F. Ryan, *Jesuhui shi zai zhongguo*, trans. Tao Weiyi (Taizhong: Guangqi chubanshe, 1965).

[15] The translation of this line is somewhat awkward if not slightly incorrect. The graphs *yanwang* 閻王 denote the "King of Hell." Thus, the line recommends its hearer to beware of the Catholic missionaries who will remove your internal organs and send you forthwith to an audience with the ruler of Hell. The graph 閻 literally means "a village gate" or the "gate of a lane," and 王 means "king," thus, the "king of the gate." In Buddhist parlance he is referred to as the 閻魔大王, the "great demon king of the gate." This guardian of Hell's gate is also called 琰魔 and 閻羅.

[16] Excrement is traditionally held in China to be a useful agent in exorcisms.

[17] With a few minor changes, I have followed Eva Hung and Tam Pak Shan, trans. "Anti-Christian Propaganda" by anonymous authors, in *Renditions: Chinese Impressions of the West*. No. 53–54 (spring–autumn 2000), 251–52.

[18] Ibid., 250. Another example of an anti-Western ditty is *"Waiguo yangren tan shi sheng"* (The Westerner's Ten Lamenting Sighs). This short verse was procured by Arnold Jacques Antoine Vissière (1858–1930) while living in Beijing and Shanghai at the French embassy and consulate from 1882 to 1899. He purchased the song as part of a Chinese chapbook. It reads, "The foreign devil preached his faith and heaved his sixth sigh, a host of Chinese converts were his desire. But the Chinese people's wits, you see, are of the finest rate, don't be hawking nursery rhymes outside Confucius' gate." Ian Chapman, trans. "The Westerner's Ten Laments: Excerpts," by an anonymous author in *Renditions: Chinese Impressions of the West*. No 53–54 (spring–autumn 2000), 248. Religion, as can be seen here, is one of the most emphatically expressed themes in antiforeign literature and songs of the late nineteenth century. One might also note that balladry in China has remained a popular form of criticism from early antiquity, even if at times it has been highly circuitous. A good study of the early uses of ballads as a source of criticism and a way to gain access to popular sentiment is Anne Birrell, *Popular Songs and Ballads of Han China* (Honolulu: University of Hawai'i Press, 1988). While Birrell's study focuses on the Han dynasty Music Bureau (*yuefu*) ballads, her discussion carries relevance into the present era.

[19] Paul A. Cohen, *China and Christianity: The Missionary Movement and the Growth of Chinese Antiforeignism, 1860–1870* (Cambridge: Harvard University Press, 1963), 45.

[20] Ian Chapman, "Introductory Note," in *Renditions: Chinese Interpretations of the West*. No. 53–54 (spring–autumn 2000), 14–15.

[21] Tam Pak Shan, trans. "Selections from *An Illustrated World Geography*" by Wei Yuan, in *Renditions: Chinese Interpretations of the West*. No. 53–54 (Spring and Autumn 2000), 14–15.

[22] Ibid.

[23] Ibid.

[24] Ibid.

[25] There are understandable antecedents to the belief that priests removed the eyes of dying Catholics while administering Extreme Unction. During the traditional rite of Holy Unction the priest arrived at the home of the dying with the Blessed Sacrament, and all Catholic faithful were expected to kneel as a sign of reverence. After the priest's arrival he would normally hear the final confession of the dying person, a practice that for obvious reasons required privacy, something quite suspect in Chinese sensibilities, especially when it involved a woman. Finally, the priest would take holy oil and anoint the closed eyes, the ears, the nostrils, the closed mouth, the hands, and perhaps even the feet. Rumor of this ritual had clearly evolved into odd accounts of eye removal and so forth. Of course the prayers would have been intoned in Latin, adding to the "magical" appearance of the ceremony.

[26] While the Hunan *Bixie jishi* may have been the most extensive treatise against Christianity, a later work by a Marxist supporter of Sun Yatsen (1866–1925), Zhu Zhixin, includes an almost equally offensive tract entitled "Yesu shi sheme dongxi?" (What Kind of Thing Is Jesus?) in 1919. See Jessie Gregory Lutz, *Chinese Politics and Christian Missions: The Anti-Christian Movements of 1920–28* (Notre Dame: Cross Cultural Publications, 1988), 19. Lutz notes, "While the *Bixie jishi* concentrates on the activities and teachings of the evangelist within the Chinese context, Zhu adds details on the role of the church in Western history and the textual criticisms of Western scholars. The nineteenth-century document denigrates Christianity with scatological accounts of church rituals, while the twentieth-century article scoffs at the validity of the Gospels and the virtue of Jesus" (19).

[27] Quoted in Cohen, *China and Christianity*, 49.

[28] Henry Blodget to N. G. Clark, October 24, 1870, quoted in John K. Fairbank, "Patterns behind the Tientsin Massacre," *Harvard Journal of Asiatic Studies* 20, no. 3–4 (1957): 480–511.

[29] Quoted in Cohen, *China and Christianity*, 51.

[30] Quoted in ibid., 51, text accompanying the fourth image. Several of the graphs are unclear; I have thus marked them with square blocks. I might note here that native Chinese reactions to the Crucifixion were almost universally negative. The

Jesuit missionary Johann Adam Schall von Bell presented a volume of forty-eight woodblock images of the life of Christ to the Ming emperor, Chongzhen (r. 1628–44), in 1640, and among them was a depiction of the Crucifixion. As this image became more widely seen, pejorative descriptions of it began to appear. For example, the Confucian official Yang Guangxian (1597–1669) produced a caustic anti-Christian booklet entitled, *Budeyi* (I Cannot Contain Myself) wherein Christ's Crucifixion is presented as a criminal act of subversion and rebellion. As David Mungello puts it, "In Yang's view, Jesus was an outlaw who deserved denunciation rather than a divine figure worthy of reverence." David E. Mungello, *The Forgotten Christians of Hangzhou* (Honolulu: University of Hawai'i Press, 1994), 86. Mungello has also included images of Schall's print of Christ's Crucifixion, which was also used in Yang's *Budeyi*. In his comments on the image of Christ crucified, Yang writes, "The pictures depict how Jesus was nailed to death by law. These pictures would make all people in the world know that Jesus was put to death as a convicted criminal, so that not only would scholar-officials not write prefaces for their [Christian] writings, but people of the lower classes would also be ashamed to believe in that kind of faith." Translated in Gianni Criveller, *Preaching Christ in Late Ming China: The Jesuits' Presentations of Christ from Matteo Ricci to Guilio Aleni* (Taipei: Taipei Ricci Institute, 1997), 393. Other anti-Christian works dating to the late Ming are may be found in the same work. Also see Anthony E. Clark, "Early Modern Chinese Reactions to Western Missionary Iconography," *Southeast Review of Asian Studies* 30 (2008): 5–22.

[31] The putative author of the *Xiyou ji* is Wu Cheng'en (ca. 1506–82). The pig character in the story, called "Pigsy" in Arthur Waley's excellent abridged translation, bears striking similarities to the crucified "pig" in the *Bixie jishi*. Zhu Bajie was originally a great commander in Heaven of over one hundred thousand heavenly troops, but he got himself into trouble with the Jade Emperor by making drunken advances toward the Goddess of the Moon while at a party. The emperor accordingly banished him from Heaven to earth, where he was born of a mother pig, assuming the two-part body of a pig and a man. In general, the story's narrative of Zhu Bajie is one of lustful improprieties. A good Chinese recension of the novel is Wu Cheng'en, *Xiyou ji* (Taipei: Sanmin shuju, 2003).

[32] Quoted in Cohen, p. 140, text accompanying the sixth image.

[33] Mengzi, *Mengzi yizhu*, commentator Yang Bojun (Taipei: Wu nan tushu chuban, 1981), 245. It was considered unfilial to prevent oneself or others from having descendants, but it is similarly unfilial to harm the body at all, as according to Confucian sensibilities the body is not one's own but the property of one's parents, from whom it was received. In the *Xiaojing* (Classic of Filial Piety), which includes an ostensible dialogue between Confucius and his disciple, Zengzi, Confucius asserts, "Now, filial piety is the root of virtue and the origin of education." *Xiaojing baihua*

zhuyi (Taipei: Guanzhong yan xie he, 1959), 2. Having established filial piety as the "root of virtue," Confucius continues, "One's body, hair, and skin are received from his father and mother, and so he would not dare [allow] his body to be harmed. This is the beginning of filial piety" (2). The rumor that missionaries were removing fetuses from pregnant women was, *first*, unfilial because it prevented them from having offspring and, *second*, unfilial because it harmed the rightful property of the other person's parents and was thus a type of usurpation. Add to this the fact that Catholic priests were celibate and had no offspring.

[34] Quoted in Cohen, *China and Christianity*, seventh image after page 140.

[35] Joseph Esherick, *The Origins of the Boxer Uprising* (Berkeley: University of California Press, 1987), 253.

[36] The Chinese "official" Catholic Church is the Chinese Patriotic Catholic Association, sometimes abbreviated as CPA, CPCA, or CCPA, a state-controlled religious association under the auspices of the People's Republic of China's Religious Affairs Bureau. Pope Pius XII (1876–1958) excommunicated any bishop who allied himself with the CPA because by doing so he declared formal autonomy from Roman pontiff. For a succinct description of the circumstances surrounding China's relationship with the Vatican through its shift to a communist state, see Richard Madsen, *China's Catholics: Tragedy and Hope in an Emerging Society* (Berkeley: University of California Press, 1998). For a more exhaustive consideration, see Sha Baili, *Zhongguo jidutu shi* (Taipei: Guangqi wenhua shiye, 2005).

[37] *People's Daily*, September 26, 2000.

[38] *People's Daily*, October 1, 2000.

[39] *Xinhua News Agency*, October 2, 2000. It should be noted that the same people who were claimed by the *People's Daily* to have raped and exploited the native Chinese, Chapdelaine, Capillas, and Crescitelli, had already been beatified in large public celebrations at the Vatican in Rome without a single comment from the Chinese authorities. Saint Chapdelaine was beatified by Pope Leo XIII on May 27, 1900; Saint Capillas was beatified by Pope Pius X on May 2, 1909; and Saint Crescitelli was beatified by Pope Pius XII on February 11, 1951. It is indeed suspicious that the Chinese media should react so vehemently in 2000 while relations with the Vatican were already quite strained. For brief hagiographies of these three men, see *The Newly Canonized Martyr-Saints of China* (Taipei: Commission for Canonization of Saints and Martyrs of China, 2000).

[40] Ibid.

[41] Ibid.

[42] *People's Daily*, October 6, 2000.

[43] Ibid.

[44] The term in French is *droit de seigneur* or *droite de cuissage*. An excellent study of this medieval mythos is Alain Boureau's *The Lord's First Night: The Myth of the Droite de Cuissage*, trans. Lydia G. Cochrane (Chicago: University of Chicago Press, 1995). While Boureau's monograph centers almost exclusively on France, his discussion traces the trope of *jus primae noctis* in both the secular and ecclesial spheres, demonstrating that the popular belief is essentially mythological.

[45] *The Epic of Gilgamesh*, trans. N. K. Sandars (London: Penguin, 1972), 62.

[46] Herodotus, *The Histories*, trans. Aubrey de Sélincourt (Harmondsworth: Penguin, 1983), 167.

[47] Quoted in Séamus MacPhilib, "Jus Primae Noctis and the Sexual Image of Irish Landlords in Folk Tradition and in Contemporary Accounts," *Bealoideas: The Journal of the Folklore of Ireland Society* 56 (1988): 103, n. 29.

[48] See Polo's description of the customs of Tibet in *The Travels of Marco Polo*, trans. Ronald Latham (London: Penguin, 1958), 172. The full text reads, "Here there prevails a marriage custom of which I will tell you. It is such that no man would ever on any account take a virgin to wife. For they say that a woman is worthless unless she has had knowledge of many men." Polo continues to narrate that when travelers pass through their area the guests are encouraged to have intercourse with the local women. He recounts, "So long as they remain, the visitors are free to take their pleasure with the women and use them as they will."

[49] The biographical data on John of Mandeville (also called Sir Jehen de Mandeville) is scant. He is the putative author of a French travelogue called *The Voyage and Travels of Sir John Mandeville, Knight*, published in 1366. The real authorship of the text has been disputed; it is variously attributed to several people. See Josephine Waters Bennett, *The Rediscovery of Sir John Mandeville* (New York: Modern Language Association of America, 1954).

[50] Cohen, *China and Christianity*, 58.

[51] Ibid.

[52] Edmund Burke expresses my point well in his comment, "The greater the power, the more dangerous the abuse." "Speech on the Middlesex Election, [1771]" in Edmund Burke, *Selected Writings and Speeches*, Peter J. Stanlis, ed. Reprint (Washington D.C.: Regnery Publishing, 1997), 363. When a culture such as that of the West wields enormous power, as it did in China, abuses are sometimes contrived by the weak to marshal contempt for the strong. Two recent works discuss the by-products of cultural intrusion/reinterpretation: Geoffrey C. Gunn, *First Globalization: The*

Eurasian Exchange, 1500–1800 (Lanham, MD: Rowman and Littlefield, 2003); and Ros Ballaster, *Fabulous Orients: Fictions of the East in England, 1662–1785* (Oxford: Oxford University Press, 2005).

[53] A *positio* is an official Church document related to one's cause for sainthood. The three documents provided by Guo's order are helpful, although they were written from within the Church structure and so are somewhat apologetic and hagiographical. These works are Mariagrazia Zambon, *Crimson Seeds: Eighteen PIME Martyrs*, trans. Steve Baumbusch (Detroit: PIME World Press, 1997) (see especially pages 33–46); Gianni Criveller, *The Martyrdom of Alberico Crescitelli: Its Context and Controversy* (Hong Kong: Holy Spirit Study Centre, 2004); and Elio Gasperetti, *In God's Hands: The Life of Blessed Ableric Crescitelli of the Missionaries of Saints Peter and Paul, P.I.M.E.* (Detroit: Missionaries of Saints Peter and Paul, PIME, 1955).

[54] The letters Crescitelli wrote to his family in Italy are held at the Pontifical Institute for Foreign Missions (PIME) archives in Rome. I might add here that a large number of these letters express his disdain for the Italian government and its leftist inclinations, thus discounting Chinese accusations that he was an Italian imperialist. The tenor of his correspondence discloses that he was interested in little more than his obligations as a missionary. There exist, however, several somewhat pejorative complaints about Chinese customs in his comments, complaints common in nearly all Western missionary letters posted from China.

[55] The English translation of the *Positio* (official Vatican documents) I have consulted is located in Criveller, *The Martyrdom of Alberico Crescitelli*, 39–42. Criveller's text appears in both English and Chinese.

[56] Ibid.

[57] The original Chinese passage from the *Ningqiang xianzhi* is included in ibid., 36, in the Chinese section of the book. The translation here is my own.

[58] Based on the *Positio* documents held in the Vatican's Secret Archives, Elio Gasperetti narrates the decapitation as follows: "When the time came to deal the final blow, no one stepped forth voluntarily to assume a task so fraught with individual responsibility. The ringleaders therefore selected two brothers who were renowned as a bad lot, got them drunk, and entrusted the work to them. The lethal instrument was a long, single-edged cutting implement with a handle at each end, used by Chinese farmers to cut hay for domestic animals. Rusty and dull, wielded by two tipsy men, the blade bungled its office very badly. Finally the two men fell to using it like a saw." Gasperetti, *In God's Hands*, 64.

[59] Zhang Li and Liu Jiantang, *Zhongguo jiao an shi* (Chengdu: Sichuan sheng shehui kexueyuan chubanshe, 1989), 555–57.

[60] Criveller, *The Martyrdom of Alberico Crescitelli*, 35. Criveller's case in favor of exonerating Crescitelli is based on a somewhat complex account of an antagonism between him and a village elder named Teng Shangxian, who lived where the missionary was stationed. It appears that since the Catholics did not pay the local temple tax, Teng refused to give them the government-issued food charities during a 1900 famine. Crescitelli complained to the local mandarin, who required Teng to release the charities and incur a loss of public face. Criveller's premise, then, is that Teng and his cohorts both plotted to murder Crescitelli and perhaps contrived fictions about the priest forcing young virgins to have intercourse with him to mitigate the charges against Teng. Criveller writes, "Teng was preparing to organize his revenge. He contacted members of the secret society called 'The Nail' to kill Crescitelli" (32). Also see Jean Charbonnier, *Les 120 martyrs de chine: Cononisés le 1er Octobre 2000* (Paris: Églises d'Asie, 2000), 194–201.

[61] Two short works on Ricci and Schall von Bell offer a quick sketch of their lives: Zhang Fengzhen, *Tang Ruowang yu zhongguo* (Tainan: Wen dao chubanshe, 1992); and Vincent Cronin, *Li Madou zhuan*, trans. Si Guo (Taizhong: Guangqi chubanshe, 1982).

[62] Robert E. Entenmann, "Christian Virgins in Eighteenth-Century Sichuan," in *Christianity in China: From the Eighteenth Century to the Present*, ed. Daniel H. Hayes (Stanford: Stanford University Press, 1996), 183. The White Lotus Sect was a Buddhist society that worshipped the Eternal Mother. Its adherents believed that there would be an advent of the Buddha Maitreya. Jonathan Spence writes, "In 1774 Chinese rebels under the leadership of a martial arts and herbal-healing expert named Wang Lun rose up against the Qing, invoking the support of an 'Eternal Venerable Mother' goddess." Jonathan Spence, *The Search for Modern China*, 2nd ed. (New York: Norton, 1999), 112. It was, of course, conspicuous that both the White Lotus rebels and the Catholic missionaries venerated a woman who was referred to as a mother. One of the Catholic Chinese names for Mary employed during the Boxer Uprising era was Sheng Mu or "Holy Mother."

[63] Quoted in André Ly, *Journal d'André Ly, prêtre chinoise, missionaire et notaire apostolique, 1747–1763*, ed. Adrien Launey (Paris: Picard, 1906), 12.

[64] Translated in Cohen, *China and Christianity*, sixth image after page 140.

[65] While most scholars presently hold that the *jus primae noctis* trope is mythological, Alain Boureau is not prepared to completely relegate the idea to the realm of fantasy. For him, the most important question is how the legend has left its mark on the modern imagination of the Middle Ages, noting that, "real or imaginary, the *droite de cuissage* had been brandished as a proof of the social ignominy of feudalism" (*The Lord's First Night*, 4).

[66] For the appearance of the word *rape* as a metaphor for colonialism, albeit one nuanced slightly differently than I am suggesting here, see Sara Suleri, *The Rhetoric of English India* (Chicago: University of Chicago Press, 1992). The word is indeed often used as a metaphor, for example in "the rape of Iraq" or "the rape of Nanjing."

[67] Quoted in Cohen, *China and Christianity*, fifth image after page 140.

[68] *Quanfei jiliie* (Shanghai: Shangyang shuju, 1903). A study by Chester Tan includes a bibliographic entry for similarly named text: Sawara Tokusuke and Ouyin, *Quanfei jishi*, 6 vols. (N.p., 1901). See Chester C. Tan, *The Boxer Catastrophe* (New York: Norton, 1971), 250.

[69] Paul Cohen, *History in Three Keys: The Boxers as Event, Experience, and Myth* (New York: Columbia University Press, 1997), 41. Also see *Quanfei jiliie.*

[70] See, for example, Tan, *The Boxer Catastrophe*; Frederic A. Sharf and Peter Harrington, *China 1900: The Eyewitnesses Speak* (London: Greenhill, 2000); Henry Keown-Boyd, *The Boxer Rebellion* (New York: Dorset, 1991); and Diana Preston, *The Boxer Rebellion: The Dramatic Story of China's War on Foreigners That Shook the World in the Summer of 1900* (New York: Walker, 1999). One must look to books by presses sympathetic to Christian missions in China for more than cursory considerations of the Christian slaughters during the Boxer Uprising. See for example, Pierre-Xavier Mertens, *La légende dorée en chine: Scènes de la vie de mission au Tchely Sud-Est* (Paris: Editions Spes, 1926); Pierre-Xavier Mertens, *The Yellow River Runs Red: A Story of Modern Chinese Martyrs*, trans. Beryl Pearson (London: Herder, 1939); M. T. de Blarer, *La bienheureuse Marie Hermine de Jésus et ses compagnes* (Vanves, France: Franciscaines Missionaires de Marie, 1947); G. de Montgesty, *Two Vincentian Martyrs*, trans. Florence Gilmore (New York: Catholic Foreign Missionary Society of America, 1925); Nat Brandt, *Massacre in Shansi* (Syracuse: Syracuse University Press, 1994); and *Les 120 Martyrs de Chine: Canonisés le 1er octobre 2000,* Études et Documents, no. 12 (Paris: Églises d'Asia, 2000), to name a few. For what appears to be the most exhaustive study of the Boxer Uprising, though with scant objective commentary on the Christian massacres, see *Yihetuan*, 4 vols., ed. Zhongguo shi xue hui (Shanghai: Shanghai renmin chubanshe, 1957).

[71] In earlier notes I have mentioned available Protestant and Catholic monographs on the martyrs of their denominations. Similar histories by Eastern Orthodox writers are scant. One interesting work that provides a brief sketch of the Eastern Orthodox experience in China during the Boxer Uprising is Hiermonk Damascene's *Christ the Eternal Dao* (Platina, CA: Valaam, 1999) (see especially pages 431–32).

[72] Mertens, *The Yellow River Runs Red*, 34–35.

[73] In this vein, Joseph Esherick states, "Any search for the social origins of the Boxer movement must include an inquiry into the impact of foreign economic penetration into China. . . . But as will soon become clear, the initial and primary target of the Boxer movement was not foreign economic imperialism, but the 'foreign religion'—the missionaries and their Chinese converts" (*The Origins of the Boxer Uprising*, 68). Paul Cohen, however, downplays the religious motivations of the Boxer movement, emphasizing rather the anxieties precipitated by the drought and starvation that plagued the areas with active Boxer societies. He quotes Lin Dunkui, who asserts, "From the time of the first outbreak of the Big Sword Society [proto-Boxers] right up to the high tide of the Boxer movement, a sizable number of peasants were prompted to take part in these movements mainly by the weather" (Cohen, *History in Three Keys*, 79). The Chinese scholar, Dai Xuanzhi, in his monograph *Yihetuan yanjiu* (Research on the Society of Righteous Harmony), also notes the influence of natural disasters on the local peasants who joined Boxer bands to avoid starvation. See his chapter "Tianzai de yingxiang," in *Yihetuan yanjiu* (Taipei: Wenhua chubanshe, 1963), 56–57.

[74] Cohen, *History in Three Keys*, 50, n. 11.

[75] See ibid., 37–38.

[76] Ibid., 51.

[77] See *Four Jesuits Martyred in China in the 20th Century* (Taipei: Commission for Canonization of Saints and Martyrs of China, 2000), 16.

[78] Ibid. Photographic images of the original church taken immediately after the massacre and the gruesome sight of the human bones in its interior are preserved in *Chine et ceylan: Letters des missionaries de la compagnie de Jésus* (Abbeville: Paillart, 1901) (see especially pages 105 and 109). A copy of this small booklet is presently held in the theological library of Fujen (Furen) University, Taipei, Taiwan.

[79] See Cohen, *History in Three Keys*, 53; and Esherick, *The Origins of the Boxer Uprising*, 307.

[80] Cohen, *History in Three Keys*, 133. A good photograph of Favier illustrating his large presence can be seen in *Jiu zhongguo lüeying, 1868–1945*, ed. Chen Yong (Beijing: Zhongguo hua bao chubanshe, 2006), 43. Casserly calls Bishop Favier "a splendid specimen of the Church Militant." G. Casserly, *The Land of the Boxers* (London: Longman, Green, 1903), 99. The trope of menstrual blood as an object of disdain or magic is widely attested in Chinese mythology. I have already mentioned the rumor that foreigners stank due to the drinking of menses, and Paul Cohen discusses popular ideas regarding menstrual fluids as a form of "female pollution." One of the methods of counteracting the perceived pollution of Western magic and religion was to employ the aid of young premarried and premenstrual virgins, called the "Red Lanterns,"

in their fight against foreigners. Cohen writes, "In an environment in which the paramount danger was thought to derive from female pollution, the Red Lanterns, unexposed to the sexual and childbirth defilement resulting from marriage and, in the nutritional conditions of the time, very likely in many instances even premenstrual, were, relatively speaking, pollution-free" (*History in Three Keys*, 143).

[81] See Cohen, *History in Three Keys*, 132.

[82] Ibid., 297.

[83] Dower, *War without Mercy*, 316.

[84] See Jacques Gernet, *China and the Christian Impact: A Conflict of Cultures*, trans. Janet Lloyd (Cambridge: Cambridge University Press, 1985), originally published in Paris under the title *Chine at christianisme* by Editions Gallimard in 1982.

[85] Jacques Derrida, *Writing and Difference* (Chicago: University of Chicago Press, 1978), 278.

[86] Michel de Montaigne, *The Complete Essays*. Michael Andrew Screech, trans. and ed., Pengiun Classics series. Reprint. (New York: Pengiun Classics, 1993), 1212.

3

In Search of a Chinese Picturesque

William Alexander, George Chinnery, and the Visual Image of China in Nineteenth-Century Britain

Catherine Pagani

Beginning in the late eighteenth century, British artists traveled to the "East" both for a source of income (good money was to be made in portraiture, for example) and as inspiration for a new vogue in painting, known as the picturesque, that featured romanticized and idealized views. India was particularly popular, attracting such acclaimed artists as Tilly Kettle (1734–86), John Zoffany (1733–1810), Arthur Devis (1712–87), John Smart (1740–1811), Ozias Humphry (1742–1811), William Hodges (1744–97), Thomas Daniell (1749–1840), and William Daniell (1769–1837).[1] It was not long before artists turned to China, a subject of great interest to the British, and whose foreign residents in South China offered opportunities for well-paying commissions.

Western artists had been present in China since the late sixteenth century with the arrival of the Jesuit missionaries; however, these artists were largely restricted to working for the Chinese court. In the late eighteenth century, other European painters began to travel to China, specifically to the southern port cities of Canton (Guangzhou) and Macao (then a Portuguese territory), which were made popular and accessible by the growing East-West trade. The most noteworthy of these were the British artists William Alexander (1767–1816) and George Chinnery (1774–1852), whose careers took them to China in the late eighteenth to mid-nineteenth centuries. Alexander visited China for a brief period as part of the well-known Macartney embassy of 1792–94, and Chinnery was a long-term resident of Macao and Canton from 1825 until his death in 1852. Their talents and prolific output captured intimate views of China at a time when interest in this empire was growing. They were, in a sense, image makers, and through their use of the picturesque they played a central role in helping to create a Western vision of China that helped fabricate what the Scottish botanist, Robert Fortune (1813–80), would later refer to as an "enchanted fairy-land."[2] This lasting image was the legacy of their manipulation of the imperial picturesque (fig. 3.1).

Fig. 3.1. George Chinnery (1772-1852), "The Praya Grande, Macau," 1825-52, oil on canvas, 26.7 × 45.7 cm. (Hong Kong Museum of Art Collection.)

The picturesque developed into a central aesthetic concept in late-eighteenth-century Britain and was applied to depictions of nature, be it in painting, literature, or the form of garden design. It represented a radical redefinition of taste from the objective rationality of the Enlightenment to the more instinctual and subjective sensibilities of the romantic period and was designed to challenge the prevailing preference for the formal proportions and symmetry seen in works influenced by classical antiquity.

The picturesque—along with the beautiful and the sublime—formed the three core aesthetic ideals of romanticism and was first introduced into the mainstream by William Gilpin (1724–1804) in *An Essay on Prints* (1768). For him, the picturesque was "a term expressive of that peculiar kind of beauty, which is agreeable in a picture."[3] In a later work, *Three Essays: On Picturesque Beauty, On Picturesque Travel, and On Sketching Landscape—to Which Is Added a Poem, On Landscape Painting* (1792),[4] Gilpin further refined his theory in response to Edmund Burke's *A Philosophical Enquiry into the Origins of Our Ideas of the Sublime and Beautiful with an Introductory Discourse Concerning Taste* (1757), which categorized the aesthetic experience as belonging to either the sublime or the beautiful. The sublime, according to Burke, was vast, rugged, dark, gloomy, massive, and violent, while the beautiful was small, smooth, light, delicate, and serene. One was "founded on pain, the other on pleasure."[5] Gilpin felt that there needed to be a third category, one in which beauty came not from natural perfection (Burke's "smoothness") but from a roughness, irregularity, and sudden variation imparted by the artist, for those elements that make a "scene beautiful in nature do not necessarily make it pleasing as a painting."[6] This roughness could come in the form of broken lines, contrasts of light and dark, rough coloring of natural elements such as stones or mountains, a richness of surface texture, the depiction of ruins and rural areas, and "a free, bold touch" that united varied objects in a harmonious whole.[7] Although difficult to define, the term came to be applied to objects (particularly landscapes) that could be depicted in a painting or to a work that had the "great power of pleasure" for the viewer.[8]

By the end of the eighteenth century, the picturesque was a familiar and well-established style of landscape painting and was employed by artists that included the great British landscape painter, J. M. W. Turner (1775–1851). With its emphasis on nonclassical subjects, the picturesque provided an aesthetic environment in which images of far-off and unknown lands could coexist comfortably with depictions of rural Britain. The "Chinese picturesque" pioneered by Alexander and Chinnery catered to two competing British notions concerning the Chinese. First, romanticized views of the Chinese people and landscape conveniently conformed to an earlier mid-eighteenth-century concept of China as an ideal society whose government, philosophy and literature, for example, were to be admired if not emulated. These images provided the perfect visual accompaniment to such ideas. Second, through the use of familiar materials, techniques, and style, Alexander and Chinnery created a China that, though far-off and unknown, was not entirely alien to Western eyes. With the notable exceptions of costume and architectural details, their vision of China differed very little from depictions of "home." China was thus fashioned into an image that appealed to the colonialist imagination: it was distant and exotic, yet it retained a certain familiarity. Like India, China could be contained within the reassuring framework of the picturesque and thus could easily be imagined as a fitting extension of the British Empire, although in the end this turned out to be only wishful thinking.[9]

Visual culture can add much to our understanding of the complex issues of power associated with colonialism and empire and has been the subject of a number of recent studies, including Geoff Quilley and Kay Dian Kriz's edited volume *An Economy of Colour: Visual Culture and the Atlantic World, 1660–1830* (2003), Beth Fowkes Tobin's *Picturing Imperial Power* (1999), and John MacKenzie's *Orientalism: History, Theory, and the Arts* (1995).[10] Read within their colonialist/imperialist context, visual images document not absolute likenesses—that it to say, the "real"—but rather the representation, however subtle, of the differences between colonizer and colonized.[11] Landscape, in particular, can serve as a means of exploring the discourses of imperialism. It has been called "an instrument of cultural power" through which "social and subjective identities are formed,"[12] and it has played a significant role in the representation of national identity.[13] Landscape functions like text: it has a semiotic meaning that can be read and interpreted within its particular cultural milieu.[14]

The period of the late eighteenth and early nineteenth centuries was particularly important in the history of Sino-British relations, marked by growing trade tensions and cross-cultural misunderstandings that would culminate in the Opium War of 1839–42. China held a unique position within the British colonial world. Unlike India, where a large proportion of territory was under British control, China never became a colony and the British were unable to gain a lasting foothold. (In fact, the Chinese limited British mercantile activities to a designated area in the southern Chinese port city of Canton.) However, because China was crucially implicated in imperial trade, the overall attitudes were imperialist in nature.

The landscapes of William Alexander and George Chinnery, therefore, provide an important means of exploring both British attitudes toward the Chinese and the British concept of China at a time when contact between the two empires was at its height.[15] While Alexander's and Chinnery's sketches, paintings, and engravings may be regarded as visual records of a far-off and little-known land, their significance as sources for understanding colonialist attitudes during this time is much greater. These images functioned within the larger cultural context by contributing to the British vision of China in the first half of the nineteenth century. In their picturesque depictions, these artists presented a China of the British colonialist imagination that had little connection to political or economic realities. This romanticized imperial image represented visually a land that the British had hoped to dominate through trade.

However, while both Alexander and Chinnery exoticized and romanticized the East, they did so in significantly different ways and with markedly different results. Alexander's detailed watercolors were influenced by his career as a military draftsman, while Chinnery's developed a delicate picturesque style that owed much to his formal training under Sir Joshua Reynolds (1723–92). Although Alexander was never as highly regarded as for his artistic skill as Chinnery was (to date there has been only one exhibition devoted solely to Alexander's works), it was his observant eye and strong sense of design that ensured his images a surprising longevity—albeit anonymous—that continued well into the nineteenth century. The demands of art and those of empire do not always run parallel, and the trajectory of these two artists' careers tells us a great deal about both.

William Alexander

In 1796, William Alexander exhibited a selection of his recent watercolors at the Royal Academy. Just two years earlier, Alexander had returned from China as the draftsman for the well-known embassy under Lord Macartney (1737–1806), and his paintings were based on his own sketches. This association would have increased interest in Alexander's work: here he offered a firsthand visual account of an unknown and exotic nation with which Britain had been trading and which had received extensive coverage in the popular press.

It was, however, a difficult artistic sell as not all of the associations with the embassy were positive. This was the first embassy sent by Great Britain to reach the Chinese court. George Macartney was sent to China in September 1792 (arriving in China in 1793), charged with negotiating a treaty that would allow a representative to reside at Beijing, increasing the level of trade at Canton and opening new ports for trade.[16] While Macartney was successful in obtaining an audience with the Chinese emperor, the overall results of the embassy were almost nil and were regarded as a national embarrassment. Not only did the embassy not achieve its intended goals, but it did little to change the Qianlong emperor's perception of England as nothing more than a tributary nation that was sending a congratulatory entourage in honor of his eightieth birthday.[17] In the end, Macartney did not reach his goal of increasing trade with the Chinese, further alienating the Chinese ruler during the infamous "kowtow (ketou) incident" when he refused to prostrate himself before the emperor.

The art critic Anthony Pasquin (1761–1818, the pen name of John Williams) referred to the venture as "the puerile embassy to the *Emperor* of *China*; a voyage which was undertaken for the amusement, not improvement, of a *beastly Public*!" Alexander's paintings met with an equally cool reception. Of Alexander's abilities as a painter, Pasquin wrote:

> We have no doubt of the faithfulness with which the objects are represented, but they are so scattered over the surface of every drawing, as to make them appear spotty, and out of harmony. The figures are drawn with more accuracy than is usual in works of this nature: his knowledge of aerial perspective is very limited, and the parts seem to ride upon each other.[18]

Pasquin's remarks suggest why Alexander was never able to secure a position among the great artists of the day and why his watercolors have largely been forgotten. Nonetheless, his "faithfulness" and linear precision made his work ideally suited to engravings. Sir John Barrow (1764–1848), the comptroller of the embassy, noted that "Mr. Alexander drew beautifully and faithfully in water-colours, and omitted nothing that was Chinese, from the human face and figure, down to the humblest plant, and so true were his delineations, that nothing before or since could be compared with them."[19] Barrow illustrated his own published account of the embassy with engravings by Alexander. It was in engraved form that Alexander's images had their greatest public impact.

Little is known about William Alexander's life. He was born in 1767 as one of three sons of a Maidstone coach builder. He moved to London in 1782, where he studied painting under Julius Caesar Ibbetson (1759–1816), and in 1784 he began his studies in the Royal Academy Schools. In 1792, on a recommendation by Ibbetson, he accompanied Lord Macartney's embassy to China as the draftsman, returning to London in 1794. It is clear that the two-year period that Alexander spent as a member of the Macartney embassy was the most significant event in his professional life; it was his first commission, and it provided him with material that he would make use of for the rest of his life. Numerous watercolors were based on these sketches, and between 1795 and 1804 he had occasion to exhibit his work sixteen times at the Royal Academy, with the first thirteen focusing on his watercolors of China.

In 1802, Alexander left London to become the master of landscape drawing at the Royal Military College at Great Marlow, a position first offered to John Constable, who turned it down. Alexander resigned in 1808 to become keeper of prints and drawings at the British Museum. He was already familiar with the museum's collections, having sketched, and then published its Egyptian works of art over the previous six years. Alexander suffered from rheumatic gout, and in 1816 he became ill suddenly and died.

Alexander was not the first choice as draftsman for the embassy, but through a series of circumstances found himself recommended for the position. In 1787, the embassy under Colonel Charles Cathcart, with Ibbetson as the artist, set out for China. Unfortunately, Cathcart died of tuberculosis en route and was buried in Java. Not wishing to make the journey again, Ibbetson recommended that Alexander accompany Macartney in his place, joining the official painter, the Irish artist Thomas Hickey (1741–1824). Although Hickey was paid an annual salary of two hundred pounds, twice that of Alexander, he was apparently a mediocre painter who did very little work.[20] As John Barrow noted in his memoirs, "Mr. Hickey, an indifferent portrait-painter, was a countryman of Lord Macartney, whose portrait he had painted; and being now out of employment, his Lordship, it was said, took him out of compassion; I believe he executed nothing whatever while on the embassy, but in conversation he was a shrewd, clever man."[21]

Alexander, on the other hand, worked diligently, producing sketches of all he saw and recording his observations in his journal. However, neither he nor Hickey appear to have been held in high regard by Macartney. For the crucial audience with the emperor at his summer retreat at Jehol, Macartney chose to leave the artists behind in Beijing, "much to [Alexander's] disgust."[22] Alexander, however, still managed to make convincing drawings of the Jehol palace complex and of the emperor being carried in a palanquin to meet Macartney, obviously based on sketches provided by another member of the embassy.[23] Alexander's general knowledge of the Chinese scene allowed him to produce convincing renditions of this portion of the trip.

After Macartney's failure to open more trade with the Chinese, the embassy left the capital. Macartney's party traveled by land southward. Alexander and some of the others made their way along the Grand Canal to Hangzhou, which was considered a less desirable route, again showing Macartney's overall disinterest in the artists.[24] From there, the party was prevented from making its way to Canton along the inland waterway and instead was sent by ship. Alexander remarked in his journal, "His Excellency saw my sketches &c. & applauded my industry, but I cannot reconcile this with preventing the exercise of my pencil in passing through such an extent of country from hence [Suzhou] to Canton through the interior of the Empire."[25]

Ironically, although Alexander considered this mode of travel a lost opportunity to record the country, his best-known images come from this part of the journey. Many of the depictions had to be done from the deck of the junk as the Chinese gave the party little opportunity to go ashore. Alexander and his group arrived at Canton one week before the rest of the embassy, giving him time to wander about and sketch. In March of 1794, the embassy sailed for England.[26] In September, after six months of traveling, the party arrived at Purfleet.

Alexander's images of China first appeared as engravings in 1797 in Sir George Staunton's (1737–1801) *An Authentic Account of an Embassy from the King of Great Britain to the Emperor of China*. Eight years later, in 1805, Alexander's best-known and most influential work, *The Costume of China*,[27] was published (some illustrations are dated as early as July 20, 1797), and in 1814 his final book, *Picturesque Representations of the Dress and Manners of the Chinese*, appeared.[28] In addition, he left behind over one thousand watercolors and color-wash drawings housed primarily in the India Office Library and the British Museum.[29]

George Chinnery

In 1830, a more sophisticated version of the Chinese picturesque arrived in Britain with the work of George Chinnery, a solid and well-trained painter who had been living in Macao since 1825. Unlike Alexander's diplomatic sojourn, for twenty-seven years Chinnery made his home in Macao, where he "penetrated into the spirit of the Chinese life and scene."[30] His outgoing nature allowed him to establish a wide social circle, and the writings of his contemporaries describe him as a colorful character who was considered to be the best portraitist of the day. Chinnery is known not only for the quality of his work but also for his competence in a variety of media. He was a gifted painter in oils, made fluid sketches in pen and ink, and was a watercolorist of renown. His subject matter included fine portraits as well as landscapes.

Born in London in 1774, Chinnery came from an affluent family and subsequently enjoyed artistic advantages well beyond those of his predecessor, Alexander. Chinnery's father, William, was a "talented amateur painter" and an East India merchant.[31] At the age of seventeen, George exhibited his first portrait at the Royal Academy and the next year entered the Royal Academy Schools. One of his primary teachers was Sir Joshua Reynolds, who had a strong influence on Chinnery. Recognized as a man of great talent by the age of twenty-four, Chinnery by that age had exhibited twenty-one oil paintings at the Royal Academy.[32] In his assessment of Chinnery's paintings exhibited at the Royal Academy in 1794 (two years before Alexander's views of China were first shown), Pasquin wrote, "Among the budding candidates for fame this rising young artist is the most prominent. His progress has been rapid almost beyond example and he has rather adopted a new style of painting, somewhat after the manner of [Richard] Cosway [ca. 1742–1821, a prominent painter of miniatures]."[33] In 1795, Chinnery moved to Dublin and, in 1799, married Marianne Vigne, whom he described as "the ugliest woman I have ever seen."[34] His dislike of her is often cited as the chief reason for his flight to India in 1802, where he lived for the next two decades. India had been brought to prominence just a few years earlier by a group of artists that included John Zoffany and Thomas and William Daniell, whose work in the imperial picturesque style must have been well known to Chinnery and influenced his own depictions of India and China.

The decision to go to India was not a surprising one; not only did Chinnery have connections in Madras through his family, but also it was expected of up-and-coming artists to travel and paint. It was no surprise that Chinnery should choose to travel there as well. However, unlike these other artists, Chinnery stayed in India for an extended period and never returned to England. In his twenty-three years there, he worked as a painter of portraits and landscapes and as a teacher of painting.

After he had been living in India for sixteen years, Chinnery's wife joined him. They had been together for seven years when, in 1825, Chinnery left for Macao without her. This move has led to speculation that Chinnery was escaping from his wife; however, he also owed a substantial amount of money to creditors in India. In his own words, he had to "bolt for China for about £40,000 of debt."[35] In Macao, Chinnery lived comfortably, supporting himself on his portraits in oils, mostly of foreign traders and Chinese merchants who conducted business in Canton, and selling the occasional landscape painting. He is known for his use of color, particularly vermillion, which he ground himself. Five years after arriving in Macao, he sent some of these portraits to the Royal Academy in London, which he continued to do until 1845–56, when he sent his masterwork, a self-portrait painted in 1840.[36]

Chinnery sketched out of doors nearly every day, capturing with his spontaneous, swift strokes the vitality of the Chinese scene. In 1947, Graham Reynolds offered a sensitive appreciation of Chinnery's work, redolent of the imperial habits of viewing.

> He records in the vivacious shorthand of his brisk drawings the inhabitants at their mobile food kitchen, the barber, the smith and the stonemason at work in the street, the Chinese mother and her child. . . . If we spend long looking at the sketch-books in which his Chinese drawings are to be found, we shall know the square dominated by the railings and the church of Santo Domingo as well as it we had lived there ourselves. We shall know also the boat dwellings of the poorer Chinese. Chinnery's technique is perfectly adapted to what he saw: his line reflects equally the roofs of pagodas and the loose clothes, bald heads and wide hats of the Chinese.[37]

Chinnery's output was considerable. He died at the age of seventy-eight in 1852, leaving behind thousands of pen-and-ink sketches, watercolors, and portraits and landscapes in oils.

Chinnery's greatest contribution, however, was seen not in Britain but rather in South China, where he was a teacher of painting. Earlier Western artists in China, such as the Jesuit missionary Giuseppe Castiglione (1688–1766), were largely confined to the court, and their work thus had limited circulation, making their influence on traditional Chinese literati painting minimal. Chinnery was able to teach European methods to his students, and countless other artists learned about Western styles from his students and by copying Chinnery's works. In fact, mention is made of a "School of Chinnery," and paintings of harbor views made from the 1840s through the 1860s by Chinese artists working in the Western idiom have been referred to as "Chinnerys."[38] Artists influenced either directly or indirectly by him include the well-known and very accomplished painter Lamqua (Guan Qiaochang, 1801–60), who in 1835 and 1845 had two paintings accepted for exhibition at the Royal Academy.[39] Guan's "A Chinese Temple by the Pearl River," Guangzhou (fig. 3.2) represents some of the best work that followed the style of Chinnery.

Fig. 3.2. Guan Qiaochang (attributed) (Lamqua, active 1830-50), "A Chinese Temple by the Pearl River, Guangzhou," mid-nineteenth century, oil on canvas, 43.2 × 57.7 cm. (Hong Kong Museum of Art Collection.)

Art and Influence

Although their work featured similar subjects, Alexander and Chinnery created very different visions of China. Four years before his death, Chinnery wrote, "I am not without some hope that I may yet be where Art is known, felt and appreciated."[40] Time seems to have borne this out. He was well regarded during his lifetime, having received a number of important commissions, and modern critics have said that "his finest portraits are quite equal to [those of] the best English masters of the period."[41] He has also been the subject of numerous exhibitions and scholarly studies in recent years.[42] The general opinion concerning Alexander has been less enthusiastic. He is regarded as "not a highly imaginative draughtsman, but he is neat, he strikes us as accurate, and he has a pleasing sense of colour."[43] He has also received far less scholarly attention.[44] However, Alexander's work is worthy of reassessment. The strong graphic design traits of his pictures of China—undoubtedly the result of his training in military draftsmanship—made them better suited to engraving, enabling them to enter popular circulation through their use in a variety of other works. It was Alexander's unacknowledged vision of China that dominated nineteenth-century Britain.

Alexander traveled to China when interest was high owing to British participation in the China trade, which began officially in 1600, when the Honourable East India Company was granted the monopoly for trade with India and China by royal charter. Although tea was the most important commodity, by the late eighteenth century a variety of other goods, including silks and porcelains, were imported as well, although they were not allowed to exceed two percent of the total value of the cargo.[45] This trade favored the Chinese. By the late eighteenth century, Britain was importing around twenty million pounds of tea annually, while the Chinese showed little interest in British goods. The British decided to balance that trade deficit with opium grown in the British-controlled areas of India. Soon opium became the most important commodity traded between the two empires.

British trade with China intensified an existing interest in that country and created a demand among the British for any information about this virtually unknown empire. Articles on Chinese social customs and culture appeared in the popular press alongside accounts of the trade.[46] Work by artists who had spent time in China was particularly sought after as it provided a visual enhancement to the verbal descriptions of this foreign land.[47] By converting his sketches into engravable forms for publication, Alexander ensured that his work would reach its widest possible audience. First utilized in Staunton's enormously successful account of the Macartney embassy (which eventually would see approximately fifteen editions published in eight countries) and followed by his own work, *The Costume of China* (that saw a French edition in 1815), these images were also borrowed and stolen by others. Engraved versions of his watercolors are found in John Barrow's *Travels in China* (1804), D. Bazin de Malpière's *La Chine* (1825), and the *Saturday Magazine* in the 1830s.[48] Thomas Allom (1804–72), who illustrated G. N. Wright's *China in a Series of Views* (1843), also appropriated Alexander's engravings. While Allom claims to have been the original artist for the book's plates, many of them are composites of selected elements taken from Alexander's work and refashioned into a new image. In Allom's "Rice Seller at the Military Station" (fig. 3.3), for example, both the soldier on the left and the tower on the right come from Alexander's "A Soldier of Chu-san" in *The Costume of China* (fig. 3.4). Allom was meticulous in borrowing these larger elements, particularly the soldier's stance, his garments, and his matchlock gun of "the rudest workmanship."[49] But Allom was careful with the smaller details as well, including the sentinel on the tower beating a gong and a number of soldiers in attendance at the base of the structure.

Fig. 3.3. Thomas Allom (1804-72), "Rice Seller at the Military Station."
(G. N. Wright, *China in a Series of Views*, 1843.)

In addition, the popular press used these illustrations in the early 1840s, long after Alexander's death and nearly fifty years after they were initially sketched. It was in this form that Alexander's views of China reached their largest audience. The weekly newspaper *Illustrated London News*, which began publication in May of 1842, made full use of Alexander's images in its reports of British progress in the Opium War that ended in late August of 1842.[50] Their subject matter and attention to detail made them visually appealing, and the fact that Alexander had sketched them while in China gave them added credibility. Most important, their prior publication as engravings in Alexander's books made them readily accessible. Examples include the newspaper's "Military Mandarin," which was copied from Alexander's "Portrait of Van-ta-zhin, a Military Marndarine (or Nobleman) of China"; "Chinese Ship of War" from "A Ship of War"; "Chinese Soldier" (fig. 3.5) from "A Soldier of Chu-san" (fig. 3.4; note that the same tower is included in the background); and "Chinese Merchantmen" from "Three Vessels Lying in Anchor in the River of Ning-po."[51] Unfortunately, Alexander was never given credit for this work.[52]

Alexander's imagery also had what for him would have been an unexpected use in early-nineteenth-century chinoiserie designs. Developed as a result of increased European interest in the East in the seventeenth and eighteenth centuries, the chinoiserie style had very little to do with China per se but rather reflected an idealized and highly decorative concept of the Far East,

Fig. 3.4. William Alexander (1767-1816), "A Soldier of Chu-san." (William Alexander, *The Costume of China*, 1805.)

CHINESE SOLDIER.

Fig. 3.5. "Chinese Soldier." (*Illustrated London News*, July 9, 1842, 132.)

Fig. 3.6. Detail of the mural in the Music Room, Royal Pavilion at Brighton.
(Courtesy of the Royal Pavilion and Museums, Brighton and Hove.)

loosely combining motifs from Chinese, Japanese, and even Indian repertoires. The artistic products of this movement have been described as results of the "European imagination" and "only tangentially based on Chinese designs."[53] While chinoiserie reached its height between 1740 and 1770 and was used to great effect in the design of garden architecture, ceramics, metalwork, interior furnishings, and textiles,[54] it reemerged full force in the interior of the Royal Pavilion at Brighton.[55] This exuberant example of late chinoiserie style was built for George IV (1762–1830), then the Prince of Wales, between 1815 and 1822. The architect, John Nash (1752–1835), adopted a "Hindoo" style for the exterior; Robert Jones designed the Chinese-style interior.

Alexander's influence may be seen in the pavilion's two-dimensional decoration, which borrows heavily from *The Costume of China*. The artists who worked on the hand-painted red and gold murals for the grand and opulent Music Room (considered to be the "dramatic finale of the decorative scheme"

Fig. 3.7. William Alexander (1767-1816), "South Gate of the City of Ting-hai."
(William Alexander, *The Costume of China*, 1805.)

of the Royal Pavilion) were fairly loyal to Alexander's engraving "South Gate of the City of Ting-hai" found in *The Costume of China* (figs. 3.6 and 3.7).[56] Here the mural has retained the overall rooflines—which "curve upwards, and project considerably" according to Alexander's description—as well as the overall architectural details. The tiled hipped and gabled roofs have upturned eaves that appear to be decorated with animals. A placard hangs at a forward-leaning angle above the central gateway draped with a cloth banner.

The figures on the Music Room's hand-painted glass gasolier (fig. 3.8) also owe their design to Alexander's *The Costume of China*, in this case his engraving entitled "A Chinese Comedian," which depicts an "enraged

Fig. 3.8. Detail of hand-painted figures on the gasolier in the Music Room, Royal Pavilion at Brighton. (Courtesy of the Royal Pavilion and Museums, Brighton and Hove.)

Fig. 3.9. William Alexander (1767-1816), "A Chinese Comedian."
(William Alexander, *The Costume of China*, 1805.)

military officer" from a performance of Chinese popular theater given before
Macartney's embassy on December 19, 1793 (fig. 3.9). This image was also
used for the central panel of the south staircase's three-part painted window.

Decorations also take their inspiration from Alexander's illustrations
for Staunton's *Authentic Account* of the Macartney embassy. The ground floor
corridor connecting the two staircases had at one time a design, ca. 1815, for
a skylight that was adapted from an engraving of "Jupiter of the Chinese"
(figs. 3.10 and 3.11). One will never know how Alexander would have felt
about such an appropriation of his work. Nonetheless, such use attests to

both the wider applications of his designs and their availability, and further strengthens his role in the creation of the British image of China in the first half of the nineteenth century.

Fig. 3.10. Early design of a skylight, Royal Pavilion at Brighton.
(Courtesy of the Royal Pavilion and Museums, Brighton and Hove.)

At no other time in the course of East-West interaction would depictions of China, such as those by Chinnery and Alexander, have had such an impact in creating a visual image of China in Britain as they did in the first half of the nineteenth century. But as image makers, they were unequal in their contributions. Chinnery's solid Reynoldsian training and familiarity with the imperial picturesque as it was deployed in India brought him critical acclaim in his Chinese works. His picturesque style even produced a "school" of followers among Chinese painters in South China. However, at this time the picturesque tradition was nearing its end, and as it fell out of fashion so, too, did Chinnery's romanticized views of China. Alexander, on the other hand, inspired no school of followers, but owing to his solid background in draftsmanship and his preoccupation with design and detail, his work had a broader and longer-lasting appeal. His drawings were better suited to engraving and thus were compatible with the Victorian era's interest in good design and craftsmanship. As engravings, his images could be used in diverse and unexpected ways, from illustrations in newspaper articles and picture books on China to the chinoiserie designs of the Royal Pavilion at Brighton. These offer strong evidence in support of the significance of Alexander's images as a primary source of visual information on China. Ultimately, it is Alexander to whom we owe the nineteenth-century British image of China.

Fig. 3.11. William Alexander (1767-1816), "Jupiter of the Chinese." (George Staunton, *An Authentic Account of an Embassy from the King of Great Britain to the Emperor of China*, 1797.)

Notes

[1] Tilly Kettle arrived in Madras in 1769, John Zoffany in 1783, and Arthur Devis in 1785. Thomas and William Daniell were in India and China from 1784 to 1794. William Hodges was the first British professional landscape painter in India, where he stayed from 1780 to 1783. He is the subject of a recent work that examines the aesthetic of the picturesque as it was employed in India, Giles Tillotson, *The Artificial Empire: The Indian Landscapes of William Hodges* (Richmond, U.K.: Curzon, 2000).

[2] Robert Fortune, *Three Years' Wanderings in the Northern Provinces of China, Including a Visit to the Tea, Silk, and Cotton Countries, with an Account of the Agriculture and Horticulture of the Chinese, New Plants, Etc.* (London: John Murray, 1847), 2–5.

[3] William Gilpin, *An Essay on Prints*, 5th ed. (London: Cadel and Davies, 1802), xii.

[4] William Gilpin, *Three Essays: On Picturesque Beauty, On Picturesque Travel, and On Sketching Landscape to Which Is Added a Poem, On Landscape Painting* (London: R. Blamire, 1792).

[5] Edmund Burke, *A Philosophical Enquiry into the Origins of Our Ideas of the Sublime and Beautiful with an Introductory Discourse Concerning Taste* (London: R. and J. Dodsley, 1757), 157–58.

[6] Charles Harrison, Paul Wood, and Jason Gaiger, eds., *Art in Theory, 1648–1815* (Oxford: Blackwell, 2000), 857.

[7] Gilpin, *Three Essays*, "Essay 1: On Picturesque Beauty," 16. Gilpin's ideas were further developed by Richard Payne Knight and Sir Uvedale Prince. For an examination of their discussions on the picturesque, see Stephanie Ross, "The Picturesque: An Eighteenth-Century Debate," *Journal of Aesthetics and Art Criticism* 46, no. 2 (winter 1987): 271–79.

[8] Samuel Johnson and John Walker, *Dictionary of the English Language* (London: William Pickering 1828).

[9] This is not to suggest that Alexander and Chinnery consciously worked in the picturesque style to play to prevailing British sentiments. Simply put, their painting styles were compatible with the changing societal notions of China, first as a kind of intellectual utopia and then as a land to be brought under the control of the British Empire. It is worth repeating as well that even though China was at the periphery of British colonial activities the nature of the attitudes concerning the Chinese can be seen as colonial.

[10] See Geoff Quilley and Kay Dian Kriz, eds., *An Economy of Colour: Visual Culture and the Atlantic World, 1660–1830* (Manchester and New York: Manchester University Press, 2003); Beth Fowkes Tobin, *Picturing Imperial Power* (Durham and London:

Duke University Press, 1999); and John MacKenzie *Orientalism: History, Theory, and the Arts* (Manchester and New York: Manchester University Press, 1995).

[11] Homi K. Bhabha, "Of Mimicry and Man," in *The Location of Culture* (London: Routledge, 1994), 89.

[12] W. J. T. Mitchell, "Introduction," in *Landscape and Power*, ed. W. J. T. Mitchell (Chicago and London: University of Chicago Press, 1994), 1.

[13] See Elizabeth Helsinger, "Turner and the Representation of Britain," in *Landscape and Power*, ed. W. J. T. Mitchell (Chicago and London: University of Chicago Press, 1994), 103–25; and Ann Bermingham, "System, Order, and Abstraction: The Politics of English Landscape Drawing around 1795," in *Landscape and Power*, ed. W. J. T. Mitchell (Chicago and London: University of Chicago Press, 1994), 77–101.

[14] W. J. T. Mitchell states that landscape is not a genre of painting but is a representation of culture that can take the form of painting, film, speech or music, for example. W. J. T. Mitchell, "Imperial Landscape," in *Landscape and Power*, ed. W. J. T. Mitchell (Chicago and London: University of Chicago Press, 1994), 15.

[15] For an examination landscape and colonial representation, see David Bunn, "'Our Wattled Cot': Mercantile and Domestic Space in Thomas Pringle's African Landscapes," in *Landscape and Power*, ed. W. J. T. Mitchell (Chicago and London: University of Chicago Press, 1994), 127–73.

[16] Ultimately, the embassy was unsuccessful. Earl H. Pritchard, in his "Letters from Missionaries at Peking Relating to the Macartney Embassy (1793–1803)," *T'oung Pao* 31 (1935): 1–57, discusses this with reference to letters sent by missionaries in an effort to reconcile the differing accounts of the event by the British and the Chinese.

[17] The emperor's birthday actually fell on September 21, 1790; by the time of Macartney's visit, the emperor was eighty-three years old.

[18] Anthony Pasquin [John Williams], *A Critical Guide to the Exhibition of the Royal Academy, for 1796, in Which All the Works of Merit Are Examined, the Portraits Correctly Named, and the Places of the Various Landscapes: Being an Attempt to Ascertain Truth and Improve the Taste of the Realm* (London: H. D. Symonds, 1796), 27. Pasquin offered a similar opinion on Alexander's contribution to the exhibition of 1797. See Anthony Pasquin [John Williams], *A Critical Guide to the Present Exhibition at the Royal Academy for 1797: Containing Admonitions to the Artists on the Misconception of Theological Subjects and a Complete Development of the Venetian Art of Colouring, as Is Now So Much the Rage of Imitation* (London: H. D. Symonds, 1797), 14–15.

[19] John Barrow, *An Autobiographical Memoir of Sir John Barrow, Bart.* (London: John Murray, 1847), 49, cited in George Macartney, *An Embassy to China: Being the Journal*

Kept by Lord Macartney during his Embassy to the Emperor Ch'ien-lung, 1793–1794, ed. J. L. Cranmer-Byng (London: Longmans, 1962), 345.

[20] It appears he made only two sketches and a thumbnail sketch. Macartney, *An Embassy to China*, 315.

[21] Barrow, *An Autobiographical Memoir of Sir John Barrow*, 49, cited in Macartney, *An Embassy to China*, 345.

[22] Graham Reynolds, "Alexander and Chinnery in China," *Geographical Magazine* 20 (September 1947): 203–11, refers to Alexander's manuscript journal in the British Museum.

[23] The image of the palace complex is often erroneously referred to as the "Potala, the great Lamaist monastery near Jehol." The Potala is in Lhasa, Tibet; at Jehol, the building is based on the Potala and was built in 1767–71.

[24] Alexander's companions included Thomas Hickey; James Dinwiddie, the mechanic for the embassy; William Scott, surgeon to the embassy; and Aenaes Anderson, Macartney's valet.

[25] Reynolds, "Alexander and Chinnery in China," 205.

[26] Coincidentally, the artists Thomas and William Daniell were in same convoy and met Hickey and Alexander.

[27] William Alexander, *The Costume of China Illustrated in Forty-eight Coloured Engravings* (London: William Miller, 1805).

[28] This is considered to be a work of lesser quality for the images are smaller and more crudely executed. This is likely owing to the fact that by this time Alexander was working for the British Museum and was fully engaged in drawing its collection of marble sculptures. *William Alexander: An English Artist in Imperial China* (Brighton: Brighton Borough Council, 1981), 13.

[29] Macartney, *An Embassy to China*, 315–16.

[30] Reynolds, "Alexander and Chinnery in China," 208.

[31] Robin Hutcheon, *Chinnery* (Hong Kong: Form Asia, 1989), 1.

[32] Qu Zhi-ren, "George Chinnery, Painter," *Arts of Asia* (March–April 1971), Vol. 1, no. 2, 34.

[33] Anthony Pasquin [John Williams], *A Liberal Critique on the Present Exhibition of the Royal Academy: Being an Attempt to Correct the National Taste, to Ascertain the State of the Polite Arts at This Period, and to Rescue Merit from Oppression* (London: H. D. Symonds, 1794).

[34] Cited in Hutcheon, *Chinnery*, 2. No source for the quotation is provided.

[35] James Orange, "George Chinnery: Pictures of Macao and Canton," *Studio*, 94, no. 415 (October 1927): 232.

[36] Chinnery painted fourteen self-portraits in forty years.

[37] Reynolds, "Alexander and Chinnery in China," 212.

[38] Referring to these paintings as a group as "Chinnerys" is inaccurate, as Carl Crossman points out. Some artists did follow closely the Chinnery, or English, style in painting harbor views, while others looked to Italian, French, and Dutch painting traditions. The followers of Chinnery and Lamqua painted buildings that were "low and stumpy"—as they actually appeared—rather than the "long, attenuated" style of the other painters of harbor views. Carl L. Crossman, *The Decorative Arts of the China Trade: Paintings, Furnishings, and Exotic Curiosities* (Woodbridge, Suffolk: Antique Collectors' Club, 1991), 96.

[39] For a detailed study of Lamqua (Lam Qua), see ibid., 72–105.

[40] Letter in the collection of the Hongkong and Shanghai Banking Corporation, cited in Qu Zhi-ren, "George Chinnery, Painter," 41.

[41] Orange, "George Chinnery, 234.

[42] The many studies on Chinnery include Henry Berry-Hill and Sidney Berry-Hill, *George Chinnery, 1774–1852* (Leigh-on-Sea: F. Lewis, 1963); Patrick Conner, "George Chinnery and His Contemporaries on the China Coast," *Arts of Asia* 23 no. 3 (May–June 1993): 66–81; Patrick Conner, *George Chinnery, 1774–1852: Artist of India and the China Coast* (Woodbridge, Suffolk: Antique Collectors' Club, 1993); Hutcheon, *Chinnery*; Francis B. Lothrop, *George Chinnery, 1774–1852, and Other Artists of the China Scene* (Salem, MA: Peabody Museum of Salem, 1967); Orange, "George Chinnery"; Richard Ormond, "George Chinnery's Image of Himself," *Connoisseur*, pt. 1, 176, no. 672 (February 1968): 89–93; pt. 2, 167, no. 673 (March 1968): 160–64; and Qu Zhi-ren, "George Chinnery, Painter."

[43] Reynolds, "Alexander and Chinnery in China," 208.

[44] Alexander has been the sole subject of one exhibition and catalog, *William Alexander: An English Artist in Imperial China.*

[45] Many of these goods arrived largely through private commerce carried on by the captains, crewmen, and officials on the company's ships, who were allowed to trade for profit.

[46] For an examination of the role the popular press played in creating an image of China in Britain, see Catherine Pagani, "Objects and the Press: Images of China in

Nineteenth-Century Britain," in *Imperial Co-histories: National Identities and the British and Colonial Press,* ed. Julie F. Codell (Madison and Teaneck, NJ: Fairleigh Dickinson University Press, 2003), 147–66.

[47] There was also a strong interest in Chinese art, particularly in the mid–nineteenth century. See for example, Catherine Pagani, "Chinese Material Culture and British Perceptions of China in the Mid–Nineteenth Century," in *Colonialism and the Object: Empire, Material Culture, and the Museum,* ed. Tim Barringer and Tom Flynn (London and New York: Routledge, 1998), 28–40.

[48] D. Bazin de Malpière, *La Chine, Moeurs, Usages, Costumes, Arts et Metiers, Peines Civiles et Militaires, Cérémonies Religieuses, Monuments, et Paysages* (Paris: Fermin Didot, 1825).

[49] See Alexander, *The Costume of China,* n.p.

[50] Circulation grew rapidly from an initial run of sixty thousand to more than two hundred thousand in less than fifteen years. Harold Herd, *The March of Journalism: The Story of the British Press from 1622 to the Present Day* (London: Allen and Unwin, 1952), 210.

[51] "Military Mandarin" and "Chinese Soldier" appeared in the *Illustrated London News* of July 9, 1842, 132, 133. "Chinese Ship of War" and "Chinese Merchantmen" appeared in the *Illustrated London News* of October 15, 1842, 356, 357.

[52] This was not the only time the newspaper reused images of earlier artists connected with a European embassy to China. Drawings by Jan Nieuhof from a seventeenth-century Dutch embassy under Pieter de Goyer and Jacob de Keyser were of great interest to the public. Images from this embassy appeared in the *Illustrated London News* of 1843. Considering the wealth of material contained in Nieuhof's work, a very small proportion of it was used.

[53] Ellen Paul Denker, *After the Chinese Taste: China's Influence in America, 1730–1930* (Salem, MA: Peabody Museum of Salem, 1985), 5.

[54] The term *chinois* first appeared in the English language as early as 1613 in Samuel Purchas's *Purchas His Pilgrims.* The term *chinoiserie,* referring to a Chinese notion of conduct, appeared much later in an 1883 issue of *Harper's* magazine. *Oxford English Dictionary,* prepared by J. A. Simpson and E. S. C. Weiner (Oxford: Clarendon, 1989).

[55] These were also used by Henry Holland at Carlton House.

[56] Madeleine Jarry, *Chinoiserie: Chinese Influence on European Decorative Art, 17th and 18th Centuries* (New York: Vendome, 1981), 195.

4

China and the Confluence of Cultures

Overcoming the East-West Mind-Set

Lionel M. Jensen

Oh, East is East, and West is West, and never the two shall meet,
Till Earth and Sky stand presently at God's great Judgment Seat;
But there is neither East nor West, Border, nor Breed, nor Birth,
When two strong men stand face to face, tho' they come from the ends of
    the earth.

—Rudyard Kipling, 1890

In a self-conscious era of globalization in which the incessant circulation of goods and peoples threatens to dissolve the very boundaries of the "nation-state," the persistence of the geopolitical category East-West is as curious as it is notable.[1] Max Weber's (1864–1920) bold question about the uniqueness of Western civilization is as good a place as any to start in establishing the evaluative ground on which the East-West dyad stands.

> To what combination of circumstances should the fact be attributed that in Western civilization, and in Western civilization only, cultural phenomena have appeared which (as we like to think) lie in a line of development having universal significance and value? . . . Why did not the scientific, the artistic, the political, or the economic development there [in China and India] enter upon that path of rationalization which is peculiar to the Occident?[2]

The very manner in which Weber's questions are posed opens us to the evaluative force of "Western," as developmentally precedental and thus superior. This is the East-West dichotomy that underwrites the persistent reassertion of a historical superiority in David S. Landes's *The Wealth and Poverty of Nations*, pithily summed up in his description of "the West and the rest," or that assumes a more ominous manifestation in Samuel P. Huntington's "clash of civilizations."[3] All of the chapters in this volume began from a premise at odds with this once common contention, and yet we must be careful not to reoccupy the confines of the same argument by contesting Weber's claim, or

Landes's, by demonstrating that the East was instead superior to the West. Such scholarship of the counterclaim has been produced with great effect in the past decade, particularly in economics, and it has reoccupied the earlier rhetorical frame of admiration of Eastern civilizations found in Friedrich Max Müller's *The Sacred Books of the East* (1879–1910) and Joseph Needham's encyclopedic *Science and Civilization in China* (1954–).

Out of a concern that the cogency of such an approach is undermined by defensiveness and reaction, I prefer to question the usefulness of the East-West dichotomy by looking at specific historical moments when the geocultural division fails to illuminate, as I did in my earlier work, *Manufacturing Confucianism*, and as a number of others have done in the last decade.[4] The arguments of these works succeed by operating against the grain of the common presumption that "East is East and West is West and never the twain shall meet," and from them one learns that this serviceable modification of Rudyard Kipling (1865–1936) is a modernist fallacy, one appropriate to an era we have left behind and one that depended heavily on interpretative tendentiousness.[5] What is disturbing to me in this dismissive reflex is how the din of its announcement at the height of the last century's imperialist experiment in Africa, Asia, and the tropics has deafened us to questions of value and moral commonality, which in our contemporary moment of "globalization" and global wars on terror we very desperately need to ask. It is difficult to understand why this errant cultural geography persists even after the relegation of "oriental civilizations" and "oriental studies" to the margins of scholarly repute.[6] So, for this reason alone, it is necessary to question this framework made from the conceptual artifacts of the Great Encounter (1600–1900), a defining event of the world's modernity, but one that is intelligible only as history not as geography.

East-West remains a keyword in the vocabulary of culture contact perhaps because of its contribution to the language of modern, enlightened selfhood or perhaps because it is the most expedient, but increasingly inaccurate, means of marking the difference between the developed and developing nations of the world. It is worth noting, however, that such judgmental and romantic differentiation of West from East, commonly identified as orientalism, may also be found in the culture of certain developing nations, where an equal and oppositely intense judgmental romance is found in the form of occidentalism.[7] Overcoming this stubborn, antagonistic logic of East-West represents a challenge for Occident and Orient alike.

Rather than exploring the possible reasons for its persistence, I seek in this chapter to reframe this East-West dyad. I suggest that we question our default orientation of the West and shift to an examination of how the categories West and East are used in a Chinese context. Here, too, we find a judgment reminiscent of our West-East habit of mind but in reverse: the West as exotic, the East as known and thus unmarked. In addition, by way of several examples from the twentieth, seventeenth, and twelfth centuries, I will argue that in some cases the view of difference that may be observed in China is not destructive or violent. The point of the particular selection of texts will become evident as I proceed toward a conclusion that urges twenty-first-century citizens to honor the curiosity in the Other, while neutralizing the fear consequent on any encounter with difference. It has been possible in another time and place; it might be possible once again.

East-West in China

This coded geopolitical language of East-West has a history in China as well as in "the West." For the cultural history of the geographic designations of East and West, one need only note that from highest antiquity, the ordinal points of the compass have always been symbolically loaded, even sacred, for Chinese. The *sifang* 四方, or four quadrates, measure the far points of creation and, from the earliest written records of the Shang period, organized the progress and worship of the ruling clan and enabled Shang rulers to chart the rising course of the baleful influences of winds and spirits.[8]

We observe a tendency toward a mythical metageography from early antiquity, such as in Warring States (fifth century BCE) works in which *Dongyi* 東夷, or "Eastern Yi," referred to people southeast of the North China Plain who were identified as culturally inferior. By the Han period, the West was recognized as a region of mysterious majesty and millenarian magic.

In popular mythology, and particularly in millenarian sects, the Kunlun Mountains, the peaks of the Western Paradise in present-day Qinghai, were an incitement to curiosity. These mountains, the purported dwelling place of the Queen Mother of the West (Xiwangmu, 西王母), marked a sacred territory, the *xitu* 西土 (western lands), as the farthest extension of civilization on the border of wilderness.[9] In the popular sixteenth-century novel *Xiyou ji* 西遊記 (*Journey to the West*, more popularly known as *Monkey* courtesy of Arthur Waley's abridged translation), the West is an acclaimed site of pilgrimage, as well as of the picaresque wanderings of folk heroes (real and imagined) in search of religious treasure.

The powerful draw of the West was also attested to in the ethnographies, geographies, random jottings, and travelogues of medieval Chinese scholars, who found there all forms of the marvelous: the beautiful, beastly, and bureaucratic.[10] Recasting the geographic paradigm in this manner from the perspective of another beholder generates a moment of "defamiliarization," as literary critics call it, once we recognize that Chinese curiosity about the West parallels quite nicely with the West's exotic imaginings of the East.

The point of this incomplete catalog is to remind the reader that these entities are not actually geographic so much as figurative; indeed, they are metageographic, which occasions one to ask: where is east and west in relation to me? It must always be in relation to the knower, and it is in this perfectly necessary context that one understands the advantage and limit of the designation. The East and West orientation artificially flattens the actual dimensions of the planet. Treating East and West as culturally definitive and substantively different entities requires us to suspend our scientific understanding of the globe and its constant revolutionary and rotational movement, accepting at the same time the imposition of a two-dimensional grid. As Martin W. Lewis and Kären E. Wigen point out in their critique of metageography, this simply makes no sense.

> [F]rom a planetary perspective, all East-West distinctions are clearly arbitrary. On a rotating sphere, east and west are directional indicators only and can be used to divide the entire planetary surface into distinct regions only if there is an agreed-upon point of reference.[11]

According to our familiar impression, then, the earth, appropriating for a moment the title of Thomas Friedman's popular work, is flat.[12] Of course, it is not flat, but the pull of such two-dimensional apprehension, even in the stark face of geographic fact, is tough to resist.

Tan Sitong 譚嗣同 (1865–98) was arguably one of China's most visionary and radical intellects and one who grasped the vital three-dimensional facts of late-nineteenth-century geography. His concept of *tong* 通 (communication, interconnection, penetration) will set the stage for the body of the chapter and its focus on the Sino-Jesuit interchange of the seventeenth century. The second half of the chapter will focus on cases in which Chinese make fine distinctions among each other and cases in which they embrace others. We'll see protest over such embrace. Some outsiders—European Jesuits—come to be seen as virtually Chinese by some and as animals by others. The distinction, then, between East and West is just another example of the convenient, but sometimes deadly, barriers all peoples erect. In the end, these ruminations should encourage us to interpret the East-West dyad as an artifact of modernity that points to a record of transcontinental curiosity long joining the peoples of the planet, some of whom were east and west of each other. Although East-West is often marked as an *essential* difference, I will argue that it is a rhetorical one.

East-West Moments in a Global Reimagining

> From around 1880 to the outbreak of World War I a series of sweeping changes in technology and culture created distinctive new modes of thinking about and experiencing time and space. Technological innovations including the telephone, wireless telegraph, X-ray, cinema, bicycle, automobile, and airplane established the material foundation for this reorientation; independent cultural developments such as the stream-of-consciousness novel, psychoanalysis, Cubism, and the theory of relativity shaped consciousness directly. The result was a transformation of the dimension of life and thought.[13]

This brief list offers a reminder of the sense of explosive possibility in the beckoning century and the promise that science could comprehend and transform the world. Such was the context for emergent conceptions of a planetary commonweal that inflamed the imagination of the Chinese reformer and revolutionary Tan Sitong, a historical figure whose vision of a new order of the world boldly proclaimed the limits of a geocultural dualism of East and West.

Writing 110 years ago, Tan completed a deeply passionate, visionary tract on the salvation of self and society that defied the established frameworks of East-West. He attracted considerable scholarly interest, as well as global popular attention, because of the spectacular events of his death by command of Empress Dowager Cixi 慈禧(1835–1908) in 1898. He was one of the luminaries of the *Wuxu bianfa* 戊戌變法 (Hundred Days Reforms), a liminal period of political experimentation that stretched from June to September of 1898, during which a small congress of political reformers from across the empire gained the ear of the Guangxu 光緒 Supreme Lord (emperor) (r. 1875–1908) and sought to convert the tyranny of Manchu overlordship into a constitutional monarchy. Tan was one of six reformers who were arrested and cashiered for their contumely act of defying the empress dowager by advancing, without her authorization, substantive procedural and structural reforms. He was sentenced to death by beheading, and, in a spectacular scene retold by an eyewitness, Hu Zhiting 胡至廷, he became a martyr for all time, one whose tragic end was indelibly etched into the fabric of twentieth-century revolutionary nationalism, if not the Chinese national character.[14]

There are at least two reasons for introducing Tan Sitong in the context of a challenge to the conventional understanding of the interpretation of the encounter of China and the West. The first is to offer tribute to the earlier work of Ronald Robel, who completed an inspired dissertation on Tan's life and work more than thirty years ago at the University of Michigan.[15] "The

Life and Thought of T'an Ssu-t'ung" remains a work whose reading pays a worthy dividend for the curious, especially those drawn to the remarkable concatenation of international and Chinese domestic events in the interval from 1889 to 1905, during which Chinese activists obtained a global vocabulary of history, politics, science, and technology, from which they drew liberally in advancing solutions to China's crisis. Second, I wish to use Tan's most celebrated work as a touchstone for my inquiry into the possibilities of harmony and eradication of distinction.

In Robel's third chapter we learn of the missionary and scholarly conduit for the transmission of the latest ideas and inventions, as well as the transformative excitement of the fin de siècle in China, and how these effected in China's politically engaged intelligentsia an imminent sense of a world beyond nations joined in a unitary moment of science and spirit.[16] Tan Sitong's "Renxue" 仁學 (The Natural Science of Love)—about agape not Eros—challenged contemporary understanding and revealed him to be a prophet of imminent global equality, an equality he believed inevitable yet attainable only by overcoming the distinction between the self and others. Tacking back and forth in the inspirational winds of his genius, one moment pushed by natural science and technology, the next by Buddhist phenomenology, but undeviatingly focused on equality, Tan delivers himself beyond the problematic dyad of our focus in several of the numerologically ideal twenty-seven explanations (*jieshuo*, 界說) that open the *Natural Science of Love.*

> 1. The most fundamental meaning of love is interconnectedness (*tong*). The terms ether (*yitai*, 以太), electricity (*dian*,電), and mental power (*xinli*, 心力) all indicate the means of interconnection (*tong*). 2. Ether and electricity are simply means whose names are borrowed to explain mental power. . . . 7. Interconnection is expressed as equality. 8. Interconnection must lead to respect for the soul. With equality, body can become soul. . . . 13. The essence of love is that it can neither be born or destroyed. . . . 15. To be born is close to being renewed; to be destroyed is close to dying away. Because there is equality between renewal and dying away, there is equality between past and future. . . . 16. Both the past and the future exist, but the present does not; for both the past and the future are the present. . . . The phenomenal world, the world of the void, and the world of sentient beings are permeated with something vast and minute, the cohesive, penetrative, connective power of which embraces all things . . . ether.[17]

What seemed to inform Tan's interpenetration of the Western self in the Eastern Other was both the advent of the technoscientific moment of European, Japanese, and U.S. expansion and the end of empire, specifically and very poignantly in China, the steady disarticulation of social and political order that followed in the wake of the Opium Wars (1839–60). In the short interval from 1839 to 1895, China and its Manchu monarchy, the Celestial Empire, became, in the parlance of the day, "the sick man of Asia" (*Yazhou bingren,* 亞州病人). Indeed, China was sick: sick with opium addiction, sick with political corruption, sick with co-optation by foreign authorities, and sick with dependence on foreign countries. In this moment of humiliation and later in the bloody nationalistic struggles for political unification under the two major anti-imperialist parties, the Nationalists and the Communists, China's representation as "Asia" made it the Other that we, in the West, were not. It was described, with a pronounced hopelessness, in the voices of Tan's young generation of reformers as *wangguo* 亡國 (lost or abandoned nation).[18]

Less than a decade before the completion of *Renxue,* Tan's first manifesto (more like a *feuilleton*), *Zhiyan* 治言 (Words on Rulership), would have revealed him, by contrast, as a defensive cultural nationalist, angry and resentful over his nation's despair at the hands of aggressive barbarians from the West, but convinced that China's salvation rested in its ability to restore the integrity of its spiritual civilization. In concert with the essentialist polemics of his contemporaries, Tan imagined a judgmental geopolitical stratigraphy according to which the globe was comprised of three culturally uneven parts: (1) *Huaxia zhi guo* 華夏之國 (The "Sinitic Nations"), Burma, Korea, Tibet, and Vietnam; (2) *Yidi zhi guo* 夷狄之國 (The "Countries of the Barbarian Peoples"), the Mediterranean, Northern Europe, North America, India, Japan, Russia, and Turkey; and (3) *Qinshou zhi guo* 禽獸之國 (The "Nations of the Beasts"), Africa, Australia, and South America. These nations were arranged in a descending order of material and cultural sophistication and so represented stages in evolution just behind China and its Sinitic partners.

> The wealth of the barbarians is not enough to deplete us, and their strength is insufficient to make us helpless. The zeal, passion, and violent rise of the barbarians is not enough to make us decline. The secret schemes and recklessness of the barbarians is not enough to endanger us. But when their government gives an order the whole nation accepts it as if from God, and when a law is established the whole world accepts it as the standard. . . . Names and reality correspond as form and shadow like our ancient king's saying that the Dao is one and its influence is uniform.[19]

For Tan in this instance, modernization did not mean Westernization because the barbarian nations were just now coming into alignment politically with the government of a more evolved China. In other words, as so many of his generation said in reaction to the new technics and teleologies of Western expansionists, *guyi youzhi* 古已有之, "this has been known since antiquity."

However, following the incendiary effects of China's defeat in the Sino-Japanese War in 1894, such cultural chauvinism became indefensible. Tan Sitong and others traded their defensiveness for a new global vision. Tan rejected his earlier East-West determinism of limits in favor of a universal vision of human fulfillment in the longing to be loved, to be connected. Tan identified the suffering of the kind wrought by his emerging nation's sickness as a requisite condition for its complete emancipation. He could imagine so radical a view because he was convinced that contemporary natural science (*xue*, 學) had disclosed the empirical foundation of global interconnection. In any instant of the everyday, the infinite and the infinitesimal, past and present, were joined through the eternal psychic conduit of ether (*yitai*, 以太).

> Throughout the realms of physical phenomena, empty space, and sentient beings, there is a substance, supremely great and subtle, which adheres to, penetrates, connects, and permeates all. The eye cannot see its color, the ear cannot hear its sound, and the mouth and nose cannot taste or smell its flavor or odor. Although there is no name for it, we shall call it "ether." As manifested in function, Kongzi at different times called it "humanity" (*ren*, 仁), "the origin" (*yuan*, 元), or "nature" (*xing*, 性). Mozi called it "universal love" (*jian'ai*, 兼愛). The Buddha called it "the sea of nature" (*xinghai*, 性海) and "compassion" (*cibei*, 慈悲). Jesus (*ye*, 耶) called it "soul" (*linggui*, 靈傀) and "loving others as oneself" (*airen ruji*, 愛人如己) and "regarding one's enemies as friends" (*qindi ruyou*, 親敵如友). Natural scientists call it "attraction" (*aili*, 愛力) or "gravity" (*xili*, 吸力); all of these are one substance. From it the realm of physical phenomena is born, on it the realm of empty space is established, and from it come forth all sentient beings.[20]

In Tan's posthumously published masterwork, *Renxue*, "a heartbreaking work of staggering genius," a universal imagining of human self-fulfillment is revealed.[21] Beyond nations and states, beyond empire, Tan conceived a world of immediate and enduring interconnection (*tong*), the realization of which depended entirely on the efforts of the knowledgeable to align themselves with the generative forces of modern industrial production and technical creativity.

> Everyone is free and is the subject of no country. The boundaries between nations will disappear; wars will cease; jealousies will end; intrigues will be abandoned; the distinction between oneself and others will vanish; equality will prevail. Even though there may still seem to be a universe (*tianxia*,

天下), there will be none. The monarchy will be abolished, and the gap between the mighty and the meek shall be bridged. Once the universal principles are made known to all, people will share their wealth equitably. Within hundreds of thousands of miles (*li*, 里), there will be only one family, one collective self.[22]

Geography in this context is real but merely contingent and certainly not determinative. But it may be more accurate to characterize geography as irrelevant. While postmodern critics may rail against the impulses of universalism/ecumenism as the romantic apprehension of a Western imagination seeking to recuperate some benefit from the disaster of the Enlightenment project, Tan Sitong here counters with a local, Chinese assertion of the equality of all peoples, the transcendence of all nations, beyond orientalism and not occidentalism.

Tan was a passionate—no, religious—convert to the universal and a future in which difference would be overcome through the all pervasiveness of "communication," a conscious overcoming of obstacles (what he commonly refers to as webs, *wangluo* 網) by "bursting through" (*chongjue*, 衝決) them.[23] In the preface to this work, he proceeds in his autocritique from local to universal, asserting that "one must burst through: the webs of vulgar learning (such as textual criticism and belles lettres), the webs of the world's learning, the webs of autocracy, the webs of human relations, the webs of Heaven, the webs of the all the world's religions," only to realize that for "those who genuinely can burst through the webs, there are really no webs."[24] The most inimical of these webs was the most fundamental and the most contrived, that of the distinction between self and other. Glossing *ren* 仁 as electricity conducted through the universal medium of ether, Tan asserts a fundamental ontology of human connectivity.

> To fail to relate to others with commonality (*xiang'ou*, 相偶) and to regard oneself as superior is the opposite of *ren*; however, this kind of distinction is sui generis and results from segregating self and others, even to the extreme of there being others and the self within my own body.[25]

From this unique activist vision of global equality through the human striving to overcome the trappings of convention, we now reverse direction to examine three instances in which the distinction between self and other is aggressively and judgmentally affirmed. These are offered as vignettes appropriate to examining the metageography, as it were, of Chinese identity. From these quick sketches we will circle back to two specific instances in which it will be demonstrated how the differences between East and West are not essential and recall the rhetorical differences commonly made between opposing groups within a given culture.

The Rhetoric of Difference and Identity

In contrast to Tan Sitong's universalist example, I now turn to selected exemplars of Chinese argumentation that have in common an exclusionary ethic wherein "mine" and "true" cannot be "thine." My interest in these arguments is in how they operate to distinguish one group from another in situations in which such a distinction may be uncertain and difficult yet preciously necessary to the representation of identity.

The first selection is taken from chapter 126 of the *Zhuzi yülei* 朱子語類 (Classified Conversations of Master Zhu) of 1263 and is one of a great many doctrinal discriminations between Zhu Xi's (1130–1200) *ru* 儒 (Confucian) self and a Buddhist *fo* 佛 other.

> Cao [a disciple] asked [Zhu Xi] about distinguishing between *ru* and *fo*. The teacher responded, "Simply take the doctrine 'What the ascendant (*tian*) bequeaths humanity is called nature (*xing*).' *Fo* do not understand this and stubbornly maintain that nature is empty consciousness. We *ru* (*wuru*, 吾儒) speak of real principles, and as we see it, then, the others (*ta*, 他) are wrong. They (*ta*) say "We will not be affected by a single speck of dust and will not jettison a single element of dharma." If they are not affected by a single speck of dust, how is it possible for them not to jettison a single element of dharma? . . . We *ru* only recognize a moral principle of real sincerity."[26]

We (*wu*, 吾) are contrasted with others (*ta*, 他).

Borrowed from a 1990s discourse analysis of Han Chinese speech about Tibetan students in Southwest China, the second text reveals a similar, albeit more striking, indigenous differentiation.

> We (*women*, 我們) didn't accept any classmates from Tibet. It (*ta*,牠) is, that is, Tibet, it (*ta*, 牠) this nationality is very bad, apparently a lot of trouble. It (*ta*, 牠) in general, now it (*ta*, 牠) is a little better. But it (*ta*, 牠) is, the Tibetan nationality, it (*ta*, 牠) is Tibetan if we're talking about Tibetans, it (*ta*, 牠) in general, it (*ta*, 牠), this ethnic conception is very strong. I don't know why. Our school (*womende xuexiao*, 我們的學校) did not accept any, that is, did not take any in. But from what I know, that is, in general, Tibetan students, if she/he (*ta*, 他/她) wants to go to a school, in general in a provincial capital, she/he (*ta*) has an exclusive school, they designate a school they can enter, that exclusively designates a class. That's how it is.[27]

Here the contrast is between we Han Chinese (*women*, 我們) and the Tibetan nationality (*ta*, 牠).

The third selection is taken from a contentious anti-Christian tract, the *Shengchao poxie ji* 聖朝 破邪集(The Sacred Dynasty's Collection Exposing Heresy), which appeared in Fujian in 1639. A little more than two decades ago, this tract served as the primary source for Jacques Gernet's arguable claim that Christianity and indigenous Chinese beliefs were ontologically distinct and their respective cultures in conflict.

> This is what the barbarians (*man*, 蠻) teach: Zisi said: "Following the nature is what is called Dao." But what they (*ta*, 他) say is: "Overcoming the nature is what is called Dao. Before the nature was corrupted, following it was consonant with morality; however, today human nature is not what it was originally. Thus, it is impossible to attain the perfection of Dao without overcoming it." In the classics and commentaries that contain the tradition of our saints (*wusheng*, 吾聖), there is not a word that does not express the heart and nature. How can these beasts (*qinshou*, 禽獸) criticize this tradition and get it all wrong? I would rather not humble myself to make even the slightest comparison, but, in fear that the unwashed will be duped by these people, I am obliged to clarify these matters in both writing and words.[28]

One observation that can be made about this diverse testimony is its instinctual, reflexive quality of the discrimination of we/they with the marked case of Otherness represented by the personal pronoun *ta* (they or them). Furthermore, a stratigraphy of evaluative judgment may be observed in the identification of "they" with *ta*. "They" gives way to *ta* (it) and, in the final text, *ta* is replaced by *man* (barbarians) and even *qinshou* (beasts). All three passages defend a sense of "us," the rightful subjects, yet the very ground that they are claiming as theirs—whether in the twelfth or seventeenth centuries or today—is not acknowledged as culturally diverse despite the evident variety of peoples dismissed by the term *they*.

From the above illustrations it is clear that difference is critical to the definition of rhetorical position and native identity. There is at work in each of these texts a logic of exclusion, of in-group/out-group distinction and the instinctual reflex of identity construction, of discrimination rather than conversation.

By juxtaposing these three very different passages, I wish to encourage reflection on the many meanings of Chineseness in order that we might see the folly of our interpretive commitment to the East-West dyad. It is not only the West that divides. It is not only the cultures of China and the West that have served, to borrow a term from Richard Rorty, as "alleviative geometries," in effect rendering the one mystical and the other rational.[29] Chinese culture has elements of both ecumenism, as in Tan's work, and anti-Other essentialism, as in the three passages just quoted. There are cases of holding apart and coming together.

Differences between cultures (Chinese and Christian, Han and Tibetan, "Confucian" and Buddhist, and in a grander sense East and West) are differences in kind. As obvious as I will show this to be, such a claim is not allowed by Chinese essentialism, whether practiced by sinologists or Chinese, at least not since Tan Sitong. Something fundamental is conveyed in the above texts (whether the difference is "native" and "foreign," East and West, or "we" and "they"). These markers of difference are most pronounced where distinction is not immediately evident and requires dramatic rhetorical exertion to identify difference as cultural incompatibility. In other words, the closer people are the more strenuously they exert their distinction. However, there are also instances of differences glossed over, where "we" and "they" are claimed to be one.

The Divergence and Convergence of Inquiry on Chinese Ground

I turn now to a seventeenth-century text, the *Poxie ji* 破邪集 (The Compendium Exposing Heresy), and the Jesuit texts that were its silent disputational Other. In their rhetoric, we see a view of Chineseness (the essential culture and race of the East) as diverse rather than singular. This shakes up the "China" we have long known through the geocultural metaphor of East-West. Although we presume that Christianity is a doctrine culturally antithetical to the indigenous religious traditions of China, it is possible to observe impressive ecumenism in how Christianity was assimilated to Chinese social practice and intellectual habit following its introduction in the sixteenth and seventeenth centuries by Jesuit missionaries.

Although it seems that the *Poxie ji,* a heterogeneous compendium of memorials, litigation records, letters, and polemics in eight parts, supports the view of the fundamental incompatibility of Christianity and the cumulative traditions of the Chinese, and, although the work's publication was prompted in an immediate sense by the 1636–37 clashes between Franciscan missionaries and local authorities over public preaching, it was not exclusively a diatribe against the Franciscans.[30]

The *Poxie ji* was a pastiche of sectarian fulminations against Christianity culled from several works composed between 1615 and 1637, which, in sum, offered evidence of an incipient organized resistance to Jesuit missionary theology and practice that nonetheless demonstrated impressive and even intimate familiarity with Christian practice. The polemics, which compose three-quarters of the *Poxie ji* (*juan* 3 through 8), were produced by critics who usually identify themselves as either *ru* or *fo*. The Buddhists especially condemn the Jesuits for their misunderstanding and deliberate misrepresentation of the teachings of Kongzi 孔子 (Confucius) and his followers.

Although this work is an anthology of multiple interested interpretations and counterclaims, its essays are focused on three principal areas of rhetorical dispute with the Jesuits. The first of these is their accommodative theology, specifically the presumption that Chinese since antiquity had believed in the one god, the Heavenly Master (*tianzhu*, 天主), a term the missionaries appropriated from a peasant convert in 1583.[31] The second issue is that of the priests' own Chinese fundamentalism. What was specifically disputed was the missionary assertion, first made by Matteo Ricci (Li Madou 利瑪竇, 1552–1610) in his Chinese catechism of 1603, the *Tianzhu shiyi* 天主實意 (The True Significance of the Heavenly Master), that the Jesuits of the China mission had obtained the transmission of the *xianru* 先儒 (primordial *ru*), a legacy from Kongzi that they called *zhengxue* 正學 (the "true teaching"). The final common area of dispute was the Jesuits' interpretations of certain classic texts such as the *Shang shu* (Book of Documents), *Shi jing* (Book of Odes), *Lunyu* (Selected Sayings of Kongzi or Analects), *Zhongyong* (Doctrine of the Mean), and their contention that the intellectual traditions, such as the *lixue* 理學 (learning of principle) and *xinxue* 心學 (learning of mind), common among sixteenth-century Chinese literati and presumed by them to be descended from Kongzi by way of Zhu Xi and Wang Yangming 王陽明 (1472–1529), contradicted the "true teaching." In short, the authors of the *Poxie ji* refuted the substance of the Jesuits' arguments, which argued against the common orthodoxy of the day, and referred not to Christianity but to their unique possession of the genuine teaching of Kongzi, the revered cultural forebear of all Chinese scholar-officials.

The *Poxie ji* authors, especially aggrieved by the Jesuit claims that they had inherited the *zhengxue* of Kongzi, anxiously reiterate what they believe is the patent fallacy of this claim and ferret out its erroneousness through demonstrations of logical inconsistency or contradiction in the fathers' arguments, as in a selection from Chen Houguang 陳候光, in which *ta* marks the difference and error of the "Other."

Kongzi speaks of serving men and rectifying daily conduct. They (*ta*, 他), contrarily, speak of serving the lord on high (*shangdi*, 上帝) and filling the mind with fantasies. Kongzi speaks of understanding life and knowing how to stay in one's place. They (*ta,* 他), in contrast, speak of knowing death and winning favors in the next world. Kongzi takes the Supernal Ridgepole (*taiji*) as the directing principle of the cosmos, considering it to be truly venerable and noble. They (*ta,* 他), however, judge *taiji* to be dependent, low, and profoundly despicable. . . . Believing care for one's parents to be of little importance, they (*ta,* 他) reject fathers and in this way show that they are more culpable than Mozi. . . . Consequently, their obedience and respect for *tian* and *shangdi* are only a pretext for advancing their own deceitful ideas. The men from the far West, using *ru* as an ally, come into our land armed with weapons. Unfortunately, half of those who esteem their teaching are prominent figures and educated men. Thus, if humble men like myself decide to stand up and fight them, there are many who will spit on us and insult us.[32]

Inasmuch as he states the problems with the Jesuits' interpretation, Chen also makes clear that they were able to represent themselves as fierce defenders of canonical ground and, more important, indicates that Chinese from the region were persuaded by the teachings of these foreigners. It is perhaps not an accident that this text originated in the southeastern province of Fujian, an area that had witnessed impressive growth in the popularity of accommodationist Christianity in the early decades of the seventeenth century, much of this due to the work of later missionaries such as Giulio Aleni (1582–1649), who were favored with both local and national attention from officials and were able to negotiate theological inroads into the kin-based ancestral cults that were the firmament of the Chinese religious universe.

Chinese of all classes, the *Poxie ji* texts complain, were much impressed with the curative effects of the Jesuits' holy water, the magical efficacy of the Latin language, and the ubiquity and omnipotence of *tianzhu*. They were particularly captivated by the poignant, filial image of the Madonna and child and assorted artifacts of Christian iconography, above all the crucifix, which Aleni permitted Chinese converts to use in conducting the familial cult of the dead so that the efficacy of prayer could be translated from the cross to the ancestral shrine.[33] Local critics were well aware of the growing presence of Christianity in Chinese life and measured it in several ways: the accumulation of more than one hundred European books in Zhangzhou and several thousands throughout the country; a total (in 1638) of seventeen Catholic churches throughout the provinces; and, according to the calculation of Huang Zhen 黃貞, the "tens of thousands of families" that had taken up the teachings of the Heavenly Master, *tianzhu jiao*.[34]

One additional, but to date unremarked, aspect of these particular anti-Christian polemics is their authors' un-selfconscious command of Christian theology, the liturgy, the "New Testament," and the mysteries associated with the *passiones* of Christ and the early martyrs as displayed in these few excerpts: "the Sovereign on High takes no visible form, consequently he cannot be represented in images";[35] "they say to drink wine is to drink the blood of the Heavenly Master [and] to eat bread is to eat the flesh of the Heavenly Master";[36] "the sutra of the Heavenly Master says, 'Our Father who is in the ascendant'";[37] "sprinkling oneself with holy water and rubbing oneself with holy oil;"[38] and "in the beginning, when the Heavenly Master fashioned the world by magic transformation, there was but one man and one woman."[39]

The text fairly bristles with resentment of the popularity of *tianzhu jiao* 天主教 among both the educated and the uneducated, for example, "In the exalted ranks they have obtained allies among officials, while below they sow discord in the hearts of the common people,"[40] and "their poison is spreading everywhere and threatens to contaminate myriad generations . . . [so that] respected literati and people of reputation follow their views, printing books of the doctrine of the Heavenly Master and composing prefaces for them."[41] Yet in these querulous reactions there is significant evidence of the foreign faith's convergence with the plural streams of local practice, if not a confirmation of Jesuit Chineseness, as they note the embrace of this new doctrine by officials and the socially exalted. Moreover, because the criticism is conveyed in the context of a common culture and language and in the very manner in which one would address the rhetorical weaknesses of any adversary in persuasion, we may read these exchanges as advocacy positions stated in a shared, though tempestuous, rhetorical context. I believe this is why in many *Poxie ji* texts the personal pronoun *ta* shifts indecisively with *man* (barbarian) and in some cases is replaced by it, as the critics of the *Poxie ji* labor mightily to exaggerate the distinctions between what is Chinese and what is not.

These concerned scholar-officials, in a spirit that recalls Sigmund Freud's (1856–1939) concept of "the narcissism of minor differences,"[42] must "expose" (*po*, 破) Christian doctrine as heresy (*xie*, 邪) and "discriminate its teachings" (*bianxue*, 辨學; *bianjiao*, 辨教) from those native to China but, in the process, show that an accommodative Christianity was grafted onto the root of indigenous practice and was syncretically joined with certain traditions of *ru* discourse. Another passage offers a tendentious but telling explanation of how Li Madou (Ricci) in particular was able to invent a Christian doctrine that was consonant with Chinese tradition. Accusing Li of deceit, Huang Wendao 黃問道 holds that:

the words and sounds of his language were not like those of Chinese and [there was a] fear that his ideas would contradict those of our *ru*. Therefore, he invited some literati to teach him the Classics. Ignoring the abstruse in these works, he fashioned his own doctrine so that there appeared to be little difference between what he was saying and [what is contained in] the writings of Yao, Shun, Zhou Gong, and Kongzi. Yet in fact he was furtively inventing his own doctrine. Renouncing *fo*, criticizing Dao, and disparaging *ru*, he, at the same time, used Yao, Shun, Zhou Gong, and Kongzi to convey his teachings.[43]

Huang could denigrate Li's motives, but there was no denying that the Italian missionary, with the assistance of very capable Chinese scholars, had made a Chinese Christianity that "complemented *ru* and banished *fo*"[44] and, according to some Chinese, was indistinguishable from *ru*. I consider these rhetorical discriminations to be the reflex of a persistent impulse to recapture the indigenous identity of *ru* teaching, for the Jesuits are never called by either of the official titles they assumed among the Chinese: *xiucai* 秀才 (cultivated talent) and *ru* 儒 (scholar). Instead they are *man* and *yeman* 野蠻 (barbarians) while, by means of a host of nativist neologisms such as *wu ru* 吾儒, (we *ru,* or our *ru,*) and *wu rusheng* 吾儒聖 (our *ru* saints), the various authors of the *Poxie ji* seek, through conscious invocation of tradition, to reclaim legitimate, indigenous ground believed lost to the Jesuits.

At every turn, rhetorical phrasings punctuate the nativist sectarian syntax of "we" and "they," the most effective of these being use of the term *xuemai* 學脈 (scholarly streams) to designate the authentic intellectual traditions of China.[45] The expression is a homophonic pun on *xuemai* 血脈, meaning "artery," and, thus, proper teachings are distinguished by an appeal to anatomy, to the ultimately inalienable: blood. The symbolic capital, as it were, of *xuemai* exceeded anatomy, reaching from local self to authoritarian state, as it was a common late Ming reference to the waterways over which coursed the sustenance of the empire.[46] In this way, the narrow differences between Jesuit *ru* and Chinese *ru* were dramatized at the same time that anti-Christian critics sought to frame their invective as an appeal for official sanction against the foreigners in the name of "love of ruler and country."

Medieval Chinese Polemics of Self and Other

Aside from the occasional appeal to authorities for intervention, the denunciations in the *Poxie ji* were not unusual by comparison with the rhetorical practices of the day, and in fact, if we push the chronology farther back in time we will see that such criticisms were virtually indistinguishable from the prose and passion of the extended confutations of Chan Buddhist doctrine by Song era (1000–1300) followers of the "learning of principle." In the late Ming (ca. 1570–1640), Buddhists and Daoists were commonly criticized vigorously for their misleading teachings, and unspecified "people" were faulted for failure to discriminate properly between *ru* and alternative traditions, thereby coming under the sway of such heresy. However, as it was in the late Ming dynasty (between 1583 and 1645) that the Jesuits enculturated and became Chinese scholar-officials, thus occasioning the fierce debates over foreign and native identity and genuine and false teachings, it is best for purposes of illustration to take up a last text. This one is from an earlier time, one that was not complicated by the presence of an uninvited Christian "Other." Here we will observe a vituperative differentiation of true and false, native and foreign, very similar to those found in the *Poxie ji*.

During the Southern Song period (1127–1279), when the practices of Chan Buddhism were becoming increasingly popular, a new, *ru*-restorative fellowship (*daoxue*, 道學) produced disputational texts within which contestation of the "correctness" (*zheng*, 正) or "foreignness" (*yi*, 異) of a doctrine was argued and interpretive positions polarized with a vigor reminiscent of anti-Christian polemics. Responding to a question from one of his disciples concerning the differences between *ru* and *chan* 禪, Zhu Xi follows the nativist instinct and "disputes" (*bian*, 辯) the doctrines, saying:

> That which we *ru* (*wuru*) nurture is humaneness, righteousness, rites, and knowledge. That which they (*bize*, 比則 [others]) nurture is only seeing, hearing, speech, and activity. For *ru*, within all of creation there are a great many moral principles each having its own distinction between true and false. They only see [the universe] as a chaotic dispersal of things and events utterly without specific segregation of true and false. For them, the horizontal is true, while the vertical is equally true; the straight is true and the curve is equally true. To see things in contravention of the principle is their very nature, as is seeing things in accordance with the principle. They are very confused and [their teachings are] without one iota of truth.[47]

Zhu goes on to lament the popularity of Buddhist learning, complaining, in a language just as appropriate to anti-Christian polemics, that Buddhism "is injurious to human affairs" and "some contemporary *ru* erroneously follow in the steps of Buddhists."[48] Elsewhere, Zhu invoked nativist metaphors of place and antiquity when discussing the history of Buddhism's "sinification," the explicit injunction being that *fo* was alien.[49]

The rhetorical similarity between this passage from Zhu Xi and Chen Houguang's denunciation of the Jesuits is as explicit as their meaning;

differences in theory in a single culture appear as cultural differences. Just as Buddhism could be made Chinese, so could Christianity. Indeed, Buddhism was engulfed within Chinese practice and added to the symbolic fund of the Chinese imagination, one from which Tan Sitong liberally drew in reconceiving the meaning of love and advocating a singular resolution of the vectors of cultural difference in the universals of ether and electricity.

From Universal Particular to Particular Universal

Looking back, the diverse testimonies of the *Poxie ji* and Tan Sitong suggest that the currents of intellectual hybridity and boundary making moved in both directions, from west to east and east to west. Similarly, in the rhetorical battles of medieval Chinese scholars, with the elaboration of doctrine in offensive or defensive terms, there was imaginative movement across a broad cultural spectrum of China. The geography, East or West, East-West, was not very relevant.

We are drawn back to the "matter-of-fact usages" of late imperial Chinese to find a universe of possibilities in the particular, conflated as often as they are segregated, as when the Chan monk Tongrong 通容 (1593–1662) says of Li Madou, the harm he has done cannot be estimated. Let us try to confute his doctrines through appeal to our *ru* saints (*wu rusheng*). According to Mengzi, body and feelings are the ascendant nature.[50]

In the heat of the discriminatory moment, vocabularies of one tradition bled indiscriminately into another so that, as in this instance, notions originating from the Chinese embodiment of a foreign Christianity were fused with traditional *ru* cosmology and articulated by a Buddhist. Even Lin Qilu 林啓陸, an outspoken opponent of Sino-Christianity (*tianzhu jiao*), could not see in his nativist criticism of Jesuit theology that the most pointed aspect of his critique bore the signal, conceptual traits of the foreign, when he said:

> Every creature possesses the law of heaven. It is because each one can conform with heaven's principle and also comply with the law of the Sovereign on High that humanity can lord over the ten thousand things, govern the universe, remove the flaws of the world, and rectify present-day teachings. That is what we *ru* (*wuru*) call Heavenly Master (*tianzhu*).[51]

To accept that native and foreign could be so un-selfconsciously intertwined in seventeenth-century China is to understand two things. First, the Western and Chinese historical imaginations of four centuries ago were more disposed toward reasonableness and tolerance and capable of recognizing in the local and particular the prophetic intimations of the absolute than are we. Second, *China* denotes an ecological complex of diverse collective representations wherein cumulative traditions such as *ru, fo, dao,* and *tianzhu jiao* were the products of a conscious selection among alternatives. Over the centuries of cultural intercourse, a common symbolic fund was created from which interpretive resources could be—and were—drawn. Christianity assumed its Chinese form through the distinct mediation of local structures, and both were enriched. The same can be said of Tan's ether (*yitai,* 以太) and electricity (*dian,* 電) as definitions of love and could just as well be extended to the circuits, virtual and real, that join the four hundred million mobile phone users accessing the Internet in China today. What holds in this contemporary instance holds for Tan and his Sino-Jesuit predecessors and even Zhu Xi; these distinctions occur in a framework of plural conversations.

Difference is the enabling condition of discourse, not its denial. East-West is the legacy of an early modern civilizing project and is meaningful only as a relation of contrast. My point in being critical of the geocultural impulse is not to argue against differences, but to emphasize that the identification of difference is the ground of all identity in cultures.

Is East-West a cultural or geographic construct? I would say that they are rather a synecdoche taking part of one for the whole of the other. This volume began with a questioning of the representational aptitude of these geocultural entities. Even in the most generous sense of a desire to expand the referents of the term *we,* there was, from the start of the exploration of the Asian Other, a misapprehension as East and West represented both geography and value. The West was what was best, and the errand into the wilderness was inspired by curiosity but transformed into contempt for the primitive.

These apparently geographic distinctions, insofar as they remain today, are the residue of the era of empires. Our academic culture today, as much as we may try to deny it, is in part an extension of past empire. It is important to recall that Asian area studies in the United States was formed in the postwar era as the handmaiden of imperial expansion, providing technicians the knowledge necessary to interpret the behavior of an inscrutable Other, in particular one in Southeast Asia with which we were at war. Area studies scholars are the between takers, entrepreneurs in acquiring local knowledge of the Asian Other and transporting it home. So this has largely been the legacy of the translation of Chinese and other texts and contexts into European languages begun more than four centuries ago.

However, rather than retracing the steps of the Sino-European cultural encounter, I have focused on the idea of difference as conveyed in the rhetoric of Chinese of various centuries. In trying to get beyond the East-West polarity, I presented two illustrations: (1) Tan Sitong's idea that local is universal, wherein love (*ren*) is defined as electricity (*dian*), thereby including all peoples and faiths in a single moment of communication, like strings of lights along a series; and (2) the local history of rhetorical differences raised to the level of cultural opposition, an opposition just as fierce on the surface as that between West and East. In the end I hope to have shown that the longer history of "East-West" cultural contact has been construed from an ongoing mutual enhancement—exchange rather than conquest—just as has been the case in China from its long pluralistic past forward.

I conclude with a thought about the planetary arc of curiosity under which we stand today as interpreters of Asia, joining as legatees those about whom I have written above. Does our urge for the Other derive from emotion or reason? It is a question long struggled over in the history of Continental epistemology that I do not dare answer, although my hunch is that it is a divine proportion of both. Head and heart are the organs of curiosity, and it is curiosity that, since the sixteenth century, has drawn this conceptually flat earth closer together, all too often at the cost of misapprehension. Nonetheless, from this moment forward we might continue to discover, and in so doing to define and discriminate, with greater consciousness of the consequences of knowing well the world and its many selves and others. In this way perhaps we can carry forward, but not follow, the meaningful but misbegotten misapprehension of East-West.

Notes

[1] I have chosen to interpret the theme of this collection of essays, East-West, a self-conscious appropriation of the title of the third part ("East-West") of Salman Rushdie's story collection about identity in translation. See Salman Rushdie, *East, West* (New York: Vintage International, 2006), 123–211.

[2] Max Weber, *The Protestant Ethic and the Spirit of Capitalism*, trans. Talcott Parsons (New York: Scribners, 1958), 13, 25. The posing of these questions by a figure whose "Protestant ethic" became a universal definition of modern development has provoked cultural defensiveness evident in decades of compensatory studies of the transformative rather than accommodative impulses of "Confucianism" that have posited a bedrock of "Asian values" responsible for this region's accelerated economic change. For examples of this compensatory anti-Weberian reading of the commercial productivity of Confucianism, see Tu Wei-ming, ed., *Confucian Traditions and East Asian Modernity: Moral Education and Economic Culture in Japan and the Four Mini-Dragons* (Cambridge: Harvard University Press, 1996); and Tu Wei-ming, ed., *The Living Tree: The Changing Meaning of Being Chinese Today* (Stanford: Stanford University Press, 1995).

[3] David S. Landes, *The Wealth and Poverty of Nations: Why Some Are So Rich and Some So Poor* (New York: Norton, 1999); Samuel P. Huntington, *The Clash of Civilizations and the Remaking of World Order* (New York: Free Press, 2002).

[4] Lionel M. Jensen, *Manufacturing Confucianism: Chinese Traditions and Universal Civilization* (Durham: Duke University Press 1997). See also Jack Goody, *The East in the West* (Cambridge: Cambridge University Press, 1996); Jack Goody, *Capitalism and Modernity: The Great Debate* (Malden, MA: Polity, 2004); Kenneth Pomeranz, *The Great Divergence: China, Europe, and the Making of the World Economy* (Princeton: Princeton University Press, 2000); André Gunder Frank, *Re-ORIENT: Global Economy in the Asian Age* (Berkeley: University of California Press, 1998); and R. Bin Wong, *China Transformed: Historical Change and the Limits of European Experience* (Ithaca: Cornell University Press, 2000).

[5] Rudyard Kipling, "The Ballad of East and West," in *A Victorian Anthology, 1837–1895,* ed. Edmund Clarence Stedman (Cambridge: Riverside, 1895).

[6] I can only imagine that this habit of mind is a consequence of the pull on our imaginations of an established framework of knowledge. Being an intellectual historian, I do not chafe at the prospect of covering grand expanses of the globe. It is as though the globe itself, its mass, matter, and physical reality, make no claim on my imagination. It is the ideas that drive me, and I am surprised often by the ease with which I travel the reaches of the planet in pursuit of intellectual curiosity. Yet these ideas are drawn for context as real as the physicality I neglect to acknowledge and yet

not in a deterministic way. Take some historical examples to provide an artifactual, as it were, friction by which we might slow the slippage into the competitive metaphorical landscape of East and West that has caused us so much grief in the past two hundred years. Modernist temper may enable us to overcome, or, if not overcome, more frequently acknowledge, the limitations while we seek to identify how one can be so different from another and yet not in conflict.

[7] Ian Buruma and Avishai Margalit, *Occidentalism: The West in the Eyes of Its Enemies* (New York: Penguin, 2004); Chen Xiaomei, *Occidentalism: A Theory of Counter-discourse in Post-Mao China*, 2nd ed., revised and expanded (Lanham, MD: Rowman and Littlefield, 2003).

[8] David N. Keightley, *The Ancestral Landscape: Time, Space, and Community in Late Shang China* (Berkeley: Institute for East Asian Studies, 2000); Sarah Allan, *The Shape of the Turtle: Myth, Art, and Cosmos in Early China* (Albany: State University of New York Press, 1991), 75–87.

[9] The belief in Kunlun as an axis mundi joining heaven to earth as well as the instinctively paired association of Kunlun and Xiwang Mu, was well attested before the Han era in the text of the *Shanhai jing*. Moreover, by Han times this geographic imaginary was associated with the figure of Kongzi (Confucius), when an entry for *qiu* 丘 (hill), the putative given name of Kongzi, in the *Shuowen jiezi* (ca. 110 CE) offers a depiction of a hill as the sacred mountain Kunlun, marking the conjunction of Heaven and earth. See Xu Shen, *Shuowen jiezi* (N.p., n.d.), 169.1. See also Nancy Thompson Price, "The Pivot: Comparative Perspectives from the Four Quarters," *Early China* 20 (1995): 93–120.

[10] Liu Yu, *Xishi ji* (An Account of an Embassy in the West) of 1263; Zhao Rugua, *Zhufan zhi* (Description of Foreign Peoples) of 1225; and Zhou Qufei, *Lingwai daida* (Instead of Replies to Friends about the Southwestern Regions) of 1178 are just a few of the works that represent this medieval curiosity about the West and convey its significance as fantastic.

[11] Martin W. Lewis and Kären E. Wigen, *The Myth of Continents: A Critique of Metageography* (Berkeley: University of California Press, 1997), 48.

[12] Thomas L. Friedman, *The World Is Flat 3.0: A Brief History of the Twenty-first Century* (New York: Picador, 2007).

[13] Stephen Kern, *The Culture of Time and Space, 1880–1918* (Cambridge: Harvard University Press, 1983), 1–2. A more detailed yet still incomplete catalog of the inventive technical production of this short interval would list the telephone, 1876; Edison's gramophone, 1877; synthetic fiber, 1883; the steam turbine, 1884; photographic paper, 1885; the Kodak box camera and pneumatic tire, 1888; the

Eiffel Tower, 1889; the cinematograph and gramophone record, 1894; Roentgen's X-ray, Freud's *Interpretation of Dreams*, Marconi's radio telegraph, the Lumière brothers' invention of the movie camera, and the Curies' discovery of radium, 1895; and Henry Ford's quadricycle (the "Thin Lizzy"), 1896. Less than a decade later, the Wright brothers pioneered powered flight (1903) and Einstein proposed the special theory of relativity (1905) from which the energy and mass of the nuclear age would evolve. The story of these inventions and their tremendous aesthetic consequences is told in chapter 1 of Robert Hughes, *The Shock of the New* (New York: Knopf, 1981).

[14] It is reported that when the sentence was carried out the executioner's blade was not sufficiently sharp to decapitate any of the six martyrs and so a saw was used. The grisly scene, as recounted by Hu—"but the skull was still connected to the neck and it was necessary to stretch the 'criminal official's' neck out and saw it"— would be long remembered by Chinese revolutionary nationalists, deepening their resentment of the Manchus and the empress dowager in particular. Hu Zhili, quoted in Tao Juyin 陶菊隱, *Xin yulin* 新語林 (Shanghai: Zhonghua shuju, 1930), 107. See also Timothy Richard, *Forty-five Years in China* (London: Fisher Unwin, 1916), 2–3. In the first installment of the wildly popular 1987 television special *Heshang* 河殤, "Deathsong of the River" (now banned), a photograph of Tan flashes across the screen in an instant of narration that calls attention to his plea for his fellow countrymen to "break through the webs" of illusion and suffering that preclude China's opening to the world. See Zhang Yuanji 張元濟, ed., *Tan Sitong quanji* 譚嗣同　全集 (N.p., n.d.), 3–4.

[15] Ronald Ray Robel, "The Life and Thought of T'an Ssu-t'ung," PhD diss., University of Michigan, 1972.

[16] One of the most memorable stories of this period is that of John Fryer's 1896 introduction of X-ray images to Tan, who took the radioactive film as evidence of an accelerating ethereality of the human body that confirmed the eschatological vision of Mahayana Buddhism.

[17] Chan Sin-wai, trans., *An Exposition of Benevolence: The Jen-hsüeh of T'an Ssu-t'ung* (Hong Kong: Chinese University Press, 1984), 61–63, 67.

[18] The term *wangguo* would be uttered with greater despair in the years following the massacre of the 1898 reformers, but it achieved a powerful adversarial, condemnatory voice in 1902 in Zou Rong's clarion *Geming jun* 革命軍 (The Revolutionary Army) (N.p., 1902).

[19] Zhang Yuanji, *Tan Sitong quanji*, 103–7.

[20] Tan Sitong, "Renxue," in *Tan Sitong chuanji* (Beijing, 1954), n.p.; Zhang Yuanji, *Tan Sitong quanji*, 9.

[21] Dave Eggers, *A Heartbreaking Work of Staggering Genius, Based on a True Story* (New York: Vintage, 2001). The title is an especially appropriate one to purloin as a description of *Renxue*, which remains to this day a work admired and repeatedly translated but not entirely understood. In this final respect, Tan's work endures without the limits of shelf life with which some believe Eggers's novel is burdened.

[22] Tan Sitong, Renxue, n.p.; Zhang Yuanji, Tan Sitong quanji, 85.

[23] For readers familiar with contemporary Chinese simplified vernacular, *wangluo* 網羅 is instantly recognizable as the preferred term for the Internet and World Wide Web, which may be the most apposite realization of Tan Sitong's vision of *tong*.

[24] Zhang Yuanji, *Tan Sitong quanji*, 4.

[25] Ibid., 14.

[26] Zhu Xi 朱熹, *Zhuzi yulei* 朱子語類 (rpt., Taipei: Zhongwen chubanshe, 1970), 8:4832–33.

[27] Quoted in Susan D. Blum, "Pearls on the Strings of the Chinese Nation: Pronouns, Plurals, and Prototypes in Talk about Identities," *Michigan Discussions in Anthropology* 13 (1998): 207–37 (special issue: "Linguistic Form and Social Action").

[28] Huang Zichen 黃紫宸, "Pixie jie" 闢邪解, in *Shengchao poxie ji* 聖朝破邪集, ed. Xu Changzhi 徐昌治 (rpt., Hong Kong: Jiandao Shenxueyuan, 1996), 265 (hereafter *Poxie ji*). For an analysis of the text and its composition, see Douglas Lancashire, "Anti-Christian Polemics in Seventeenth-Century China," *Church History* 38, no. 2 (1969): 218–41. For a suspicious scholarly hermeneutics of the Christian mission that relies on generous excerpts from the *Poxie ji*, see Jacques Gernet, *Chine et christianisme* (Paris: Editions Gallimard, 1982); or Janet Lloyd's English translation, *China and the Christian Impact: A Conflict of Cultures* (Cambridge: Cambridge University Press, 1985). The *Poxie ji* was the first of several denunciations published between 1639 and the accession of the Supreme Lord Kangxi in 1662 that ultimately aimed at expelling the missionaries from China.

[29] Richard Rorty, "Relativism and Pragmatism," Tanner Lectures, University of California, Berkeley, January 31, 1983. What Rorty means by this term is that the concepts of cultures East and West presume a relativism that alleviates the need for empirical study or, as well, reflection.

[30] It does contain a reference to the infamous 1616 persecution of Christians on the order of Shen Que, vice minister of the Nanjing Board of Rites. See Ad Dudink, "Opposition to the Introduction of Western Science and the Nanjing Persecution (1616–1617)," in *Statecraft and Intellectual Renewal in Late Ming China: The Cross-Cultural Synthesis of Xu Guangqi (1562–1633)*, ed. Catherine Jami, Peter Engelfriet, and Gregory Blue (Leiden: Brill, 2001), 191–224. The memorials represented a grave

attack on the offices of the Jesuits in both Nanjing and Beijing for the damage they had allegedly caused to Chinese belief and practice. Twelve Jesuits and a few Chinese converts were arrested and tried for their heinous offenses (particularly the successful introduction of Western astronomical science at court), and by the winter of 1617 four of the fathers were, by imperial proclamation, banished from China.

[31] The story of the invention of *tianzhu* by a young Chinese convert is reconstructed in Jensen, *Manufacturing Confucianism*, 72–74, 324.

[32] Chen Houguang 陳候光, "Bianxue chuyan" 辨學芻言, in *Poxie ji*, 244. See also the translation of this same passage by Gernet in *China and the Christian Impact*, 53. Chen actually slanders Li's (Ricci's) interpretation of *taiji* 太極 in this instance; Ricci merely pointed out Master, *tianzhu*. On the Jesuit contestation of the divinity *taiji*, see Li Madou [Matteo Ricci], *Tianzhu shiyi* 天主實意, in *Tianxue chuhan* 天學初函, ed. Li Zhizao 李之藻 (rpt., Taipei: Xuesheng shuju, 1965), 1:406–7.

[33] This sort of magical efficacy of contiguity was common among the early missionaries and is described in Li Jiubiao 李九標, *Kouduo richao* 口鐸日抄 *Li Jiubiao's Diary of Oral Admonitions: A Late Ming Christian Journal*. Ed. Erik Zürcher. Vol 56 of Monumenta Serica Monograph Series (Institut Monumenta Serica, 2007). Aleni's encouragement of this practice is discussed in Erik Zürcher, "Giulio Aleni et ses relations avec le milieu des lettres chinois au XVIIe siècle," in *Venezia e l'Oriente*, ed. Lionello Lanciotti (Florence: Leo S. Olschki, 1987), 105–35. The Chinese fascination with holy water, Christian icons, and other mysterious objects of the missionaries is well documented throughout the *Poxie ji*.

[34] Huang Zhen 黃貞, "Qing Yan xiansheng pi Tianzhu jiao shu" 請顏先生闢天主教書, in *Poxie ji*, 152.

[35] Chen Houguang, "Bianxue chuyan," 246.

[36] Xie Gonghua 謝宮花, "*Lifa lun*" 曆法論, in *Poxie ji*, 308.

[37] Xu Dashou 許大受, "Shengchao zuopi zixu" 聖朝佐闢自序, in *Poxie ji*, 192.

[38] Huang Zhen, "Qing Yan xiansheng pi Tianzhu jiao shu," 152.

[39] Xu Congzhi 徐從治, Huishen Zhong Mingren deng fan'an 會審鐘鳴仁等犯案, in *Poxie ji*, 111.

[40] Li Weiyuan 李維垣, "Rangyi baoguo gongjie" 攘夷報國公揭, in *Poxie ji*, 292.

[41] Huang Zhen, "Qing Yan xiansheng pi Tianzhu jiao shu," 152.

[42] The term was first formulated in Freud's 1918 paper "The Taboo of Virginity" but more fully developed in Sigmund Freud, *Civilization and Its Discontents*, trans. James Strachey (New York: Norton, 1961).

[43] Huang Wendao 黃問道, "Pixie jie" 闢邪解, in *Poxie ji*, 267.

[44] This is the celebrated formulation, *buru yifo* 補儒易佛, of Xu Guangqi 徐光啓, Preceptor of the Hanlin Academy and a Christian convert. See Xu Guangqi, "Bianxue zhangshu" 辨學章疏, in *Tianzhu jiao dongchuang wenxian xubian* 天主教東創文仙續遍 (Taipei, 1965), 1:25.

[45] See Huang Zhen, "Qing Yan xiansheng pi Tianzhu jiao shu," 150, 152.

[46] On the arterial metaphor for the fluid concourses that joined the imperial center and the bucolic periphery, see Frederic E. Wakeman Jr., *The Great Enterprise: The Manchu Reconstruction of Order in Seventeenth-Century China* (Berkeley: University of California Press, 1985), 1:1–31.

[47] Zhu Xi, *Zhuzi yulei,* 8:4832–33. See also Li Jingde 黎靖德, ed., *Zhuzi yulei*, Chuanjing tang edition (N.p., n.d.), *juan* 126, 13b.

[48] Li Jingde, *Zhuzi yulei*, 12.6a–b.

[49] Zhu Xi 朱熹, "Shishi lun xia" 釋氏論下, in *Hui'an xiansheng Zhu Wengong wenji xuji* 晦庵先生朱文公文集續集, Sibu congkan chubian jibu edition (Shanghai: Shangwu chubanshe, n.d.), 10:1935.2–1936.1.

[50] Tongrong 通容, "Yuandao pixie shuo" 原道闢邪說, in *Poxie ji*, 384.

[51] Lin Qilu 林啓陸, "Zhuyi lunlüe" 誅夷論略, in *Poxie ji*, 282. Because *tianzhu* was at this time inextricably linked with the "men from the west" and their curious doctrine and practice, the appropriation of the term by an avowedly *ru* scholar-official such as Lin signaled how mutually entailed Chinese and Jesuit discourse on religious matters had become. *Tianzhu* was now a Chinese philosophical term liberated from its Christian religious context.

5

(Mis)conceiving the Self in Early China
Memory and Truth in Early Chinese Autobiographical Writing

Matthew V. Wells

The comparative study of early China and early Europe is often a specious enterprise. Though stimulating and at times illuminating, most scholars must admit that the relationship between early Chinese and European philosophy, literature, or history is both a tenuous one and largely academic. But the study of early Chinese autobiographical prose presents us with an opportunity for meaningful comparisons between two traditions of autobiographical writing, as the Western tradition has, over time, shaped our understanding of and approach to this body of literature in its modern and traditional forms. Scholarship of autobiography in both English and Chinese has been dominated by an expectation for a narrative that accurately discloses either the inner life or historical experience of a distinct, autonomous individual. This view of autobiography begins with the confessional requirements for an autonomous, historical subject found in the narrative of Augustine of Hippo (354–430), for whom the tropes of autonomy and individuality were paramount. For this reason we might regard Western autobiography at its core as Christian autobiography, for ultimately the kind of self-definition required of Augustine for his confession of faith has become, over time, the standard by which subsequent autobiographies are measured. Because our modern notion of autobiography is rooted in Augustinian religious discourse (be it accepted or rejected), it provides us with an opportunity for comparative study between early European, confessional autobiography and early Chinese autobiographical prose if only to explore how our understanding of the former has shaped and even distorted our interpretations of the latter. Conversely, early Chinese autobiographies also allow us to interrogate the tropes of individuality, agency, and verisimilitude that permeate the Western tradition of self-narrative. Such tropes are widespread among authors and critics alike, for they allow authors to lay claim to an individual identity that possesses considerable cultural capital in modern societies and they allow critics to reinforce false dichotomies between Western "individuality" and Eastern "collectivism."

The persistence of the Augustinian model in the study of early Chinese autobiographical prose reflects the importance of these early texts for modern scholars as precedents for late imperial and twentieth-century Chinese autobiography, which heretofore has been the subject of most, if not all, scholarship on the topic. Such studies generally regard early Chinese autobiographical texts as the antecedents of a modern genre taken to be the narrative of the individual author's experience; early autobiographies are seen thus as stages in the development of modern subjectivity and modern autobiography.[1] As a result, early self-narratives are characterized in two ways. The first is to reduce the texts to a series of literary tropes designed to link the historical author to written works or individuals from history. In extreme cases, the reticence required by traditional society resulted in the erasure of the individual. According to this view, the demands of traditional literary culture limited self-expression in early self-narratives, and so the *individual* author remains lost within literary allusion such as in the "Biography of Mr. Five Willows" by Tao Qian (365–427). The second is to evaluate the texts based on their formal features. In other words, the more the texts conform to biography or impart historical, biographical detail, the more likely they are to be antecedents to modern forms, which share these formal features. This often leads to cherry-picking from other genres those texts that conform to a modern sensibility of memory as verisimilitude, texts whose primary concern seems to be the fidelity between the life narrative and the author's lived experience. The resulting "genre" of early Chinese autobiography includes an odd cross section of texts, including Tao Qian's "Biography" for its etymological and stylistic link to biography (even though it imparts no real biographical information), but ignores others, such as Ban Gu's (32–92) "Biographical Postface" to the *History of the Former Han*, for its lack of conformity to modern expectations of subjectivity and biographical narrative.

Studies of late imperial and modern autobiographical texts remain influenced by the formulation of the genre during the late nineteenth and early twentieth centuries when interest in autobiography experienced something of a surge worldwide. In China, as in most nations, the intellectual and political currents of modernity fueled the fascination of the reading public for autobiographies. Intellectuals inspired by the new culture movement asserted modern identities that eschewed traditional culture and affirmed the self-worth of the author. These authors simultaneously invoked the patriotism and nationalism of a generation of Chinese students and activists, linking their personal stories to the larger narrative of China's struggle to emerge as a modern nation. In addition to the proliferation of autobiographies, memoirs, and autobiographical fiction during this period, a few scholars sifted through the traditional literary canon in search of an indigenous genre of autobiography, attempting to make universal both the genre and its assumed statement of individual identity. From this modernist perspective, the tradition of early Chinese autobiography consists of the "Authorial Postface of the Grand Astrologer" of the Han dynasty historian Sima Qian (ca. 145–90 BCE), the *Lunheng* "Chapter of Self-Record" of the Eastern Han philosopher Wang Chong (27–97), the "Authorial Postface to the Discourse on Literature" by Cao Pi (187–226), the "Authorial Postface" to the *Baopuzi waipian* (Outer Chapters of the Master Embracing Simplicity) of the Jin dynasty official Ge Hong (283–343), and the "Biography of Mr. Five Willows" of the Liu-Song (420–78) author Tao Qian (365–427).[2] Except for Tao Qian's "Biography," all of these texts are authorial self-narratives, or *zixu*, a postface attached to another work with which the author explains the creation of the masterwork in the context of his or her life. Their inclusion betrays a wider, modern emphasis on a preponderance of biographical information, the historical accuracy of this information, and its resemblance to historical biography.

This essay builds on these previous studies of early Chinese autobiography by addressing the different relationships between truth and identity that underlie self-narratives in China and the West. In this way, I hope not only to clarify our understanding of early Chinese self-narratives but also to ask how early Chinese texts challenge our understanding of the trope of verisimilitude the Western and modern tradition. We will first examine Augustine of Hippo's *Confessions* in order to outline the underlying paradigm of self and self-narrative that, in the main, has come to dominate the Western tradition. Second, I shall provide briefly some background on the author who is the focus of my own research, Ge Hong, and the autobiographical chapter that concludes his text. Ge Hong's work is one example of how a lack of verisimilitude or a strong, autonomous subject challenges our definition of the genre. Third, I would like to show how early Chinese autobiographical writing can be better understood in terms of *zhi*, a term frequently translated as "the will," which denotes one of many facets of the psychophysical person. This interpretation has the advantage of engaging Chinese literary theory and early notions of subjective experience that were contemporary to the authors in question rather than interpreting these texts in terms of modern or postmodern notions of autobiography, author, and text. Ironically, while this approach tends to devalue biographical detail as a tool for understanding the author, a reading of the tropes and conventions of these stylized texts suggests a deeper and more complete understanding of the author and, more generally, the genre of self-narrative.

Augustine and Western Self-Narrative

Augustine's *Confessions* is commonly regarded as a milestone in the development of autobiography and subjectivity in the West. Most significant, the centrality of memory to the *Confessions* and its subsequent expression in art as a life narrative has had a lasting impact on critics of autobiography and modern interpretations of the genre both in China and in Europe and in North America. The most pertinent feature of Augustine's work for later autobiographers is his vivid, narrative account of his own life up to his conversion to Christianity (ca. 386 CE). The life narrative created by Augustine in *Confessions* would become the model for Western autobiography, which seeks to impose a pattern on life experience that provides coherence and, more important, a comprehensible meaning.

The organization of *Confessions* as a detailed and lengthy narrative reflects the centrality of accurate memory to Augustine's text, while distinguishing his confession from acts of contrition in early Daoism.[3] By fashioning his life narrative as an act of penitence, Augustine elevates the importance of memory, which must accurately and completely recall sins in order to seek forgiveness for them. Indeed, Augustine suggests in several places that memory lies at the core of confession.[4] The organization of *Confessions* reflects this idea by describing the moral transgressions of his youth until the moment of his conversion, with considerable reflection by the author on the role that memory plays in constructing his narrative. I suggest that the centrality of verisimilitude in the Western autobiographical tradition begins in Augustine's Christian discourse. Augustine ostensibly defined autobiographical accuracy in terms of memory and historical factuality, which are important because having made an accurate confession is a requisite condition for divine redemption.

We should also note that the act of confession is at once a path to union with the divine and the source of individuation. In Augustine's view, the true self emerges along the path to redemption, for the hope of losing oneself in the divine is predicated on knowledge of the self as an individual soul. Indeed, Augustine rejects the importance of the physical body in favor of a narrative history of interior life, thus breaking sharply with those classical thinkers, such as Aristotle, who defined the person in terms of physical categories.[5] Instead, Augustine sought to emphasize the importance of the human soul as the fundamental level of individual identity. "And I know that my soul is the better part of me," he wrote, "because it animates the whole of my body. It gives it life, and this is something that no body can give to another body."[6] For Augustine, the body and its relationship to the material world are largely inconsequential for describing an individual. Instead, individual identity must be seen in terms of the immortal soul, which draws meaning from beyond corporeal existence. Augustine's lasting influence on autobiography lies in the durability of his idea of subjective experience, that the life narrative records the inward journey of the individual soul or self.

Because an accurate memory of one's transgressions would seem necessary for a true and faithful confession, defending the accuracy of memory is critical to Augustine's narrative. For him, the act of memory is entirely limited to the mind, and so the act of memory is intimately bound up with thought.[7] Memories are initially formed through sensory contact with the outside world only to reemerge in the mind, where they are organized and collected. It is important to note that, although the mind plays an active role in organizing memories, Augustine never questions the accuracy of the memory itself.[8] Indeed, memory is so accurate a faculty that events may be seen in the conscious mind as they actually occurred.[9] The life narrative of the individual is thus the result of the collection and organization of memories, the accuracy of which are determined by a mind that weighs the relevance and position of the memories relative to each other.[10]

Despite the persistent challenges of recent critics to the notion of verisimilitude, the Augustinian model continues to dominate our contemporary understanding of autobiography. We need look no further than the controversy that erupted over James Frey's "memoir," A Million Little Pieces, published in 2003. Frey's sordid tale of drug abuse and redemption went largely unnoticed by the general public until Oprah Winfrey chose it in September 2005 for her monthly book club. On October 26, Frey even appeared as a guest on the Oprah Winfrey Show to discuss his account with her viewers, and the example of his life narrative was put forward as an inspirational example for others. Less than three months later, on January 8, 2006, the guerrilla journalism website The Smoking Gun rebutted several of Frey's claims as exaggerations or entirely fictional, paying particularly close attention to his account of an alleged arrest in Ohio in 1992.[11] Although Winfrey initially defended the author, on January 26 Frey again appeared on the Oprah Winfrey Show and addressed the inaccuracies in the volume, this time with his publisher at Random House, Nan Talese. Talese addressed the issue of verisimilitude by arguing that her responsibility as an editor was to assess the authenticity of the account.

> A memoir is an author's remembrance of a certain period in his life. Now, the responsibility, as far as I am concerned, is does it strike me as valid? Does it strike me as authentic? I mean, I'm sent things all the time and I think they're not real. I don't think they're authentic. I don't think they're good. I don't believe them. In this instance, I absolutely believed what I read.[12]

The heart of the controversy consisted of an assumed, transparent relationship between verisimilitude and the authenticity of the author's self-representation. By calling into question the accuracy of details in the text, the very authenticity of Frey's self-representation became unstable, and the value of his confession, both to himself and to others, was negated, at least in Winfrey's estimation.[13]

Problems Defining Autobiography in Early China

The Augustinian, Western definition of autobiography as a detailed, historically accurate life narrative of an individual subject has long dominated approaches to early Chinese self-narrative. But prior to the early twentieth century, Sima Qian's text was not considered to be a particularly revealing of the author and, together with those of Sima Qian, Wang Chong, Cao Pi, and Ge Hong, was regarded as belonging to the genre of the authorial postface. Scholars who uphold the position that these texts are the progenitors of Chinese autobiography acknowledge the defensive or explanatory purpose of such chapters to justify the work as a whole, but define them as autobiography in terms of their biographical content and the precedent they established for self-narrative.

Some, though not all, modern scholars consider Sima Qian's "Authorial Postface to the *Grand Astrologer's Record*" to be the progenitor of early Chinese autobiography and in so doing illustrate the influence of the Augustinian model. For example, Zhao Guoxi writes:

> We recognize that the "Grand Astrologer's Authorial Postface" is Sima Qian's autobiography . . . [and] its publication not only shows that the genre of autobiography had formed by the Han period but also reflects Sima Qian's affirmation of the value of his self-identity. . . . After Sima Qian's era, people continued to express their self-identity, and many people imitated Sima Qian and used autobiography to build up their own prestige.[14]

Here Zhao recognizes the function of the postface as an introduction to and table of contents for Sima Qian's seminal work, the *Shiji*, yet at the same time he interprets the text in modern terms by asserting that one of its primary functions was the "affirmation of the value of his [Sima Qian's] self-identity." More important, according to Zhao, Sima Qian established the genre from an early period as largely concerned with self-expression or self-narrative, a truism about the authorial postface that persists in most studies of early Chinese autobiography. Even more interesting is Zhao's claim that Sima Qian's postface is representative of a genre of autobiography that had already taken shape by the early Han dynasty. But we should note that Sima Qian's focus on familial ties and the writing of the *Shiji* makes the text far less revealing or detailed than we might expect, which potentially undermines the work as an example of autobiography by modern standards. The presence of biographical detail does not in and of itself imply that the postface was intended to express self-identity; indeed, at times the identity of the author seems secondary to an account of Sima Qian's family and the genesis of his unprecedented work. The inescapable conclusion becomes a characterization of early Chinese self-identity as one that exists strictly within social relationships.

But using the authorial postface to disclose individual self-identity was less important to these authors than disclosing their *zhi* (meaning "ambition" or "what's on the mind"), which often depended on interpersonal considerations. The notion of *zhi* was central to Liu Zhiji's criticism on the subject in chapter 9 of his *Shitong,* entitled "Xu zhuan" (The Authorial Postface). Liu is highly critical of those authors who he feels engage in self-description to the point of impropriety, defined as narrating their own ambitions and accomplishments at the expense of familial or social bonds. In contrast, he lauds the work of several writers whose narratives are so reticent that they would fall far short of modern expectations for autobiography.[15] Liu Zhiji singles out Wang Chong, Cao Pi, and Ge Hong and takes them to task for their immodesty by invoking the *Analects.*

> Now when the sages set forth their words, at times they also demonstrate their own talents. Sometimes [they do this] by relying on indirection to show their feelings, or [they] select artful words and reveal their tracks. But they never pose and brag of themselves or stir up public talk. Moreover, when he commanded his disciples [by saying] "Each [of you] speak to your own ambition," Zi Lu was not modest and was criticized by Confucius for impropriety.[16]

According to Liu, too much information, particularly in the form of self-promotion, is a social faux pas that verges on the "criminal." But we should also note that Sima Qian is not included in Liu's criticism, and so, although modern scholars read much into the autobiographical qualities of this text, unlike Ge Hong's "Authorial Postface," it was not considered to be revealing of the author's subjective experience.

Ge Hong's postface does indeed seem to meet many of the modern expectations for autobiographical narrative; it is a detailed narrative of the author's life that makes certain claims to be an accurate account of the subject. Such portrayals obviously resonate more strongly with the sensibilities of modern readers of autobiography, for they resemble the mode of self-confession, inaugurated with

Augustine, to which modern readers have become accustomed. However, the notion of autonomous subjectivity so familiar to modern readers was a concept of personal identity largely incongruous with early Chinese concepts of the self. As I argue below, Ge Hong's very careful process of self-creation and his selective demarcation of the authorial postface as a genre was a result of his needs as an author rather than the product of a radically antisocial stance or a climate of individualism during the Wei-Jin era.[17]

The Life and Dubious Autobiography of Ge Hong

Ge Hong was a minor official during the early Eastern Jin dynasty (317–420), and is best known for his interest in Daoism, alchemy, and techniques of longevity. There are only a few studies of Ge Hong and his writing in English, but it should be noted that all save one deal exclusively with the religious content of his work. In Chinese and Japanese we find a similar situation, with the majority of scholarly activity dedicated to his sectarian writing. Yet religious and esoteric writing represents only a portion of Ge Hong's literary productivity, which reflects the broad range of his education and experience.

Ge Hong was born during the turbulent period that saw the reunification of China by the Western Jin dynasty (265–317), founded by the Sima clan, after decades of war and division. Sinified Turks would eventually divide China again in 317 and establish the Zhao kingdom north of the Yangzi River, destroying the Jin after the empire had declined due to a lengthy contest between rival claimants to the throne. By Ge Hong's own account, his family was once extremely close to the Wu court, but his father's death and social dislocation at the turn of the fourth century diminished the promise of his birth. Ge Hong briefly distinguished himself in military service by helping to quash a local rebel, but shortly thereafter the murder of his benefactor in 306 forced him into premature retirement, and he spent nearly a decade in seclusion away from the traditional political and cultural centers of the empire. During this time he composed a significant body of writing and immersed himself in the religious traditions of his family, which emphasized canonical Daoist texts and *waidan*, techniques of longevity that share some features with European Renaissance alchemy.

Ge Hong probably reentered public life around 314, receiving honors for his prior military service and most likely filling official positions under the patronage of the powerful minister Wang Dao (276–339), who was the adviser of the future emperor Yuan (r. 318–23). At the time, Yuan was still prime minister, but with Wang Dao's assistance he sought to consolidate his position south of the Yangzi River by patronizing southern families around the area of Jianye. Around 331, Ge Hong retired again, moved to the south, and avoided public life until his death; his official biography states that he left in search of the raw materials for concocting elixirs of transcendence, and I've never seen compelling evidence to doubt this. Ge Hong died while living in the southern reaches of the Jin state; religious tradition holds the date of his death—and subsequent transcendence—to be 363, while most modern scholars place the date of his death at 343.

What first drew my attention to Ge Hong's autobiographical writing was the occasional, pronounced disjuncture between the subject of the self-narrative and the biography of the historical author. Contrary to what we might expect, in many ways Ge Hong's autobiography is a very bad source for biographical details about the author's life. Indeed, we might go so far as to say that he fabricates a kind of Henry Chinaski alter ego, the Master Embracing Simplicity, who shares a few of Ge Hong's biographical details but differs from him in several important ways. The clearest example is Ge Hong's claim to poverty early in life, which is considerably more pronounced in the autobiography than we could realistically expect. In Ge Hong's account, his father's death results in a state of poverty so severe that he is reduced to chopping and selling firewood to buy ink and paper with which he studies and copies the classics; a poor farmer, he also personally engages in plowing and planting his fields from dawn to dusk. This image of the poor farmer chopping wood to support his scholarship is without doubt an exaggeration. When Ge Hong's family was divested of its former power under the Sun clan, it marked a demotion in authority and status, but wealth and position continued for Ge Hong's father under Sima rule; Ge Hong's family may have lost power and prestige, but it was not likely reduced to abject poverty in one generation.[18] The activities of scholarship would have been out of reach for a person in the abject poverty described by Ge Hong.

Evidence within Ge Hong's own writing supports the logic of this conclusion, as he contradicts this account of his early life and studies in the autobiography itself, as well as in the rest of the *Baopuzi*. In several instances, he is very clear that at an early age—perhaps fourteen—he came under the tutelage of Zheng Yin, who had been a student of Ge Hong's uncle, Ge Xuan. Zheng Yin not only taught Ge Hong esoteric texts and techniques of *waidan*, but he was also a scholar of the Shu (Documents) and tutored Ge Hong in canonical Han literature. In his account of his studies with Zheng Yin, Ge Hong describes how he also swept the floors and gathered firewood for his teacher, activities that would have been expected of a student. Thus, it may have been this work that Ge Hong later described in his autobiography as the task of an impoverished young man who could ill afford books or a teacher.

These disagreements between the narrative and the author's life result in part from the fact that the postface chapter was intended to promote a view of the subject as author of the text to which it was appended. In a sense, the author's life provides the hermeneutic for reading the primary text, which in Ge Hong's case was a multivolume study of esoteric practices and political philosophy.[19] The postface, along with the rest of Ge Hong's work, would in turn have been composed to boost his reputation and ultimately gain employment in an official post. In this regard, the text serves Ge Hong's political ambitions, not an abstract purpose of self-discovery. Once the text was written and a measure of success had been achieved, there would have been no reason to go back and amend it, for the chapter was never really considered autobiography in the sense we mean it today but as a kind of extended resume attached to the larger work. Thus, the life narrative serves to provide the context for the composition of the text; in a real sense we see the life of the subject (the author) leading inextricably to the act of writing. In Ge Hong's case, this happens at a relatively young age, probably around thirty-five, which confronts us with two issues: first, the short narrative arc of the subject in terms of time; and, second, the fact that the work of the narrative is to explain why the larger text was written not to recount the life of the author. A further factor may be that, while the text does reflect the author, like most literary endeavors, it is a record of his "ambition" made manifest in the text, and any demand for verisimilitude was with regard to such ambition not to the historical (i.e., factual) details of his life. Regarding the text as a manifestation of the *zhi* suggests that in the postface Ge Hong cast his subjective experience in terms of tropes and literary archetypes, many of which he borrowed from verse. Stepping back from the biographical details of the text and viewing them as tropes ironically provides us with a much firmer understanding of the historical person.

The Psychophysical Category of *Zhi*

What, then, is *zhi*? Donald Munro, citing Mencius (II. I.2/9, 10), describes *zhi* as the "active aspect of the mind"; it is that which mediates the heart/mind (*xin*) and the *qi*, the material of the body, ensuring that no violence is done either to the *qi* or to the mind.[20] In the context of Mencius, *zhi* seems to be related to qualities of self-control; the *zhi* seems to govern the *qi*, but both seem subsequent to the mind.

Portions of the *Lushi chunqiu* chapter "Concentrating Aims" seem to agree with Mencius's assessment of *zhi* as that which governs the *qi*.[21] Indeed, the *zhi* may focus the *qi* to the point of strengthening the material body—and indirectly the mind—and allowing the individual to perform extraordinary feats of mental acuity. For example, in *The Annals of Lü Buwei* (24/5.3), Confucius, Mo Di, and Ning Yue studied furiously to overcome their deficiencies, and "they did anything that facilitated their studies but were unwilling to do anything that might impede them. . . . . Using their will thus with such vigor, what task could they not accomplish? What action could they not fulfill?"[22]

In the next portion of the chapter (24/5.4), we learn that Ning Yue was originally a rustic who, weary of farm work, once asked a friend, "What does one have to do to avoid this drudgery?"

> "Nothing beats studying," replied his friend. "If you study thirty years you can succeed." "Let me do it in fifteen. When others rest, I will not dare do so; when others sleep, I will not dare do so." In fifteen years he became the tutor to Duke Wei of Zhou.[23]

Insofar as the *zhi* in these two instances can govern the self to make possible extraordinary feats of scholarship, it does lend itself to the English term *will*. A person may use (*yong*) their *zhi* for discipline and self-control, pursue a goal, and achieve it to the utmost. However, according to the *Lushi chunqiu*, the *zhi* is more than the sum of self-control and concentrated effort. It also exists innately as part of the self, and its disposition from within the body toward the material world is instrumental for orchestrating the mind and body toward some potentiality. The author of the chapter asserts that a certain Yang Youji "had the ability to hit his target [with an arrow] before actually hitting his target."[24] The passage seems to imply that the innate quality of the *zhi*, one's "single-minded intention," makes possible what may be impossible for others.

The definition of *zhi* takes on the added dimension of "intention" when we turn to parallel discussions in early Chinese literary theory, where we encounter the idea that "verse expresses *zhi*," first expressed in the *Book of Documents* and elaborated on in the "Great Preface" of the *Classic of Poetry*. "The poem is that to which the *zhi* proceeds. In the mind it is the *zhi*, emerging in words; it is verse." The *zhi* emerges within the context of the mind and is expressed in the material world; in Mencius, *zhi* governs the activity of the *qi* or the material body; in literary theory, it emerges in words as poetry. Presumably some combination of thought, feeling, or desire emerges in the heart as the *zhi*, which we may once again think of as a form of potentiality, something that *may* be expressed through the body and in the material world. The *zhi* may influence *qi*, propelling the body into action, or it may be expressed in other ways such as poetry specifically or literature more generally.

The will may refer to something abstract or concrete, but it must refer to something unrealized or not yet attained. At the risk of being trite, one oft-quoted illustration of this point may be found in *Analects* 11.26, in which Confucius asks three of his disciples to imagine what it would be like if their abilities were well appreciated. One by one, the disciples answer the question with regard to their abilities to govern states of various sizes and conditions. Finally, Confucius must prod a reluctant Zeng Xi ("styled" Dian) to speak, saying, "What harm is there in it? You should also speak of your intention as they did." Zeng Xi replies, "In late spring in the third month, wearing clothing fit for spring, with five or six lads who had reached capping [twenty years of age] and six or seven youths, [I would like to] bath in the Yi River, dry off in the breeze at Wu Yu, and return home singing." To this idyllic expression of Zeng's will, Confucius famously replies, "I'm with Dian!" *Analects* 1:11 more succinctly illustrates this point when Confucius says, "[If someone's] father is alive, observe his will; [after his] father is dead, observe his actions; if for three years there is no change from his father's way, then he may be called filial." Presumably, when his father is alive a man's actions would not deviate from his father's way; thus, to know him it is necessary to examine his will, which might not find an avenue for expression. Since the focus of this passage is filial piety (*xiao*), we may assume that in this instance we examine the will of the man in order to determine the quality of his fealty toward his father. However, when a man's father dies he might feel unrestrained by such obligations and might express his will in action. The upshot of this, according to Confucius, is that we may ultimately judge the extent of a child's fealty after his father's death when the individual will may emerge in action. In other words, is the will of the child to hold fast to the way of the parents or deviate from it once they are dead? In the context of the *Analects*, we may regard the will or intention as more than desire, casual wishes, or "what's on one's mind" but as a tendency toward action that reveals something of one's character. Early theories of literature assumed that the author expressed intention (*zhi*) but not the *self* (*zi* or *ji*), which was not a synonymous category but rather the totality of what was demarked by the physical body.

Zhi as Both Action and Literature

The idea that the will can be expressed in writing was later combined with the notion that literature is inferior to action, producing the concept that stymied intention leads to writing as a last, desperate resort. This paradigm of writing had its beginning in antiquity with figures such as Confucius and Qu Yuan, the quasi-historical poet immortalized by his work, "Encountering Sorrow."

By the Three Kingdoms era, it had become a poetic cliché, as exemplified by Cao Zhi's poem "Jiao zhi" (Determined Will), which was written soon after his brother Cao Pi's (187–226) ascent to the throne as Emperor Wen of Wei in 220 CE.

> Although the cassia is fragrant[25]
> It is hard to use as bait
> Neglecting duties while taking pay[26]
> It is hard to make a name
> The loadstone attracts iron
> It does not join to gold
> The great court appoints officials
> Yet fools hear no summons from it.

The poem is unusual for its straightforward commentary on its own allusions, but clearly it seems to express Cao Zhi's disappointment at being shut out of government by his brother.

By the Jin dynasty, writing had acquired more importance among social elites as a way to distinguish oneself through literary talent and erudition.[27] Ge Hong viewed his own work in similar fashion, arguing that one needs to separate worthy writing from meritorious action.[28] According to him, writing after nearly a decade of unexpected reclusion, his work ought to be considered a virtuous action in its own right.

> Virtuous action is a concrete action, good and bad are thus easy to distinguish; writings are subtle and mysterious, their relative worth is difficult to comprehend. Now that which is easy to see is coarse; that which is difficult to comprehend is delicate. . . . I therefore forsake the coarse and easy to see and discuss the delicate and hard to comprehend; can this not also be done?[29]

The importance of writing lay in its usefulness as a tool for ethical and moral instruction in an age of social dislocation and political fragmentation. Ge Hong compares erudite writing to Zhuangzi's fish trap. When the fish is caught, the trap may be discarded, but "when the Way has not yet been put into practice, we cannot do without writings."[30] Although writing was viewed with some suspicion during the Warring States era and was subordinate to virtuous action, for literati of the Wei-Jin era, the production of literature took on increasing importance as a virtuous act in itself.

Early authors of the postface such as Ge Hong were frequently at pains to justify their literary accomplishments and typically resorted to ambition—or an analogous concept—to explain their writing. In such instances, the author frequently cited some goal or fate deferred by circumstances beyond the author's control. Having no means with which to exert his will, the author expresses it in writing. Beginning with the postface of Sima Qian, it became fashionable for an author to describe his or her work in terms of the trope of unrealized potential. Ge Hong draws on this trope and describes his text in similar terms with a fictitious dialogue at its conclusion.

> Hong wrote the chapter of his autobiography and someone criticized him, saying, "In earlier times, when Wang Chong was sixty years old, his ideals could not be carried out and his hopes were cut off. He was fearful that both his body and his name would be extinguished, so he wrote a postface to conclude his work. Now, you are but thirty years old . . . [and about to assume high office]. . . . [H]ow can you deplore the fact that your glory has not been made known and work so studiously on an 'old man's occupation' [i.e., a postface]."[31]

While it was a formal demand of the genre to defend the act of writing in conversation with a fictitious interlocutor, here Ge Hong seems to focus explicitly on the issue of why he wrote the self-narrative and defends his postface rather than the work as a whole. In other words, the issue is not the writing of *Baopuzi* but the postface itself and why he wrote it at that particular moment of his life. In this sense at least, Ge Hong's work is without precedent, as he was the first to address overtly the issue of self-narrative and subjectivity in Chinese literature.

For our purposes here, we may note that Ge Hong also alludes to the convention of stymied will or intention by referring to the work of Wang Chong, who never achieved high office despite his literary talent. According to Ge Hong, the postface provides some consolation to the unsuccessful literatus, whose name would be recorded for posterity even if he were successful in public life. Here the interlocutor questions whether Ge Hong, who has just received honors for previous military service, has any call to worry about the durability of his name for posterity. In this regard, the dialogue lays bare the difficulties of using the narrative as a source of biographical detail by acknowledging that Ge Hong has cooked the raw material of his lived experience to create an image with little, if any, verisimilitude. While many literati experienced the frustration of an obstructed public career, we should not count Ge Hong among them. Like his claim to poverty and lack of education, so, too, his air of frustration and disappointment seems an exaggeration or at worst a literary pose. Such tropes should not be dismissed as mere artful self-creation and therefore useless for understanding the author's biography, for it is through the tropes that we may come to understand Ge Hong's *zhi* and resolve many of the tensions between the realities of his lived experience and his carefully crafted self-image.

How to be a Genuine Fake (Hermit)

The trope of reclusion and disengagement permeates Ge Hong's autobiographical account and augments his image as an obstructed, unsuccessful official who manifests his *zhi* in writing while living in seclusion from society. The virtuous, reclusive sage is perhaps the most prevalent literary trope in the *Baopuzi*, but it is important to note that the hermits of Ge Hong's work do not live in splendid isolation. Rather, in candid debates with visiting officials, they express their motives in clear moral terms and critique the ethical failings of society. In this regard, those who laid claim to the aesthetic of reclusion did so as a form of public engagement and social criticism, not out of an interest in solitude per se. Understanding how Ge Hong regarded the phenomenon of reclusion is the key to understanding his self-image in his autobiographical account and to understanding the role of *zhi* in the process of self-narrative.

Six hermits in the "Outer Chapters" defend their reclusion to interlocutors and outsiders such as government officials, and, although all of them are encouraged to return to public life, they are ultimately unwilling to return to society. The officials criticize the actions of archetypal recusants such as Bo Yi and Shu Qi—both of whom starved to death in the wild rather than serve a conquering state—as futile and suicidal, and they appeal to the reclusive official on the grounds that social and political order has finally returned: "I hope [you] will give up the caves of dragons and serpents,[32] advance on the path of opportunity, [and] abandon your residence of solitary purity. . . . Bo Yi was only one man; how is plucking ferns sufficient to bring admiration?"[33] But the recusants of the *Baopuzi* refuse to return and serve as state officials, and they justify their continued reclusion by casting the role of the recluse as one of a social and political critic for whom a return to public life is largely irrelevant.

Ge Hong thus invests the hermit with a much larger political role than he might expect to wield at court, for by occupying a position of moral purity on the periphery, the hermit retains the paradoxical authority to "serve" as a teacher to the wisest rulers. Conversely, the ruler who understands the position and function of hermits in this way will honor them as teachers rather than pressing them to return to court. This argument is, naturally enough, cast in historical terms with reference to political icons of the past.

> The recluse said, "As for the Duke of Zhou, he was a great sage; although he was of high rank, he put himself below the common people. Spitting out the food in his mouth and holding his wet hair, he was afraid of losing talented men.[34] He followed seventy scholars from poor families and received ten scholars wearing commoner's clothes, he personally met them with gifts as if receiving a teacher, and he treated twelve scholars in commoner's clothes as friends, and in all of these instances they were not forced to appear at court. Hypothetically, assuming that Lu Shang had lived in the Duke of Zhou's land, all such people would become bodies displayed in the market or the court or rotting flesh in ditches and ravines!"[35]

According to Ge Hong's interpretation of reclusion, the relationship between ruler and subject is comparable to the relationship between teacher and student. The ruler's ostensible subordination to the wisdom of the recluse demonstrates the elevated status of the latter within this model relationship. However, the example above also reaffirms the status of the ruler by stressing the wisdom of his judgment. In this scenario, the ruler may indeed lose corporal power over a single subject, but he acquires the broader authority of enacting the outward signs of virtuous rule. In a sense, the ruler appropriates the moral authority of the distant recluse and in turn acquires greater authority over the center of his domain.

> Although [recluses] are of no practical quality, and their talents are not equal to outstanding officials at court, is this not better than shrugging their shoulders and lowering their brows [so as to act humble], flattering the powerful, bearing gifts and concealing valuables, traveling at night to the homes of the powerful, to race one another for access to the powerful, to buy famous treasures in the marketplace, abandoning the basis of virtuous action and the basis of study and knowledge while proceeding to the gratuitous end of forming cliques among their own kind?[36]

Here Ge Hong clarifies the link between physical isolation and moral authority, for the recluse is able to remain unblemished by the cliques and factionalism of court life. The argument that a recluse has no "practical use" recalls the ostensible uselessness of objects, such as the *shu* tree in the *Zhuangzi*, that ultimately upend conventional notions of utility by enduring through time. Thus, the statement above advocates unequivocally for the moral superiority of recluses and the rulers who understand their utility.

This notion had practical implications for Ge Hong during the Wei-Jin era, when enacting the role of recluse was essentially a vocation. The duration of Ge Hong's reclusion was more than a decade and may have subsequently benefited his official career by allowing him to cultivate a literary image that corresponded to the ideal of reclusion as outlined above. This may have permitted him to move away from his early military career into the more prestigious appointments befitting a member of the literati. One must admire the way in which he cultivated an air of virtuous eremitism and promoted it with a body of philosophical work and other literature, emerging from his abrupt retirement, which began with the violent end of his benefactor, Ji Han, around 306. As Alan Berkowitz has observed, "During the Six Dynasties the nomination of candidates whose sole forte was dissembling the lofty conduct of a man-in-reclusion continued as a sort of mutated vestige of the earlier recommendatory system. And a sizable number of aspiring officials did in fact gain recognition and suitable employment through a stint 'in reclusion.'"[37] The attention paid to recluses was not isolated but was part of a larger policy to create cohesion within literati society—atomized and ravaged by years of conflict—under the auspices of the emperor's court. In *A New Account of Tales of the World,* 18.15, we read:

> Every time Chi Chao heard of someone living in lofty retirement, he would always put up a subsidy for him of a million cash and in addition would build a residence for him.[38] While he was living in the Shan Mountains he once constructed a house for Dai Kui (d. 396) that was extremely refined and genteel.[39] When Dai first went there to live he wrote letters to all his intimate friends saying, "Recently when I arrived in the Shan Mountains, it was like coming to an official mansion.'[40]

Like Chi Chao after him, Ge Hong's benefactor, Wang Dao, seems to have patronized many famous recluses, perhaps out of a desire to project an image of virtuous authority. Scattered through several sources are accounts in which Wang attempts to lure various officials out of retirement. In *A New Account of Tales of the World* (18.4), we read how Wang Dao appointed Li Xin (d. ca. 350) to the position of clerk, as Sima Rui had earlier appointed Ge Hong. When Li received the summons, he reportedly laughed and exclaimed, "Wang Dao is once more conferring a title on a man." [41] The *Jin shu* biography of Ge Hong's friend and contemporary Guo Wen is more remarkable, claiming that Wang constructed a facsimile of a garden abode in which Guo could reside as his hermit in residence, all the while entertaining Wang Dao's entourage with philosophical debate and clever conversation.

> Wang Dao had heard of Guo Wen by reputation and sent someone to extend an invitation. Wen steadfastly refused boat or carriage, but, shouldering his pole, he walked there. When he arrived, Wang placed him in the Western

courtyard, in the middle of which the fruit trees had grown into a [veritable] forest, and there lived birds and beasts and elk and deer, and so [Wang] housed Guo Wen there. Thereupon the court gentlemen all came together to see him, but Guo Wen sat limply with his legs sprawled, as if there were no one present.[42]

We must acknowledge the possibility that Ge Hong's brief period of reclusion and subsequent literary self-image may have spoken to his ambitions for public office. In this sense, we might regard his autobiographical postface, which he probably wrote while relatively young, as a resume of his good character that helped contribute to a laudatory reputation that ultimately resulted in recognition and an official position granted by the new rulers of southern China. Ge Hong's stance of seclusion and disengagement was ironic testimony to his suitability for office. This adds a new wrinkle to the tradition of early Chinese autobiography, for rather than a text meant to convey the life story of the author, we are confronted with a self-narrative that did not insist on the historicity of the author other than to testify to elusive qualities of character that would be useful for advancement in office. Ge Hong's autobiographical account, written at a young age and for public consumption, required verisimilitude only in terms of the author's family history and was not burdened by the requirements for realistic biography.

Conclusion

The desire for verisimilitude was the fundamental characteristic of the confessional autobiography of Augustine of Hippo, who claimed to possess a memory that was both accurate and available on demand. The ostensible, religious purposes of the text assumed an accurate memory as a prerequisite for confession, and the accurate rendition of these memories was not only implicit in the act of confession but also necessary to sway the reader from a life of sin. It is this demand for verisimilitude, born out of the act of Christian contrition, that molded early-twentieth-century efforts to categorize autobiography within the Chinese tradition as it persists in shaping the expectations of the general reading public.

Early Chinese autobiographers such as Ge Hong defined themselves through reference to literary tradition by invoking canonical figures such as Confucius alongside specific authors of self-narrative and alluding to significant cultural archetypes such as the rejected official or recluse. In his autobiographical account, Ge Hong set aside the question of whether or not he conveyed biographical details that were faithful to his lived experience; he was instead consumed by the question of which archetypes were the most useful for his own self-creation. Moreover, it seems clear that one of the primary functions of this text was to create a narrative self that conveyed suitability for office in terms easily recognized by his contemporaries, rather than achieving an accurate confessional narrative along the lines of Augustine of Hippo's, in which the author casts himself as a model of spiritual development for future readers.

We may conclude by asking whether or not early Chinese autobiographies can challenge the verisimilitude so readily assumed in the European tradition of self-narrative. One is left to wonder what other purposes of Augustine were served by his autobiographical account. Augustine became coadjutor bishop of Hippo at roughly the same time that he wrote *Confessions*. What role might such a work of contrition have played in the appointment or his moral and spiritual authority as a bishop? Did he exaggerate his account in order to better serve the purpose of setting an example for his reader? This question is also about the cross-purposes that might be served by biographical detail, where the factual accuracy demanded by contrition and the moral or spiritual representation of the author coincide or diverge. James Frey, in defending his self-narrative, stated, "[What] I developed was sort of this image of myself that was greater, probably, than—not probably—that *was* greater than what I actually was. . . . When I was writing the book . . . instead of being as introspective as I should have been, I clung to that image."[43] However, while attempting to evade Oprah's wrath, Frey inadvertently paralleled early Chinese autobiographers by asserting the utility of the image even when the biographical details are inaccurate or falsified. "I don't feel like I conned everyone," he said, "because I still think the book is about drug addiction and alcoholism and nobody's disputing that I was a drug addict and an alcoholic. And it's about the battle to overcome that."[44] For Ge Hong, biographical detail did not need to conform to a standard of objective veracity based on the act of Christian contrition; instead its purpose was to conform to literary and cultural archetypes that conveyed his character, acumen, and qualifications to his audience, the court literati of the Eastern Jin. While other features of Ge Hong's autobiography without doubt reflect a concern with the historical legacy of the author, it cannot be denied that his fictionalized account speaks with a purpose and to an audience unimagined by the modern reader. In the end, his personal account represents an altogether different kind of historical truth than that entertained in the autobiographical genres anticipated in the West.

Notes

[1] Studies that take these early works as precedents of modern or twentieth-century Chinese autobiography are Janet Ng's *The Experience of Modernity: Chinese Autobiography of the Early Twentieth Century* (Ann Arbor: University of Michigan Press, 2003); and Wendy Larson's *Literary Authority and the Modern Chinese Writer: Ambivalence and Autobiography* (Durham: Duke University Press, 1991). Pei-yi Wu's *The Confucian's Progress* discusses late imperial autobiography and links Ming (1368–1644) and Qing (1644–1911) autobiography to these earlier texts.

[2] This literary grouping is found in Kawai Kouzô's *Ch goku no jiden bungaku* (Tokyo: Soubunsha, 1996); and, with some variation, in Guo Dengfeng's *Lidai zixu zhuan wenchao* (Taipei: Taiwan shangwu, 1965), first published in the 1930s.

[3] For details on early Daoist confession, see Tsuchiya Masaaki, "Confession of Sins and Awareness of Self in the *Taiping jing*," in *Daoist Identity: History, Lineage, and Ritual*, ed. Livia Kohn and Harold Roth (Honolulu: University of Hawai'i Press, 2002).

[4] Augustine of Hippo, *Confessions*, trans. R. S. Pine-Coffin (New York: Penguin Classics, 1961), IV.1/71.

[5] Ibid., IV.16/88.

[6] Ibid., X.6/213.

[7] Ibid., X.11/219.

[8] Ibid., V.6/98.

[9] Ibid., X.8/216.

[10] Ibid., X.8/214.

[11] http://www.thesmokinggun.com/jamesfrey/0104061jamesfrey4.html (accessed February 23, 2007).

[12] http://www2.oprah.com/tows/slide/200601/20060126/slide_20060126_350_113.jhtml (accessed February 23, 2007).

[13] Winfrey concluded the show by stating, "I believe that the truth matters." http://www2.oprah.com/tows/ slide/ 200601/20060126/slide_20060126_350_209.jhtml (accessed February 23, 2007).

[14] Zhao Guoxi, "Sima Qian xie 'Shiji Taishigong zixu' wei ziji shubei lizhuan," *Jilin shifan xueyuan xuebao* 9 (1996): 6–9, 6.

[15] Indeed, for modern scholars of early Chinese autobiographical writing, the most troubling aspect of Liu Zhiji's treatment of the subject may be his inclusion of certain texts in the genre of the "authorial postface," in which the author is not the ostensible

subject of the narrative, for it is from this genre that modern critics draw most of their early examples of Chinese autobiography.

[16] Liu Zhiji, *Shitong*, (Taipei: Wenhai chubanshe, 1953), 9.3b–4b/330–31. Here Liu refers to *Lun yu,* 11.26.

[17] Liu Dajie's *Wei-Jin sixiang lun* (Shanghai: Shanghai guji chubanshe, 2000) has just one example of a very typical argument that Wei-Jin literature "departed from real social norms and fully expresses a kind of transcendent romanticism" and individualism (145).

[18] See Jay Sailey, *The Master Who Embraces Simplicity: A Study of the Philosophy of Ko Hung* (San Francisco: Chinese Materials Center, 1978), 279–80.

[19] The same is true of the postface of Ge Hong's predecessor, Sima Qian, who attempts to explain the circumstances that led to the writing of his masterwork, the *Shiji* or *Grand Astrologer's Record.* Given the unprecedented nature of such a monumental history, and the fact that during Sima Qian's time the post of *taishi gong* (grand astrologer or, more commonly, grand historian) was actually responsible for the imperial calendar and not state historical writing, an explanation was probably in order. One of Sima Qian's goals in the postface was to equate his life with literary production and demonstrate the necessity for writing the *Shiji* in terms of the author's personal history. In the context of this explanation, Sima Qian uses biographical detail as a way to ground his text within a tradition of literary production by focusing on his filial duty to his father, Sima Tan, who allegedly began the work that was completed by his son. See Larson, *Literary Authority,* 13–15.

[20] Donald Munro, *The Concept of Man in Early China* (Ann Arbor: Center for Chinese Studies, University of Michigan, 2001), 153.

[21] See Mark Edward Lewis, *The Construction of Space in Early China* (Albany: State University of New York Press, 2006), for a thorough genealogy and alternate interpretations of the concept of *zhi* during the Warring States era.

[22] John Knoblock and Jeffrey Riegel, *The Annals of Lü Buwei* (Stanford: Stanford University Press, 2000), 24/5.4 (p. 618).

[23] Ibid., 24/5.4 (pp. 618–19).

[24] Ibid., 25/5.5 (p. 619).

[25] Zhao Youwen indicates that the fragrant cassia in the first line have been linked by earlier commentators to a story about a fisherman from Lu who used cassia as fish bait. See Zhao Youwen, *Cao Zhi ji jiao zhu* (Beijing: Renmin wenxue chubanshe, 1998), 317.

[26] For an explanation of this expression, see Wang Chong, *Lunheng jiao shi,* 4 vols. (Beijing: Zhonghua shuju, 1996), 2:12.35/547.

[27] Wang Yunxi, *Wei-Jin nan bei chao wenxue piping shi* (Shanghai: Shanghai guji chubanshe, 1989), 133.

[28] Pu Youjun, *Zhongguo wenxue piping shi lun* (Chengdu: Ba-Shu shu she, 2001), 251.

[29] Yang Mingzhao, ed., *Baopuzi waipianjiaojian*, 2 vols. (Beijing: Zhonghua shuju, 1997), 2:32/107 (hereafter *BPZWP*). See also Sailey, *The Master Who Embraces Simplicity,* 177.

[30] *BPZWP,* 2:32/109. See also Sailey, *The Master Who Embraces Simplicity*, 177.

[31] *BPZWP,* 2:50/715.

[32] *Zhouyi*, "Fan ci xia." See Zhou Zhenfu, ed., *Zhouyi shizhu* (Beijing: Zhonghua shuju, 1999), 260.

[33] *BPZWP,* 1:19/474.

[34] See Sima Qian, *Shiji*, 10 vols. (Beijing: Zhonghua shuju, 1999), 5:33/1518.

[35] *BPZWP,* 1:2/71.

[36] Ibid., 1:2/72.

[37] Alan Berkowitz, *Patterns of Disengagement: The Practice and Portrayal of Reclusion in Early Medieval China* (Stanford: Stanford University Press, 2000), 136.

[38] Chi Chao (336–77) was an official who served under Huan Wen. See Fang Xuanling et al., *Jin shu.* 10 vols. (Beijing: Zhonghua shuju, 1998), 6:67/1802.

[39] Dai Kui's (d. 396) biography is found in the collective biography of recluses in ibid., 8:94/2457.

[40] Liu Yiqing, *Shishuo xinyu jiaojian* (Beijing: Zhonghua shuju chubanshe, 1999), 18.5. The translation is from Richard Mather, *A New Account of Tales of the World* (Ann Arbor: Center for Chinese Studies, University of Michigan, 2002), 361.

[41] Liu Yiqing, *Shishuo xinyu jiaojian,* 18.4. The translation is from Mather, *A New Account of Tales of the World,* 357.

[42] Fang Xuanling et al., *Jin shu,* 8:94/2440.

[43] http://www2.oprah.com/tows/slide/200601/20060126/slide_20060126_350_105.jhtml (accessed February 23, 2007).

[44] http://www2.oprah.com/tows/slide/200601/20060126/slide_20060126_350_107.jhtml (accessed February 23, 2007).

6

From Beat to Hardcore

A New Twist on Phony Zen

Eric P. Cunningham

In 2003, the world received a new transmission of the Buddha dharma in the form of something called "hardcore Zen." An expression of Zen experience that claims direct roots to the American punk rock scene, hardcore Zen is best characterized in Brad Warner's *Hardcore Zen: Punk Rock, Monster Movies, and the Truth about Reality.* Among the assertions transmitted by Warner, a punk rocker turned Buddhist priest, is this commentary on the state of the world right now.

> The world is in deep shit right now. The only thing that can possibly save us from our own self-induced destruction is direct knowledge of the truth. And I say this without any reservation at all. Mankind cannot survive unless the truth dawns—from within—in each and every one us. No political solution, bellicose *or* peaceful, will ever save us. No law. No pact. No treaty.[1]

Fortunately, *Hardcore Zen* shows us the way to the truth—the truth about reality—and reality, according to Warner, is "you—naked, stinky and phony as all get-out." Moreover:

Reality doesn't know a damned thing.
Reality has doubts and insecurities.
Reality gets horny sometimes and sometimes reality likes to read the
    funny papers.
Reality is an old guy in Cleveland Heights complaining that his grandkids
    have stolen his dentures again.
Reality is five guys trying to tune three guitars and a Farfisa compact
    organ to the same pitch and failing miserably.
Reality is the source of every star, every planet, every galaxy; every dust
    mote, every atom; every klepton, lepton, and slepton.
Reality is the basis of every booger up your nose, every pit-stain in your
    dad's T-shirts, and every dingleberry on your ass.
Reality is this moment.[2]

One online reviewer called *Hardcore Zen* "an engrossing and entertaining Chicken Soup for the Anarchist Soul," praising its philosophy as a means of "opening the possibility to spiritual stability for people who, in this enlightened age, simply can't allow blind faith in a mystical deity to run their lives."[3] Another, while warning that *Hardcore Zen* was "not your grandmother's Zen book," introduced Warner's rant as a "refreshing spiritual voice in the Zen tradition."[4] Indeed, one labors in vain to find anything but high praise for *Hardcore Zen* in the blogosphere, suggesting that Zen Buddhism, in its latest, postmodern incarnation, has reclaimed its place among the spiritual powers seeking to overcome the modern world. This is a defining moment in history's march toward its own end, and it needs to be recognized as such if we want to understand the evolving role that popular Zen has played in both modern history and postmodern reality. The appearance of hardcore Zen in contemporary culture signals the presence of a new stage in the historical development of modern Zen and, arguably, a new stage in the crisis of modern historical consciousness. The object of this essay is to reflect on the manifold nature of hardcore Zen and point out some of its broader historical implications.

I should make it clear at the outset that I am not technically a Buddhist scholar and thus have no real stake in demonstrating how faithfully or unfaithfully hardcore Zen represents the authenticity of historical Zen tradition. Arguments over the difference in quality between traditional and modern Zen have long occupied Buddhist scholars, and they seem to follow the pattern of the arguments that have taken place in each of the world's great historical missionary religions. Buddhism, Christianity, and Islam have all confronted those moments when success in "spreading the word" has led to conflict between protecting the orthodoxy of core teachings and promoting the positive aspects of growth and ecumenism. Since the appearance of Zen Buddhism in the Western world near the turn of the twentieth century, the argument over what *does* and *does not* constitute the genuine Zen experience has spread beyond the confines of Japanese sectarian debates into the domains of academics, pop culture, psychology, and even historiography.[5] As a historian, I claim no authority to comment on either the academic or the doctrinal orthodoxy of hardcore Zen. Accordingly, in evaluating the assertions contained in the blurb on the back of Warner's book ("This is not the same old crap you've seen in a thousand books you don't want to read. This is Zen for people who don't give a rat's ass about Zen. This is the real deal"), I have no qualified judgments to offer.

Nevertheless, because my research is concerned with modern Japanese thought and its relationship to the eschatological unfolding of the modern world, I do *sincerely* give "a rat's ass" about Zen. My chief interest in Zen, though, lies in trying to understand how this very old East Asian practice has been reinvented in the modern West as a discursive means of achieving two specific historical ends. These ends are (1) fusing the spiritual traditions of "East" and "West" and (2) revitalizing or even redefining Western spirituality. When books such as *Hardcore Zen* and its generic companion, *Dharma Punx* by Noah Levine, make their respective splashes in pop culture and spark the enthusiasm of so many contemporary readers, we might take it as evidence that postmodern Buddhism and its antileaders have abandoned any interest in achieving these "traditional" modern ends.[6] The authors of *Hardcore Zen* and *Dharma Punx* have seemingly very little invested in the project of integrating the spiritual traditions of East and West and appear to exhibit equal measures of contempt and ignorance for the spiritual traditions of the Western civilization from which they themselves hail. This is as much a historical problem as a religious one.

In one sense, hardcore/punk Zen carries on the high modern Zen function of providing a mirror for the "failed" aspirations of Western spirituality. Surprisingly, though, this new Zen offers no positive or systematic substitute for a civilization in need of light.[7] Warner, for one, is as disdainful of the religiosity of "orthodox" modern Zen practitioners as he is of the "sugar-coated imitations of truth" and "vapid platitudes" of the formal religions of the West.[8] Of course, Warner gives no evidence of having maintained any prolonged association with mainstream faith, so his judgments on the impoverishment of Western religion seem to be based largely on his own prejudices. The only "gods" to which he professes any degree of devotion are monster movies and punk rock. Levine, whose dharma entails the rejection of both material consumer culture (the online "Dharma Punx®" shop notwithstanding) and drug use, seems to bear no allegiance to any path but his own adopted "Buddhist" lifestyle. This includes an eclectic meditation regimen embracing the twelve-step recovery process, *zazen* (intense sitting meditation), and Sufi mysticism, held together and validated by a lifelong love affair with the rebellious energy of punk rock.

Given that hardcore Zen has nothing to do with advancing the ends of conventional religious consciousness, its apparent popularity gives rise to a number of questions for the historian. Specifically, what exactly *is* this thing called hardcore, or punk, Zen and where did it come from? What does it stand for? What does it stand against? What are its terms, parameters, assumptions, and logical outcomes? What exactly is the relationship between hardcore Zen and "mainstream," modern Zen? What do the stated and implied differences in these varieties of Zen allow us to learn about the phenomenon of postmodern spirituality? Finally, what does it all mean from the standpoint of modern historical consciousness? This chapter will not be able to explore all of these questions, but it will offer a few definitions and some observations on the historical significance of hardcore Zen.

Modern Zen

Before defining the specific postmodern phenomenon of hardcore Zen, it may be useful to discuss the general historical development of Zen in the modern West. I have made several references to *modern Zen*, which is the term that seems best for naming that specific form of Japanese-influenced Buddhism that came to the West at the end of the nineteenth century and so strongly influenced Western religion and culture throughout the twentieth century. The success of modern Zen as a cross-cultural phenomenon can be attributed chiefly to D. T. Suzuki (1870–1966), the charismatic Japanese Buddhist professor who spent over sixty years promoting Zen in the West. When we consider the remarkable teaching, speaking, and writing career of Suzuki and make even a cursory inventory of the Western thinkers his works have influenced, we might see him as a latter-day Boddhidharma, a man who single-handedly bridged two cultures and transformed the "post-Christian" West into a mission field for Buddhism.

As many religious studies scholars have observed, the popular, Suzuki-mediated Zen so familiar to Western Buddhists is several degrees removed from the traditional practice of Zen (*dhyana* in Sanskrit or *ch'an* in Chinese) as it has been known in Japan for roughly a thousand years. The Zen sect, which locates its doctrinal origins in such Mahayana classics as the Prajñapāramitā and Vimalikīrti sutras, follows a tradition grounded in meditation and extraintellectual insights into the "suchness" of reality and the "void" of nothingness wherein the essence of truth is said to lie. The Zen tradition has always valorized the personal experience of transcending the phenomenal world; its practitioners seek "passage" from the delusions of transitory materialism into the Buddha fields of metaphysical emptiness. Through *zazen* and deep concentration on nonlogical riddles known as *kōan,* the linear mind is pushed to a point of crisis, resulting in a breakthrough of "first awakening" or *kenshō.* With the attainment of *kenshō,* a disciple is certified as having attained a valid personal experience of the Buddha mind. Suzuki equated *kenshō* with *satori,* or enlightenment itself, which represents "the unfolding of a new world hitherto unperceived in the confusion of a dualistically-trained mind."[9]

While these features remain central to contemporary understandings of Zen in the West, many Buddhist scholars maintain that the wider culture of

Zen popularized by laymen such as Suzuki bears little substantial resemblance to the traditional practice of Zen Buddhism in Japan. Robert Sharf calls modern Zen a "twentieth-century construct" that not only fails to transmit the fullness of Zen tradition but may also cause great damage in nonreligious contexts.[10] The language of Zen, conspicuously abstract and transcendental, is open to manipulation by those who would exploit the ambivalence of such terms as *void* and *nothingness* for political, social, and cultural aims. "Once wrenched from its institutional and ethical context," Sharf writes, "this free-floating Zen [can] be used to lend spiritual legitimacy to a host of contemporary social, philosophical and political movements."[11] When we note the degree to which Zen has been invoked as an organizing principle for such varied things as Japanese militarism, psychoanalysis, psychedelic drug use, archery, basketball coaching, "motorcycle maintenance," corporate management, Christian contemplative practice, and now hardcore punk resistance to "the machine," Sharf's judgment seems very much on the mark.

Using Zen to signify "anything and everything" can lead to great confusion in representation. From a positive standpoint, if "Zen is everything" then all phenomena, from the Engakuji temple to a used oil filter, must possess some kind of Zen nature; if so, Zen becomes validated as a kind of universal absolute. From a negative standpoint, the kind of pantheism that notions such as "Zen is everything" promotes quickly degrades the meaning of all particular things, especially Zen itself. It seems necessary, if one seeks to make an absolute out of an inherently supersensible entity (as all mystical religions do), that one should be able to point to clearly articulated theologies, canons, and teleologies that give believers a sense that their absolute holds some unifying intelligibility in time and space if only for the purpose of creating a coherent religious culture for the worship of that absolute in the historical world. In the case of modern Zen—and especially in the case of postmodern hardcore Zen—the lack of any unifying intelligibility and the refusal to admit to one opens the door to a kind of spiritual anarchy if not spiritual nihilism. Practitioners of "conventional" modern Zen might see this conclusion as somewhat alarmist (as admittedly all warnings against anarchy and nihilism are), but since most modern Zen practitioners operate from within the well-defined and readily identifiable structures of modern culture, they do not generally question whether these structures might come unglued. They are, in a sense, modernists first and "Zennists" second. Moreover, harboring anxieties about the degradation of spiritual value tends to violate the Zen ideal of taking things as they are and going with the flow; modern Zen, like modern anything, is always open to novelty. Hardcore Zen practitioners, on the other hand, who see themselves as outside the pale of all conventional structures, might call the possibility of spiritual anarchy a "no brainer" and even welcome its appearance. For these people, the fact that reality is manifestly unknowable is neither a hazard to avoid nor a mystery to be embraced, but rather a harsh truth that one had better get used to. As Warner tells us, "Buddhism won't give you the answer. Buddhism might help you find your own right question but you gotta supply your own answer. Sorry."[12]

Modern Zen, which has become radically far-flung in its expressions, was originally grounded in a grand historical project to promote a unified and progressive world civilization. For early Western followers of Zen, the whole point behind the movement of Zen "from West to East" was to bring a new light to a benighted West desperately in need of a new revelation of truth and to do so in an expressly dialectical, historically self-conscious way. We might consider the propagation of modern Zen as taking place in three loosely defined stages: from 1893 to the outbreak of World War II, from 1945 through the early 1970s, and from the 1970s up to the present-day dispensation of hardcore Zen.

In the first stage, Zen was not distinguished from other forms of Buddhism and was only vaguely differentiated from other foreign religions. It was understood as an "oriental" path to wisdom that joined and complemented a larger historical process of unfolding world religious consciousness. We can locate its beginning in the summer of 1893, when the Japanese monk Shaku Sōen (1859–1919) delivered a paper entitled "The Law of Cause and Effect as Taught by Buddha" at the World Congress of Religions. At this glittering convocation of world religious leaders sponsored by the Chicago Columbian Exposition, Sōen spoke of Buddhism in terms that were readily understandable to American listeners. Making no reference to "nothingness" (*satori*) or even meditation, Sōen forthrightly explained Buddhist causality in natural, not mystical, terms and hailed the Buddha as "the first discoverer" of "the law of nature."[13] Buddhism, in this representation, could be seen not only as the first cause of global religious consciousness but also as a historically valid way to bridge the gap between science and religion, a rift that defined the spiritual crisis of the late nineteenth century.

Among those Western thinkers who saw Buddhism as the answer to this crisis were Dr. Paul Carus (1852–1919), editor of *The Monist* and *Open Court Press*.[14] Carus befriended Sōen at the world congress and invited him to take part in a project to publish canonical Buddhist texts for Western readers. While Sōen declined to join Carus in this work, he did nominate in his stead one of his lay students, Suzuki Daisetsu, the young man who had translated his address to the congress. Thus, in 1897, after Sōen returned to his duties as abbot at the Engakuji temple in Japan, D. T. Suzuki came to Illinois to help Carus with Open Court's series on oriental texts. For nine years, Suzuki diligently worked to produce translations of Ashvaghosha's *Awakening of Faith in the Mahāyāna*, the *Tao Te Ching*, and his own *Outlines of Mahāyāna Buddhism*.[15] As Suzuki began to publish more of his own works on Buddhism for the West, his reputation as a scholar spread worldwide and his books and articles attracted the attention of the people who would become the first generation of Western Zen devotees.

The early Western Zen disciples were, like Carus, generally earnest, scholarly people who exhibited ecumenical sensibilities and a wide-ranging intellectual curiosity. Dissatisfied with early-twentieth-century modern society, they identified materialism as a historical disease and a degenerate organized Christianity as chief among its symptoms. Rather than trying to revitalize Christianity, though, these Western Buddhists redefined themselves as members of an international religious community that transcended sectarian and national boundaries. By becoming religious citizens of the world, they could continue to pursue their modern lives while adopting their own preferred form of religious expression. In this way, they were able to promote religion as a means—and religious open-mindedness as a principle—of pushing the material world past its existing level of historical stagnation. They were not necessarily after renunciation or even enlightenment. What they wanted, it seems, was a more sensible, more rationally "spiritual" world. Perhaps the greatest exemplars of this type were Ruth Fuller (Sasaki) of the United States and Christmas Humphreys and Alan Watts of Great Britain, all of whom approached Zen with decidedly modern, middle-class sensibilities and a well-honed, well-educated, intellectual curiosity.

Yet even as Zen was being hailed by English-speaking interlocutors as the answer to the West's spiritual malaise as early as the 1930s, it was being reshaped by Japanese scholars to fit into a larger discourse of anti-Western cultural nationalism. While the Englishmen Humphreys and Watts gushed about the universal light of the Buddha, Japanese nationalists (including Suzuki) were focusing on the essential Japaneseness of Zen. "Imperial Way Zen," a jingoistic ideology that invoked ancient associations of samurai culture with Zen Buddhism, was conflated with modern state Shinto practice and used as a means of justifying Japan's military expansion in Asia.[16] The unpleasant facts of the mutually supportive relationship between institutional Zen and the Japanese imperial war machine were largely unknown to postwar Zen followers in the West, who resumed the project of promoting Zen in Western culture, again under the guidance of Suzuki, very soon after the war.[17]

The second historical phase of modern Zen began during the postwar Occupation, when a new generation of scholars, Philip Kapleau, Robert

Aitken, and Richard De Martino, to name only a few, took up the study of Zen Buddhism and helped revive it in the United States. Suzuki also came to the United States in 1949, eventually landing in New York, where he was invited to hold public seminars on Buddhism at Columbia University. His lectures were an enormous hit, and he soon found himself being toasted by the city's cultural elites. Before long he was being featured in popular magazines and on television, and as his celebrity grew, new editions of his translated works achieved the status of "required reading" for East Coast intellectuals and literati. Within a few years of his arrival in New York, Suzuki's message of Zen had spread throughout the academic and artistic communities of America.

While Suzuki remained the front man for Zen during the 1950s, the "evangelical" strategy in the postwar West changed somewhat. In the aftermath of World War II, Zen became not just a universal path to intellectual illumination but also a historically timely cure for the pathology of modern civilization. Zen increasingly came to be seen as the answer to the worsening of the spiritual crisis of modernity, which had evolved from a mere "rift" between materialism and spiritual aspirations into a full-blown case of humanity's alienation from nature.[18] Arguably, the rise of an antimodern ideology such as fascism in Germany, Italy, and Japan was the mutation of romantic attempts by these nations to inject a spiritual quality into a world overdetermined by bourgeois materialism, but the rift was not resolved by the war and indeed may have been exacerbated by it. The triumph of modern civilization over European and Japanese fascism had been achieved at horrific cost, including the advent of the atomic age and the possibility that the human species might annihilate itself with nuclear weapons. Moreover, while the empires of Germany, Italy, and Japan had been crushed by free modern states, the Allied victory seemed to bring only a new arrangement of great power rivalry and did little to end Old World patterns of violence, exploitation, and imperialism. For many observers, modernity was anything but a triumphant and robust ideology; it was, rather, a form of historical sickness. Accordingly, when Zen appeared on the American scene in the 1950s, it was welcomed as a cure for modern material history and the kind of linear, discriminating, conflict-based thinking that had created it. Social critics as diverse in outlook as the Catholic monk Thomas Merton, psychologist Erich Fromm, and poet Gary Snyder all looked for ways to cure the pathology of modernity and, in their various ways, invoked Zen as a means of recapturing spiritual healing for a sick world.

Among the more interesting therapeutic expressions of Zen in the 1950s was the fusion of *satori* and psychedelic consciousness, a phenomenon that developed rapidly after the war as drugs such as LSD and mescaline became available for use in the treatment of mental disorders. Psychoactive drugs, loosely regulated in the 1950s, made their way into the artistic and literary worlds and were used by a wide variety of people trying to expand their consciousnesses beyond the limits of mundane reality. Zen students such as Watts, Snyder, and the poet Allen Ginsberg were also pioneers in the psychedelic movement and did much to foster the idea that Zen enlightenment was analogous with, if not equivalent to, the "void" one experienced while under the influence of hallucinogens. Owing to an interesting correspondence of language and core ideas, among them "the destruction of the ego," the "dissolution of subject-object boundaries," "illumination," and "nothingness," the hallucinogenic experience was assigned religious value by a growing number of users of psychedelic substances.

By the late 1950s, Zen was being used as a code word for every conceivable kind of movement that sought to critique or question modern bourgeois society. Beat poets, avant-garde composers, and abstract expressionists all claimed to be making Zen art, and LSD users were claiming to have attained Zen enlightenment. Suzuki, who had encouraged the early propagation of many of these "Zens," began to caution against "gross misrepresentation" and tried to keep Zen from being "absurdly caricatured."[19] In 1958, Alan Watts wrote "Beat Zen, Square Zen, and Zen," offering his own observations on the various ways Zen was experienced in the West and the real problem of using it to justify an "anything goes" approach to life. According to Watts, "beat Zen" was a "complex phenomenon" that ranged from "a use of Zen for justifying sheer caprice in art, literature and life" to "a very forceful social criticism."[20] Square Zen, on the other hand, was "the Zen of established tradition in Japan, with its clearly defined hierarchy, its rigid discipline, and its specific tests of *satori*."[21] Watts, true to his nature, was cautious about both extremes and did not see one as being necessarily worse than the other; indeed, he expressed the hope that "beat Zen and square Zen will so complement and rub against one another that an amazingly pure and lively Zen will arise from the hassle."[22] When Watts refers to something called "phony Zen," though, it is clearly in the context of the false bohemian aesthetic practiced by self-styled urban Buddhists.

> To some extent, Zen is used in the underworld which often attaches itself to artistic and intellectual communities. After all the Bohemian way of life is primarily the natural consequence of artists and writers being so absorbed in their work that they have no interest in keeping up with the Joneses. It is a symptom of creative changes in manners and morals which first seem as reprehensible to conservatives as new forms in art. But every such

community attracts a number of weak imitators and hangers-on, especially in the great cities, and it is mostly in this class that one now finds the stereotype of the "beatnik" with his phony Zen.[23]

According to Watts, the key to authenticity and success for anybody trying to pursue Zen authentically from the Western tradition was to acquire a thorough knowledge of his or her own tradition so that the pitfalls of an overly eclectic beat Zen and an overly dogmatic square Zen could be avoided.

> [T]he Westerner who is attracted by Zen and would understand it deeply must have one indispensable qualification: he must understand his own culture so thoroughly that he is no longer swayed by its premises unconsciously. He must really have come to terms with the Lord God Jehovah and with his Hebrew-Christian conscience so that he can take it or leave it without fear of rebellion.[24]

In stressing the need for a thorough knowledge of one's own religious culture as a prerequisite for exploring Zen, the notoriously progressive Watts seemed to be issuing a decidedly square verdict on the authenticity of Zen practices. His conservatism in this case was not entirely unexpected. Because Watts *did* know his own religious traditions thoroughly, he possessed the ability to interpret Zen in a formal religious context and knew the difference between phony and well-informed judgments. Also, as one of the architects of Zen studies in the West, he must have felt some proprietary concern over what so many lesser-informed people were recklessly defining as Zen. It is interesting, though, that he would go to such lengths to establish boundaries of correctness around a tradition that he himself borrowed largely because it offered him so much freedom of expression. This would not be the last time Watts would side with the squares when Zen was challenged by more "heterodox" forms. In 1971, the journal *Eastern Buddhist* published a collection of papers dealing specifically with the topic of drugs and enlightenment. In response to what they felt had been an inappropriate equation of religious experience with psychedelic pleasure seeking, a number of celebrated Zen scholars, including Watts, decided to "circle the wagons" around "real" Zen illumination and condemn psychedelics as a false path to enlightenment.[25] Despite previous endorsements of psychedelic experience in *The Joyous Cosmology* and *The New Alchemy*, Watts had obviously come to feel that without prerequisite knowledge and preparation the use of drugs could only produce what he called "ecstasies without insight."[26] The "Drugs and Buddhism" symposium marks something of a turning point in the development of modern Zen. Not only would Zen elites officially endorse the path of "the ordinary mind" for the next several decades, but they would also increasingly deemphasize the power of Zen as a transformational religious experience. A new stage in the development of modern Zen appeared when it broke free of its entanglement with beatniks, hippies, and drug users and became available as a user-friendly spiritual path to masses of people who were not especially interested in following a real one.

This third stage, which began in the mid-1970s and continues into the present, is something of a "high modern" period for Zen, one in which Zen is more an expression of material culture than a cure for it. While Suzuki is still well known and widely read, the average person is just as likely to have been introduced to Zen by reading *Zen and the Art of Motorcycle Maintenance* (a book that says very little about Zen) or reading in *Sports Illustrated* about "Zen Master" Phil Jackson, the legendary professional basketball coach who credits much of his success to his adherence to Zen principles. In this most recent phase, Zen is the center of an enormously active merchandising project that churns out calendars, books, desktop gardens, videos, clothing, statues, management guides, investment software, furniture, incense, tea, yarn, and perfume. As this stage has matured, Zen has become increasingly uncoupled from any traditional understanding of Buddhism or formal religious practice. Zen is essentially whatever lifestyle-enhancing attitude, product, or activity the authors of endless books or directors of workshops want it to be, complete with instructions on breathing, mind control, and some form of meditation that does not necessarily require sitting in the difficult full lotus position.

Given this trajectory, the appearance of hardcore Zen in the new millennium is hardly surprising. With each stage in its development, modern Zen has become not only better advertised but more alienated from formal Western religion, more indifferent to its historical Japanese roots, more insistent on declaring that it possesses the essence of truth, and less concerned with defining what that truth might be. Hardcore Zen brings us farther along this developmental path in every way and takes Zen, finally, from a high modern mode to a more postmodern one.

With that, let us take a closer look at the phenomenon called hardcore Zen. As strangely gratifying as it would be to consider Warner's entire book line by line and illuminate every bit of inanity masquerading as Zen wisdom, such an exegesis would not serve the aims of this study and would surely be little more than the academic "head trip" of somebody playing the role of Buddhist scholar; as Warner warns his readers, "[I]t's hard to find a group of people who misunderstand Buddhism more thoroughly than Buddhist scholars."[27] Warner's book will most likely never become one of the great books of Buddhist literature; some narrow-minded gatekeeper of Buddhist studies, who has his head "firmly wedged in his ass,"[28] will see to that. Nevertheless, the book is important for the unsettling evidence it provides us of what Zen has become in the new enlightened age of postmodern consciousness.

Hardcore Zen: What Is It?

Despite marketing *Hardcore Zen* as "the real deal," Warner never defines Zen or explains Buddhism in any formal way. For Warner, Zen is neither a religion nor a belief system nor even a ritualized way of life. "Unlike religions," he writes, "Zen doesn't have a set system of beliefs for you to adopt."[29] In fact:

> Zen replaces all objects of belief with one single thing: reality itself. We believe only in this universe. We don't believe in the afterlife. We don't believe in the sovereignty of nations. We don't believe in money, power or fame. We don't believe in our idols. We don't believe in our positions or our possessions. We don't believe we can be insulted, or that our honor, the honor of our family, our nation or our faith can be offended. We don't believe in Buddha. . . . Zen is the complete absence of belief. Zen is the complete lack of authority. Zen tears away every false refuge in which you might hide from the truth and forces you to sit naked before what is real.[30]

Sifting through these various pejorative pronouncements, the reader is left with the task of trying to glean from a disjointed narrative of autobiography and reflections on life what the subject of this book really is. The closest Warner comes to defining Zen is perhaps this assertion.

> Zen Buddhism is direct pointing to the truth. It's cutting through the crap and getting to the ground of things as they really are. It's getting rid of all the pretense and seeing what's actually here right now.[31]

Since there is no clear explanation of what the "pretense" is or where the "crap" is located, one has to assume that they are everything and everywhere. This would not be completely inconsistent with the standard Buddhist worldview, which sees the phenomenal world as illusory, but Warner's Zen is not, in the classical sense, "world denying." In fact, Warner tells us that "Zen teaches that we are living in paradise right now, even amid all the shit that's going down."[32]

> This world is the Pure Land. This world is paradise. In fact, this world is *better* than paradise—but all we can do is piss and moan, and look for something better. . . . But it's not just "Buddhism" or "Zen" that says that. It's me, right now to you. And I'll say it again. This world is better than any paradise, better

than any Utopia you can imagine. I say that in the face of war and starvation and suicide bombings and Orange Terror Alerts. This world is better than Utopia because—and follow this point carefully—*you can never live in Utopia.* Utopia is always somewhere else. That's the very definition of Utopia.[33]

"The only thing Buddhists believe in," Warner explains, "is the reality of the world in which we are all living right now."[34] The paradox of living in a world that is simultaneously flawed and perfect is resolved by Zen practice, which in Warner's view consists entirely of *zazen*, and a Zen lifestyle, which consists of an endless process of questioning.

> Question authority. Question society. Question reality. But you've got to take it all the way. Question punk authority. Question punk society. Question your own rules and question your own values. Question Zen society. Question Zen authority. Question other people's values on reality and question your own.[35]

The process of questioning received constructs of reality, combined with sustained effort in *zazen*, will bring a moment of "truth" *not* to be confused, as will be discussed below, with "enlightenment." Warner writes that "if you really thoroughly question *everything*, if you pursue your questions long enough and honestly enough, there will come a time when truth will wallop you upside the head and you will *know.*"[36] Of what does this truth consist? According to Warner:

> Truth screams at you from billboard cigarette ads. God sings to you in Muzak® versions of Barry Manilow songs. Truth announces itself when you kick away a discarded bottle of Colt .45 Malt Liquor. Truth rains on you from the sky above, and God forms in puddles at your feet. You eat God and excrete truth four hours later. Take a whiff—what a lovely fragrance the truth has! Truth is reality itself. God is reality itself. Enlightenment, by the way, is reality itself. And here it is.[37]

Warner's equation of enlightenment with reality in this passage is probably the most positive thing he has to say about this fundamentally important Zen concept. According to Suzuki, enlightenment, *satori* in Japanese, is the "most significant and most essential, and most fruitful part of Buddhism."[38] Suzuki also maintains that enlightenment *is*, in theological terms, the "Chinese interpretation of the Buddhist Doctrine of Enlightenment,"[39] which suggests, as most Zen practitioners would probably agree, that the purpose of "doing" Zen is to attain enlightenment. For Warner, though, the pursuit of the "e-word" is one of the great pitfalls of Zen experience.[40] Operating apparently from the Sōtō tradition of Zen Buddhism, which places less emphasis than the Rinzai tradition on the idea of "sudden awakening," Warner seems almost dismissive of the idea of enlightenment and even argues that "the Rinzai school believes in enlightenment and the Soto [sic] school doesn't."[41] Warner's reading of this distinction seems to be somewhat at odds with other modern interpretations. The most common understanding of the difference between the approaches of these two schools is well summarized by Thomas P. Kasulis, who points out that while Rinzai "stresses the personal identity crisis resolved only by the achievement of satori, a sudden enlightenment," Sōtō "is often referred to as the gradual enlightenment school."[42] Essentially then, the Rinzai school works toward a sudden, reality-shattering illumination and the Sōtō school favors enlightenment achieved through years of consistent *zazen* meditation.

While interpreting the fine points of this difference is a matter perhaps better left to more specialized Zen scholars, it seems that Warner's reluctance to admit to the reality of enlightenment stems from a refusal to admit to the existence of any kind of authentic spiritual reality. This is curious because Warner refers to an episode that bears all the marks of a real spiritual awakening. One day, apparently, while walking toward a bridge over a river in Tokyo, Warner experienced a moment of unexpected bliss and complete peace of mind. As he recalls:

> I was walking along the road and just about to cross that bridge when all my problems, all my complaints, all my confusions and misunderstandings just kind of untwisted themselves from each other and went *plop* on the ground. I'm not talking some of my problems, I'm talking about all of them, every last one. *Plop!*[43]

At this moment, Warner writes, "The universe was me and I was it."[44] Immediately after the experience, he continued on to work and assigned no lasting importance to the event. A year later, though, he began to experience profoundly vivid dreams, dreams that were lucid to the point that he was actually fully conscious as he was having them. Some weeks after these dreams began, he experienced "the big one," a mystical awareness of unity with the cosmos, which included witnessing the evolution of the universe as he became one with it.[45] Warner's description of this event is very similar to accounts given by religious mystics who have dropped their egos, left their bodies, and joined with the fullness of the universe during periods of ecstasy. It seems that by any "objective" standard of mystical experience, Warner was given the grace of a true glimpse into the nature of the Absolute.

When he told his master, Nishijima, about his experience of "merging with the Mind of God,"[46] he was chastised for indulging in fantasy and was told that what he imagined had happened had not happened and would "never come true in the future."[47] After reflecting on the matter, Warner decided that *if* his enlightenment had been real then nobody could take it away from him. Yet he also concluded that it had not been real because it was already in the past—"it wasn't here and it wasn't now"—therefore it had been a "dream."[48] Ultimately, Warner decided, the mystical experience was an impediment to his ability to live in the here and now. To underscore the point, he relates an episode immediately following the whole bittersweet event; this was the act of eating a Japanese tangerine, or *mikan*, at his desk at work. Every stage in the act of eating the tangerine, from observing its color to removing the peel to tasting the sweetness of the fruit, took on a sublime existential importance. When Warner e-mailed Nishijima about this event, the master wrote back to him, suggesting that "eating a tangerine is real enlightenment."[49]

For Warner, the point of reporting this prolonged unfolding episode of awareness is to show the folly of attaching any real importance to things that appear to be divine illumination and to demonstrate the paradox that the truly enlightened man knows there is no enlightenment. Having read through the passage several times, I cannot help but think that this is really the narrative of a certain tragedy. If Warner had had any acquaintance with the mystical or philosophical traditions of the West, he might have interpreted his experience along the river or with his larger than life dreams—or even with the tangerine—in very different terms, and, while acknowledging their transitory nature, he might have at least been able to ponder from another angle the difference between "real" and subsidiary forms of enlightenment.

The problem is reminiscent of what C. S. Lewis refers to as "transposition," the attempt to reconcile the gap between higher and lower modes of experience, in this case the gap between spiritual reality and natural reality. Lewis argues that lower modes of experience can give us a glimpse into the true nature of the higher reality, but they should not be confused with the real thing. Just as drawings on paper reflect the true form of the object drawn and written words reflect the true essence of the signified original, the delights attained through the joys of life experience reflect the sublime nature of the intangible yet real origin of all delights. In this sense, the eating of the tangerine would have to be seen as something of a copy of the enlightenment that Warner had achieved, not the real thing. In Christian terms, the tangerine would be seen as a sacramental reminder of the true, though unfortunately fleeting, joy of enlightenment but certainly not the enlightenment itself.

I am not saying that the natural act of eating somehow blossoms into the Christian sacrament. I am saying that the Spiritual Reality, which existed before there were any creatures who ate, gives this natural act a new meaning, and more than a new meaning: makes it in a certain context to be a different thing. In a word, I think that real landscapes enter into pictures, not that pictures will one day sprout into real trees and grass.[50]

Warner's conclusion that eating a tangerine is real enlightenment, while dismissing a possibly authentic ecstatic experience as fantasy, seems to indicate either a limitation in Warner's ability to judge such matters or possibly a deficiency in the way "Zen" categorizes spiritual experience. Assuming provisionally that the latter case is true, the deficiency itself provides a very good argument for the historical necessity of an ongoing dialectical exchange between the spiritualities of East and West. To use the idiom of Nishida Kitarō (1870–1966), the phenomenon of enlightenment may very well be a "mutually contradictory self-identity," that is, a universal concrete that comes to its historical fulfillment through the dialectical interaction of different spiritual traditions. From a historical standpoint, it may be the case that westerners such as Warner need Zen to understand that simple acts of everyday life, such as eating a tangerine, can indeed be moments of divine grace. Conversely, westerners can bring to Zen their own understanding of sacramentality or their sense that even though time is a fleeting thing it is still the mode in which God operates on our puny consciousnesses and that just because an experience took place in the temporal past this does not mean that its traces are *gone*. Maybe Zen is supposed to acquire from the West some sense of the idea that the Absolute, however unknowable, is real and that the transitory nature of life should lead us not to the conclusion that this world is an illusion but rather to the conclusion that this world may be a transposition of the kingdom of God into a lower modality. Of course, if westerners do not possess such understandings, they can bring little to the dialectical exchange and can only offer such observations as, "[T]hese so-called enlightenment experiences just really aren't all that and a bag o' chips."[51]

Warner sees himself as a true Zen man and is actually quite dogmatic in his pronouncement of the Sōtō teaching that *zazen* is itself the primary "end" of Zen practice and is thus as close as one can get to anything like enlightenment. "Do a lot of zazen," Warner tells us, "and you'll see for yourself."[52] "The only enlightenment that really matters," he concludes, "is right here and right now. You have it right in the palm of your hand. It shines from your eye and illuminates everything you see."[53] In considering the scant religious understanding that Warner appears to exhibit in his definition of Zen and Zen experience, comments such as these beg the question "Says who?"

The question of authority is addressed repeatedly in the pages of *Hardcore Zen*. True to his punk origins, Warner claims to be an anti-authoritarian and sees Zen as the perfect path for people with rebellious natures. He also acknowledges that rebellion against authority can be childish and immature and concedes that "every mature person accepts some amount of authority."[54] Warner's conflicts with authority and authority figures seem to be rooted in a fundamental confusion between the concepts of authority and power.

> We have, buried within us, an unspoken, unacknowledged belief that there are some people who are somehow better than others, more deserving than ourselves—that authorities are somehow *worthy* of the authority they wield.[55]

Obviously authority, which includes author*ship*, emerges from the reality that some people are indeed better, stronger, smarter, more qualified, and undeniably more "worthy" than others. The Buddha himself was a natural authority figure, and he achieved his authority not through the imposition of power over his disciples but by serving as the kind of example they chose to follow. Warner, who recognizes the superior qualities possessed by his teacher Nishijima, to say nothing of his monster movie idol Eiji Tsuburaya (1901–70), gives freely to them the authority they possess, sometimes even to the point of obsequiousness. The authority he fears and despises is the authority of those who hold arbitrary power over him, yet he fails to distinguish between authority and arbitrary power. Accordingly, he never explains why some authority is worthy of acceptance and other authority is simply wrong. True to his view of Zen, he simply leaves the contradiction unexplained. In one of his many invectives, he equates submission to authority with a relinquishing of responsibility.

> No matter what authority you submit to—your teacher, your government, even Jesus H. Christ or Gautama Buddha himself—that authority is wrong. It's wrong because the very concept of authority is already a mistake. Deferring to authority is nothing more than a cowardly shirking of responsibility. The more power you grant an authority figure the worse you can behave in his name. That's why people who take God as their ultimate authority are always capable of the worst humanity has to offer.[56]

Leaving aside for the moment all critiques of Warner's non sequitur—the common yet rarely challenged charge made against all people of faith that because some religious people misuse religion all religious people will do so eventually—we can see that his Zen is unabashedly anarchist, and in this sense it is unabashedly "punk." With no reference whatsoever to his own virtues or qualifications, he assumes a position of superiority and judgment over those individuals society has placed over *him*. "My teachers and school administrators," he writes, "had by and large shown themselves to be hardly worthy of my contempt let alone my respect."[57] Arguably, the punk insistence on the absolute sovereignty of the self is the most dangerous form of authority in existence. It is based on little more than the ego and acknowledges no order of moral hierarchy but preference. If the punk ego, which defines the world in terms of a dichotomy of (1) things that "suck" and (2) things that "rock," finds Zen to be an accommodating spiritual path, it must be because Zen has relinquished *its* responsibility to define such simple things as authority or the reasons for it.

As a student at Kent State University, Warner attended a cooking class sponsored by a local Hare Krishna community. There he met "Terry," a Krishna convert who impressed Warner with a "rare state of inner with-it-ness,"[58] although apparently he later became a fugitive from justice in relation to a "bizarre murder." "I gave up on Holy Men after that," Warner writes.[59] It is unfortunate, though perhaps not uncommon, that one negative experience is enough to spoil young people on religion permanently, but it is a testament to Warner's deep spiritual curiosity that he remained open-minded to the pursuit of truth.

> I'd pretty much ruled out religion as a path to truth. So I thought about science for a while. The idea that there could be a sensible mathematical or scientific solution that we *just haven't quite figured out yet* seemed pretty appealing. But looking into that a little further, it was clear that scientific answers were never really going to do it either, because the best science can ever hope to do is represent reality in some way. But that's not enough. Truth has to be bigger than theories, bigger than explanations, bigger than symbols. It has to *be* everything.[60]

For a number of years, the punk rock scene served as the "everything" for Warner. When he first heard the band Zero Defex in his hometown of Akron, Ohio, he felt as if he had experienced a "religious revelation."[61] He auditioned for the band, became its bass player, and enjoyed some success in local gigs and one nationally recognized recording, "Drop the A-Bomb on Me."

If Warner's account is any indication, his college experience was largely devoid of transformative moments except for the term he enrolled in a class on Zen Buddhism. The instructor, Tim McCarthy, was down to earth and accessible and gave Warner his first exposure to *zazen* and the Heart Sutra. It is unstated but fairly obvious that this exposure to Japanese culture was at least partly responsible (along with his love of Japanese monster movies) for Warner's decision to apply for the Japan Exchange and Teaching (JET) program when he graduated from Kent State. A government-sponsored exchange program, JET sends American college graduates to Japan to assist in public schools as English instructors. Through the JET program, Warner was able to move to Japan, work, and pursue more formal Zen training with Nishijima. He was also able to make contact with Tsurubaya Productions in Tokyo and arrange a job interview with the chief executive officer, Noboru Tsurubaya. Within a few years of arriving in Japan, Warner had succeeded in combining all of his diverse passions into one expatriate lifestyle, giving us the synthesis of Zen, punk rock, and monster movies that defines this new dispensation of Buddhism.

In expounding his hardcore dharma, Warner frequently adopts the false humility of the "don't listen to me, what do I know?" variety, yet he speaks authoritatively throughout the book. Some Zen masters, Seung Sahn to name only one, succeed in making a lighthearted detachment from authority and hierarchy the core of their teaching, and they consistently refer all questions of power, order, and discrimination back to basic dharma principles such as "only don't know!"[62] Warner, though, presents himself as ponderously moralistic, critical, irreverent, in-your-face, and profane. His is the self-proclaimed authority of the punk who respects nothing, not the revealed authority of the Zen master who has attained nonattachment. If not for the fact that Warner has decided to define his punk lifestyle as Zen, complete with *shiho* (dharma transmission) from a certified Japanese master, he would have no authority whatsoever.

I confess to wondering what kind of ordination Warner received and on what criteria he was evaluated. Again, I am not qualified to judge the criteria that constitute the attainment of that state of "something like enlightenment but not enlightenment" that leads to fitness for dharma transmission, but, by Warner's own admission, "Guys who've received Dharma Transmission are a dime a dozen." His certifying master, Gudo Nishijima, is portrayed as the typical fierce, idiosyncratic Zen monk who combines intelligence, superciliousness, and the ability to win arguments almost through the sheer force of his personality. Nishijima obviously won Warner's loyalty by judging that punks are good because they "dress the way they want to, not the way society tells them how to dress."[63] I have no doubts that Warner is a dedicated practitioner of *zazen*, and I suspect that on the basis of his exegesis of the

Heart Sutra he has acquainted himself with other classic texts of the Zen tradition.[64] The degree to which he might really understand Zen tradition, however, is not evident in *Hardcore Zen* because what he has chosen to transmit is much more autobiographical than doctrinal.

Warner's life formation prior to receiving dharma transmission was, as noted above, apparently devoid of any serious religious or academic training. On the question of religion, Warner gives no indication of having grown up in any church community, but he admits to having been a "spiritual-minded kid" who speculated frequently on the problem of existence, that is, wondering where he came from. [65] Among the possibilities he sifted through were theories that he was a "brain in a jar somewhere" or a "space alien being raised by human parents."[66] An empiricist through and through, Warner realized that the lack of special powers or antennae excluded that possibility, but obviously there was nothing like catechism classes, Sunday school, or any home-based religious education to provide him with an alternative paradigm. Nevertheless, Warner's search for the truth went on.

> Religions and social institutions aside, I've always felt a need to understand the way things are. It's hard for me to say why. In fact, it's always been far more puzzling to me that more people *don't* feel such a strong need to know. Most of the folks who say they want to understand these things seem to settle for explanations that, as far as I can see, explain things about as well as my childish ideas about being a brain in a jar or a space alien.[67]

In reflecting on the unlikely relationship between Zen and punk rock, Warner observes that "in its early days, punk had a lot in common with Zen."[68]

> People have taken exception to my equating a noble tradition like Zen Buddhism with a scrappy upstart like punk rock. Zen Buddhism is ancient and venerable. Punk is trash. But punk is a cultural movement that was made possible only because of the increased understanding of reality that emerged in the twentieth century, the so-called postmodern worldview. The punks understood that all social institutions and socially approved codes of dress and behavior were a sham. This is one of the first steps to understanding. It's unfortunate that not many punks actually followed through to what punk really implied: that *all* of our values need to be questioned.[69]

This brings us, finally, back to the issue of questioning values and to Warner's ultimate conclusion that Zen is essentially the questioning of everything. Moreover, because Zen points to the truth and truth *is* reality and reality *is* God and so on, we find ourselves left with the conclusion that everything is the *questioning* of everything and the only thing that matters is the questioner and the questions. If this were the "landing place" of Warner's gospel, that is, if he wanted to do nothing more than celebrate the fusion of punk, Godzilla, and his preference for sitting meditation, then hardcore Zen might take its place among other modes of postmodernism and attain the status of a logical, if somewhat rough-edged, addition to the genre of New Age Zen that has dominated popular Zen experience in the West since the mid-1970s. For better or worse, though, Warner takes hardcore Zen beyond the vapidity of middle-class "anarchy," beyond the pastiche revolutions of bad rock and roll, and even beyond the angst of rapidly aging Gen Xers. In a gesture that is neither punk nor Zen but strangely secular and bourgeois, Warner launches one critical salvo at the traditional understanding of good and evil that informs all spiritual morality and another at the practitioners of psychedelic Zen. In dismissing both religious ethics and the possibility of psychedelic illumination, he reinforces an inherently materialistic worldview while at the same time certifying bourgeois psychologism as a "real deal" spiritual teaching.

On the issue of conventional morality, that is, those standards of behavior and ethics that have emerged in human history as a result of persistent questioning about the nature of good and evil, Warner has this to say.

> All of our religious and social codes come down to us from human beings who made connections between certain actions and their results. Sometimes their deductions were correct and sometimes they were dead wrong. But correct or not, they were passed down from generation to generation, each time gathering more psychological and social weight. Thousands of years later, one man's supposition about the connection between something he did last Thursday and some good luck he had the following weekend has become a Rule of God that none shall violate lest he be damned for eternity.[70]

Without explaining how the historical transition took place, the moral rules of humanity stop being the product of "one man's supposition"—are we to guess this man is Jesus between the Last Supper and Easter?—and become products of the "traumas we've all carried around in our heads since before we were three years old."[71] It is normal for modern secular scholars to attribute the existence of morals and social codes to any number of material causes. As we know, entire methodologies have been built around biological evolution, repressed infantile sexuality, aggressive patriarchy, economic determinism, and so on. Anything that *can* be put forth as a replacement for divine truth as the organizing principle of history *has* been put forth. That being said, it is also not uncommon for modern religious believers to make connections between various elements of modern social sciences and what they believe to be divine truth. In most cases, this occurs as a case of what I have identified earlier as transposition. The "Oedipus complex," for example, as explained by psychoanalysis, can make intuitive sense, even for people of faith, but the myth of Oedipus that makes the "complex" intelligible is not mistaken for literal truth, nor is it mistaken for divine truth. It is, rather, understood as a reflection of divine truth that has entered into the body of world mythology, into the body of cultural knowledge, and into the body of science.

In an historical understanding of morality that admits the objective reality of both matter and spirit, myth and history can reinforce each other, as can science and religion. Yet Warner's reading of the origins of moral conduct comes from an unexamined modern psychological model that separates the branch of moral behavior from the root of any objective spiritual reality. According to Warner's understanding, "a lot of religious teachings sprang from the genuine understanding of certain fundamental things that had to be done in order to preserve society."[72] He then extends this sociohistorical understanding of ethics to the realms of spiritual beings. "Gods and demons," he asserts, "are culturally bound."[73]

> What the ancients called visions of gods and demons and visits to heavens or hells are what we now call hallucinations, manic states, depressive states—even psychosis. . . . Visions and auditory hallucinations, whether you're seeing four-armed buddhas doing the Hippy Hippy Shake or hearing talking wallabees tell you to buy an AK-47 and wipe out the office are signs of faulty processes within the brain. Nothing more.[74]

Leaving aside for the moment the fact that Warner is perhaps less qualified to discuss psychology or neurobiology than he is religion, his comments on "gods and demons" are especially interesting.

> Zen Buddhism speaks of *makyo* [*sic*] or "the world of demons." Of course there isn't any actual realm that is the world of demons. But disturbing psychological states can seem so real that people react to them just as if they were absolutely real and that is a problem.[75]

This is indeed a problem—one also better left to a Buddhist scholar, but I have been long under the impression that Mahayana Buddhism acknowledges the existence of a profusion of Buddha fields, Buddha wombs, hells, and demonic regions and argues that it is this phenomenal world of matter that does *not* exist. While the Zen tradition has often been elusive about admitting the objective reality of the spiritual world and its inhabitants, it has at least been coherently and self-consciously elusive. The Zen dialectic, which seeks a way through dichotomies, in particular the dichotomies of subject and object, world and self, I and thou, heaven and hell, and so on, is a dialectic of transcendence. The subject and object exist only provisionally to collapse into a higher unity; accordingly, the "Otherness" of spiritual entities is deliberately downplayed because overweening attachment to that Otherness poses a barrier to the spiritual unity that the self must attain through enlightenment. It seems best to say that on the topic of subject-object relationships, including the relationship between the self and the spirit world, Buddhism is speaking of entirely different categories of experience, categories that cannot be reduced to material phenomena or even material psychology. Yet Warner insists that the spiritual Other is merely a network of repressed thoughts. On the subject of demons in particular, Warner asserts that they are repressed thoughts that seem so "alien" that "they take on abstract shapes or appear in the form of hallucinations, things literally experienced 'out there.'"[76]

If, as Warner suggests, all of our concepts of good are socially constructed and our concepts of evil are psychologically produced, there is no room for any objective spiritual reality and little room for any objective material reality outside the self. The logical conclusion of this judgment is that it removes the foundation of truth, reality, goodness, badness, and of course Warner's own authority to speak on any of these matters. Although he says, "[Y]ou can only do good when you know what bad really is and where it comes from," he acknowledges no objective standard by means of which bad or good can be identified as such.[77] While it is unlikely that Warner is aware that his judgments on the fundamentally subjective nature of spiritual reality render every other judgment he makes in his book invalid, it is likely that he would not care. He is, after all, an "anarchist." The historical encounter between the nonattachment of Zen and the rebellious anarchy of punk seems to be one that transforms Zen's well-known lighthearted avoidance of logic into an in-your-face repudiation of any obligation to be coherent.

There exists a fundamental difference between transcending the world and dismissing it as a false reality, because the latter judgment implies the reality of both a perceiver and a perceived. Modern Zen has avoided having to weigh in decisively on this fundamental epistemological problem because it was formed in the same cultural climate that gave birth to post-structuralism, postmodernism, and every conceivable form of social, historical, and cultural deconstruction. For over a century Zen has been involved in a healthy critique of the assumptions of modernity even as it has participated in the modern project of internationalism and cultural exchange, increasing knowledge and synthesizing world religious traditions. Now that the modern world has moved from self-critique to self-undoing, Zen continues to lend spiritual justification to the enterprise. Ironically, though, Zen no longer attempts to rescue history by holding up "spirit" as the solution to a materialistic civilization gone wrong. Instead, through such "expedient means" as hardcore punk, it deals the final blow even to spirit, invoking psychologism as the basis for reality and the perceiving subject as the only standard for measuring reality. If future disciples of hardcore Zen intend to look to people like Warner for spiritual leadership, they need to recognize that these masters are not following a technically spiritual path; they are following a path of subject-centeredness that fails to rise even to the level of coherent solipsism. The ethical and historical problems that lie at the base of this reality are alarming to say the least.

Despite the rejection of objective standards of value in hardcore Zen, Warner himself is a relentless moralizer, and directs a good deal of his Zen master wrath to the question of psychedelics. His discomfort with psychedelic Buddhism follows a formulaic pattern of condemnation on the basis of partial experience. It is clear that he has used drugs and known many users of them, and his experiences with psychedelic substances have left him unimpressed. Nevertheless, his denunciation of psychedelics is shrill, puritanical, and uncompromisingly hostile; it also betrays the common but one-dimensional Generation X attitude toward psychedelics that generally sees them as only a means of recreation and devoid of any potential spiritual use.

The debate over the use and misuse of psychedelic drugs in the context of religion, specifically Zen Buddhism, is now over fifty years old. In a 2005 article, "Ecstatic Treks through the Demon Regions," I traced the contours of this debate all the way through the criminalization of hallucinogens in 1966, and suggested that from this year forward, and especially in the mid-1970s, Zen relinquished whatever potential it may have once had for world-historical transformation and traded it in for genteel respectability.[78] I also speculated that perhaps Zen's transformational agency had even been assumed by psychedelic experience, which, despite a dynamic and seemingly symbiotic association with Zen in the 1950s and early 1960s, was ultimately dismissed as a false form of consciousness by a quorum of celebrated Zen scholars. At the point where Zen experience and psychedelic experience parted ways, Zen became a full-fledged consumer commodity. From the 1970s on, Zen spirituality became a species of New Age psychology and was redefined as a progressive mode of relaxation and self-actualization for an overstressed bourgeoisie. Psychedelic experience, on the other hand, after being criminalized in 1966, was banished from decent society and demonized for its association with drug addicts, subversives, and counterculture lowlifes.

Interestingly, psychedelic experience has made something of a comeback since the 1990s, reclaiming the road to acceptance as a result of the persistence of medical and social research organizations such as the Multi-disciplinary Society for Psychedelic Studies (MAPS). Psychedelic culture was also reinvigorated during the 1990s due to the efforts of the ethnobotanist Terence McKenna (1943–2000), whose prolific output of books, interviews, lectures, and articles helped raise awareness of psychedelic consciousness not only as a cultural and historical phenomenon but also as a potential spiritual path. In terms of its spiritual aspirations, though, McKenna's psychedelic experience acknowledged and even affirmed the rift between Zen and psychedelic culture. McKenna had little use for simple meditation and believed that the only valid path to spiritual gnosis was through the ingestion of hallucinogenic substances such as mushrooms and dimethyltryptamine (DMT).

The appearance of *Zig Zag Zen,* edited by Allan Hunt Badiner and Alex Grey in 2002, marked something of a return of psychedelic conscious to the world of Zen experience. This richly illustrated and well-written book, in a variety of interviews, essays, and works of art, reopens the old question of whether Buddhism and the psychedelic experience are mutually reinforcing. The editors also call for an "intelligent and compassionate debate" on the various problems of drug use and abuse in American society.[79] Warner's contribution to this debate is clearly spelled out in the chapter "Pass Me the Ecstasy." On discovering the book, he wrote:

> I was deeply disappointed to find a putrid little book called *Zig Zag Zen.* . . . I picked up that lump of turd and read it. Near as I can come to making any sense out of it, Badiner's argument goes something like this: (A) Buddhism is about enlightenment; (B) enlightenment is some far-out, trippy mystical brain-fuck kind of state; (C) drugs will screw up your brain too; therefore (D) doing drugs will get you enlightened.

There would be no point in making a detailed defense of the content of *Zig Zag Zen* against such charges here, but those who read the book will find that the statements of such contributors as Rick Fields, Peter Matthiessen, Huston Smith, Charles Tart, and Terence McKenna are both eloquent and well conceived. It is unfortunate that Warner does not give these authors a fair hearing—the dialogue that the editors invite is historically pertinent and well worth having—but Warner opts out, and perhaps this is where a conclusion to the subject of hardcore Zen finally becomes clear.

Hardcore Zen does not give or respond to invitations to debate, it does not engage in dialogue, it does not seek to unify, it does not seek deeper knowledge of history or culture, and ultimately it does not think. Hardcore Zen, in the final analysis, seems to be little more than the self-congratulatory reflections of the ego that has taken tentative steps away from modern disillusionment and for that effort has declared itself wise. The hardcore Zen ego does not seek the fullness of any absolute good, nor does it even recognize any absolute good. It merely abandons what it sees as absurd or useless to itself, and for that effort, too, declares itself wise. The hardcore ego is ultimately disengaged from any reality but the world of experience immediately known to itself at any moment. If what it knows is monster movies, then reality is monster movies; if what it knows is punk rock, then reality is punk rock. The idea that there might exist some greater objective truth, some deeper history, some more complex set of circumstances than those that are obtained at the moment the ego gazes out upon the world and judges, is a power trip of some kind, and the power trips of the Other are to be resisted, especially those power trips that go by the name of knowledge, education, or tradition. Human beings have always been ignorant, but they have rarely celebrated ignorance, and they have never defined ignorance as a spiritual path. With hardcore Zen, ill-mannered ignorance becomes dharma itself.

Conclusion: What Does It All Mean?

In assessing the historical significance of hardcore Zen, perhaps we can begin by revisiting Alan Watts's article on beat and square Zen. I believe Watts was correct when he said that a person seeking to understand Zen should first gain a thorough understanding of his or her own culture and religion. I would add that all people under all circumstances should gain a thorough understanding of their own culture; the means by which this occurs has traditionally been known as education. From the standpoint of education, at least as it is displayed in the pages of *Hardcore Zen*, Warner falls short of any objective qualification that might encourage us to take him seriously as a master or scholar of Zen, his *shiho* notwithstanding. More unsettling than Warner's lack of scholarly depth, though, is the attitude of resentment that pervades *Hardcore Zen*. On this matter, too, Watts has some pertinent observations to review and consider. At one point in his article, he criticizes the beats, Jack Kerouac in particular, for lacking a true Zen spirit. Watts suggests that Kerouac is "always a shade too self-conscious, too subjective and too strident to have the flavor of Zen."[80]

When Kerouac gives his final philosophical statement, "I don't know. I don't care. And it doesn't make any difference"—the cat is out of the bag, for there is a hostility in these words which clangs with self-defense. But just because Zen truly surpasses convention and its values, it has no need to say "To hell with it," nor to underline with violence the fact that anything goes.[81]

If beat Zen had trouble concealing its "hostility" and "violence," hardcore Zen makes no such attempt. If anything, the philosophy of hardcore Zen has turned these attitudes into core principles. Hostility, a spirit of violence, anger, rebellion, and resentment—those qualities that have defined punk rock since its inception as a radically angry, anti-establishment aesthetic in the 1970s—are also the defining qualities of hardcore Zen. In a society already wracked with nonspecific but widespread rage and obsessed with "respect" and self-validation, hardcore Zen could very well become a new wave of religious consciousness for disillusioned young people. If this happens, it will, as I have suggested, signal as great a collapse in modern historical consciousness as it will in authentic Zen consciousness.

Viewed through the lens of popular Zen, maybe this is just the way the cookie crumbles. It seems regrettable that the rich and insightful work started by Suzuki and carried on for over a century by people like Humphreys, Watts, Aitken, Kapleau, Bernard Glassman, Maurine Stuart, Ray Jordan, and so on, should, by hardcore Zen's "standards" of value, become simply a meaningless pile of paper—or worse—in the postmodern world. I suppose it goes without saying that in the context of hardcore, great historical Zen masters such as Dōgen, Hakuin, and Bankei, all the way down to the Buddha himself, have nothing really valid to tell us about anything either. All that matters is to sit and question reality—that is, Zen—and as long as this happens Zen is Zen and the rest is "crap." According to Zen, as it has evolved in Western pop culture, there are no judgments to make about anything. What *is* simply *is*, and what was does not matter anymore.

Viewed through the lens of history, the problem is more complicated, but we can break it down into broad modern and postmodern interpretive components.

From the standpoint of the modern, punk Zen is, as I have suggested, a kind of derailment from the synthetic track that "Eastern" philosophy and "Western" religion had opened for the world-historical evolution of human consciousness. As a good postmodern historian, I recognize that mentioning things like "East" and "West" and some narrative called "world-historical evolution" will draw ridicule from readers well trained in detecting essentialism and totalizing strategies at long range. Fine. This postmodern historian, while duly incredulous about constructed essences and *modern* narratives, has yet to renounce the notion of essences and metanarratives per se. I would agree with Richard Rorty that there is "nothing wrong with the hopes of the Enlightenment," and I would think that the attainment of "common ground," or at least authentic tolerance in matters relating to religion, could still be among these hopes.[82] The hard work of sincere and unabashedly reverent people such as Suzuki, Humphreys, Merton, Watts, and Snyder—indeed, *all* of the "Western Buddhists" and "Christian Daoists"—is both evidence of and grounds for hope that religious tolerance based on mutual knowledge and veneration, rather than merely state-sanctioned "freedom of worship," may yet be possible within the historical process. Yet the punk reduction of Zen to a radical and irreverent individualism not only diminishes the potency of Zen as a bearer of objective religious truth; it also marks a dialectically retrogressive jump, detaching a historically evolving Zen from its acquired modern function.

From the standpoint of the postmodern, hardcore Zen fails to deliver on the great and perhaps only promise that postmodernism offers for redeeming the historical world, which is the reopening of the last historical escape route to the realms of spirit. In questioning the assumptions of modern civilization, postmodernism has succeeded in rendering all forms of constructed truth officially "destabilized." The most pervasive and well-concealed assumption of modernization, materialism itself, is especially vulnerable to postmodern critique, and those rare academics who still embrace a spiritual worldview have found a space in which to insert a critical but positive wedge into this keystone of modern civilization. By invoking postmodernism, believers are able to pry open a wormhole to the premodern and exalt, among the various diversities of voice and multiplicities of discourse, odd things such as faith, religion, and belief in the spiritual world. The only way a *truly* subversive project like this can avoid being branded as absurd or "reactionary" is to keep the postmodern terrain open, free, and receptive to the process of real thinking. Throughout the entirety of a history that goes back at least to 1893, modern Zen has prefigured postmodern Zen, providing the very kind of freshness, freedom, and intellectual stimulation that has characterized the best in postmodern thought. Zen has indeed been a great leavening for Western materialism, even to the point of intimating its full transformation into something posthistorically nonmaterial. Zen has indeed helped to revitalize Western spirituality, and it may yet succeed in contributing to a posthistorical synthesis of spirit and matter that could provide humanity a reason to be optimistic about the future. Hardcore Zen, though, in rejecting intellectual endeavor for the sake of an egocentric "feel-good" experience that no longer even feels good, has robbed Zen even further of its power to transform the historical world in any positive way. In this sense, hardcore Zen, though it masquerades as a spiritual path, represents a real setback to any strategy of recapturing the discursive ground for the spirit in history.

Notes

[1] Brad Warner, *Hardcore Zen: Punk Rock, Monster Movies, and the Truth about Reality* (Boston: Wisdom, 2003), 4.

[2] Ibid., 81–82.

[3] Evan Dashevsky, review of *Hardcore Zen,* http://contemporarylit.about.com/cs/currentreviews/fr/hardcorezen.htm (accessed September 22, 2007).

[4] Jon Zuck, review of *Hardcore Zen,* http://www.frimmin.com/books/hardcorezen.html (accessed September 22, 2007).

[5] See Masao Abe, *Zen and Western Thought* (Honolulu: University of Hawai'i Press, 1989), 25.

[6] See Noah Levine, *Dharma Punx: A Memoir* (San Francisco: HarperCollins, 2004).

[7] Christmas Humphreys, *Zen Buddhism* (London: Diamond, 1996), 139.

[8] Warner, *Hardcore Zen*, 5.

[9] D. T. Suzuki, "On Satori: The Revelation of a New Truth in Zen Buddhism," in *The Essentials of Zen Buddhism*, ed. Bernard Phillips (New York: Dutton, 1962), 154.

[10] Robert H. Sharf, "Whose Zen? Zen Nationalism Revisited," in *Rude Awakenings: Zen, the Kyoto School, and the Question of Nationalism,* ed. James W. Heisig and John Maraldo (Honolulu: University of Hawai'i Press, 1995), 44.

[11] Ibid., 43–44.

[12] Warner, *Hardcore Zen,* 83.

[13] Shaku Sōen, "The Law of Cause and Effect as Taught by Buddha," in *The World Congress of Religions: The Addresses and Papers Delivered before the Parliament and the Abstract of the Congress,* ed. J. W. Hanson (Chicago: W. B. Conkey,1894), 390.

[14] Rick Fields, *How the Swans Came to the Lake: A Narrative History of Buddhism in America* (Boston: Shambala, 1992), 128.

[15] Ibid., 139.

[16] Christopher Ives, "Ethical Pitfalls in Imperial Zen and Nishida Philosophy," in *Rude Awakenings: Zen, the Kyoto School, and the Question of Nationalism,* ed. James W. Heisig and John Maraldo (Honolulu: University of Hawai'i Press, 1995), 17.

[17] See Brian Victoria, *Zen at War* (New York: Weatherhill, 1997), for a study of the relationship between Zen Buddhism and the Japanese imperial military.

[18] See Suzuki's introduction to D. T. Suzuki, Erich Fromm, and Richard De Martino, *Zen Buddhism and Psychoanalysis* (New York: Grove, 1963).

[19] D. T. Suzuki, "Zen in the Modern World," in *The Essentials of Zen Buddhism*, ed. Bernard Phillips (New York: Dutton, 1962), 371.

[20] Alan Watts, "Beat Zen, Square Zen, and Zen," in *This Is It and Other Essays on Zen and Spiritual Experience* (New York: Pantheon, 1958), 93.

[21] Ibid., 103–4.

[22] Ibid., 106.

[23] Ibid., 100.

[24] Ibid., 91.

[25] See D. T. Suzuki, Alan Watts, Ray Jordan, Robert Aitken, and Richard Leavitt, "Drugs and Buddhism: A Symposium," *Eastern Buddhist* 4, no. 2 (October 1971): 138–40.

[26] Alan Watts, "The New Alchemy," in *This Is It and Other Essays on Zen and Spiritual Experience* (New York: Pantheon, 1958), 129.

[27] Warner, *Hardcore Zen,* 8.

[28] Ibid.

[29] Ibid., 17.

[30] Ibid., 191.

[31] Ibid., 14.

[32] Ibid., 7.

[33] Ibid.

[34] Ibid., 18.

[35] Ibid., 29.

[36] Ibid., 9.

[37] Ibid., 3.

[38] D. T. Suzuki, "History of Zen Buddhism from Boddhidharma to Hui Neng (Yeno), in *Essays in Zen Buddhism, First Series* (New York: Grove, 1961), 165.

[39] Ibid., 164.

[40] Warner, *Hardcore Zen,* 8.

[41] Ibid., 89.

[42] Thomas P. Kasulis, *Zen Action, Zen Person* (Honolulu: University of Hawai'i Press, 1981), 104.

[43] Warner, *Hardcore Zen,* 96.

[44] Ibid.

[45] Ibid., 178.

[46] Ibid., 183.

[47] Ibid., 180.

[48] Ibid., 181.

[49] Ibid., 183.

[50] C. S. Lewis. "Transposition," in *The Weight of Glory and Other Addresses* (San Francisco: Harper, [1949] 2001), 112.

[51] Warner, *Hardcore Zen,* 94.

[52] Ibid., 98.

[53] Ibid.

[54] Ibid., 139.

[55] Ibid.

[56] Ibid., 29.

[57] Ibid., 138.

[58] Ibid., 12.

[59] Ibid.

[60] Ibid., 15.

[61] Ibid., 22.

[62] Seung Sahn, *Only Don't Know: The Teaching Letters of Zen Master Seung Sahn* (San Francisco: Four Seasons Foundation, 1982).

[63] Warner, *Hardcore Zen,* 29.

[64] Warner's latest book, *Sit Down and Shut Up* (Novato, CA: New World Library, 2007), a "plain language" essay on Dōgen's *Shōbōgenzō* (Treasury of the Right Dharma Eye), is indeed evidence that he has read other Buddhist texts. While it is similar to *Hardcore Zen* inasmuch as it is profane, inarticulate, and largely incoherent, it is also evidence that punk Zen is increasing rather than decreasing in popularity.

[65] Warner, *Hardcore Zen,* 14.

[66] Ibid., 13.

[67] Ibid., 14–15.

[68] Ibid., 28.

[69] Ibid., 30.

[70] Ibid., 114.

[71] Ibid., 115.

[72] Ibid., 113.

[73] Ibid., 117.

[74] Ibid., 116–17.

[75] Ibid., 116.

[76] Ibid.

[77] Ibid., 119.

[78] Eric Cunningham, "Ecstatic Treks through the Demon Regions: Zen and the *Satori* of Psychedelic Experience," on *E-ASPAC*, an Electronic Journal in Asian Studies, at http://mcel.pacificu.edu/easpac/2005/cunningham.php3. (accessed September 22, 2007).

[79] Allan Hunt Badiner and Alex Grey, eds., *Zig Zag Zen* (San Francisco: Chronicle, 2003), 10.

[80] Watts, "Beat Zen, Square Zen, and Zen," 93.

[81] Ibid.

[82] Richard Rorty, "Solidarity or Objectivity," in *From Modernism to Postmodernism: An Anthology*, ed. Lawrence Cahoone (Malden, MA: Blackwell, 2003), 454.

7

The Elusive Middle

Between Romanticism and Condemnation in the Buddhist Imaginary

Mark T. Unno

A master teaching a disciple is like the blind leading the blind.

—Zen proverb

There is only misinterpretation.

—Anti-Nietzsche

Although the present volume largely represents an effort in the academic fields of history and literary criticism, my own field is religious studies, I find myself quite at home here, first because I am an historian of religion and second because virtually all of the chapters included in this effort deal with religious themes. Whether by design or not, the presence of religion as a central concern should not come as a surprise, not only because religion has often played a pivotal role in history but because it has arguably been the source of so much misinterpretation as well as interpretation.

From the perspective of religious studies, there are certain methodological and theoretical issues of particular interest whose examination will hopefully make a meaningful contribution to this volume. Three areas in particular stand out when considering East-West studies involving religion: (1) the history of interpretation, (2) the interpretation of history, and (3) instantiations of interpretation in the study of Asian religions. Common to all of these dimensions of inquiry is the problem of interpretation considered in the process of globalization, that is, in the context of religious diversity and the global economy. In the global context, religions often tout ideologies that oppose the process of commodification driving the global economy, a process propelled by the desire for acquisition, consumption, and material gain. At the same time, religions are also often beholden to the same process of commodification even, or especially, as they attempt to support and sustain the institutions that promulgate ideologies of virtue and transcendence. Thus, histories of religions often depict complex narratives involving the tension between commodification and anticommodification, between the logic of consumptive desire, on the one hand, and the logic of duty, virtue, relational care, and transcendence on the other.

Indeed, the history of the study of religion also exhibits this tension. Religious studies arose in part as a reaction against and critique of the chauvinistic, imperialistic tendencies of religion, particularly in the West. Yet its growth as a discipline has been entangled in these same tendencies, in some cases dependent on and replicating social, political, and economic hegemonies. As Anthony E. Clark demonstrates in his essay in this volume, chauvinistic, prejudicial views of religion are certainly not limited to representatives and scholars of religions in the West. However, since the academic discipline of religious studies is a product of the West, the present essay begins with (1) an outline history of the interpretation of religion in the Western academy, goes on to (2) address the dynamics of interpretation within the context of postmodern globalization, and (3) illustrates some of the methodological issues with historical instances taken from the study of Asian religions, culminating with cases from modern Japanese Buddhism. From this kind of analysis it will become evident that misinterpretations East and West often involve problems of globalization and the commodified representation of religion in dynamic tension with the avowed interest of religious ideologies.

This will show just how difficult it is to be true to discourses of religious ethics and transcendence and to face the challenges of cross-cultural interpretation and misinterpretation with regard to religion. This difficulty is due in part to the epistemological complexities of postmodern scholarship on religion.

First, even within the postmodern context, we continue to be influenced by a kind of Newtonian scientific modernism that valorizes, indeed demands, a critical, distanced objectivity. Such an attitude is reflected in the work of scholars such as Jonathan Z. Smith.

Second, however, one strain of postmodern scholarship, in contrast, holds as an ideal, and demands, intersubjective engagement, as epitomized by the slogan "the personal is the political." This might also be reworded "the academic is the political," a view that has at various times been enunciated by, for example, the scholar of Tibetan Buddhism, Robert Thurman.

Third, many scholars find themselves caught between the demands of modern critical objectivity and postmodern intersubjective engagement, resulting in various permutations. A scholar such as Russell McCutcheon critically analyzes the nexus of ideological and sociological influences and assumptions that undercut the phenomenological claims of religionists, yet he does not situate himself within the same nexus, calling only for others' self-reflexivity without claiming a normative or constructive standpoint for himself.[1] Others, such as the Buddhist legal scholar Suekawa Hiroshi, have been socially and politically activist in their own normative engagement with scholarship, as well as critical of those who have failed to be sufficiently self-reflexive about the political influences on and of their scholarship.

The strands of this tension between the demand for distanced objectivity and engaged subjectivity have been interwoven into a complex tapestry in the history of interpretation, the interpretation of history, and instantiations of interpretation and misinterpretation in the study of religion East and West.

History of Interpretation

As the field of religious studies has matured, at various points scholars have undertaken self-reflexive surveys of its development. Some notable recent efforts include Frank E. Reynolds, "Reconstructing Liberal Education: A Religious Studies Perspective" (1990); Sumner B. Twiss, "Shaping the Curriculum: The Emergence of Religious Studies" (1995); and Jeffrey Kripal, "The Critical Study of Religion as a Modern Mystical Tradition" (2007).[2] Twiss's essay serves as a particularly useful point of reference for our purposes, as he identifies four phases in the development of religious studies in the United States: early modern theological (roughly 1800–1900), transitional ethnocentric (roughly 1900–1950), late modern critical scientific (roughly 1950–75), and postmodern hermeneutical (roughly 1975 onward). The trajectory that Twiss traces for the American study of religion is one that begins (following European practice) centered on Christian theological assumptions; gradually moves away from this in an attempt to place the center in a less-biased, more globally centered, pluralistic, model; and then goes on to further displace the center such that cultural history, not religious doctrine, becomes the basic framework within which the study of religion is considered.

Thus, of the early modern theological phase, Twiss states that the majority of faculty members were professors of divinity with Christian (Protestant) college seminary training. The transitional ethnocentric phase developed under the pressures of globalization: World War I, immigration, and the development of psychology and the social sciences. Yet most professors of religion continue to be trained in Christian divinity schools or seminaries, and the majority of professors and students are white Christians being prepared for social and professional life in the wider world. The third phase—late modern critical scientific—corresponds to the United States taking a dominant role in world affairs politically, economically, and technologically. The previous preeminence of the humanities began to give way to the natural and social sciences, in which institutions of higher education self-consciously considered themselves to be preparing an increasingly diverse student body (in terms of religion, race, ethnicity, class, gender, sexuality, and so on) to enter into active engagement in global society. Applying historical, textual, and social scientific methods to study the "world's religions," the ethnocentric and Judeo-Christian-centric approach to the study of religion was broken in principle, though perhaps not in practice. Where previously faculty came overwhelmingly from divinity schools and seminaries trained almost exclusively in New and Old Testament studies to teach in departments of religion, now, for the first time, there appeared positions in Judaic studies, the Hebrew Bible, and "world religions" to cover the rest. It is easy to forget that full-time positions devoted to Japanese or Chinese religions, religions of South Asia, Buddhism, or Islam have become widespread only in the past three dozen years or so and that this was a self-conscious development of the post–World War II period. The fourth phase—postmodern hermeneutical—"involves the vivid self-conscious awareness of pluralization within American society," of the existence of women and minorities, of global interdependence, of environmental issues, and so forth. The study of religion in "colleges and universities must take account of a student body shaped by such self-conscious pluralization, global sensitivity, and historical and social awareness." New areas have opened up in the study of the history of religions related to such areas as women and gender studies, African American studies, and Latino and Latin American studies, with attendant, interdisciplinary methodological developments in feminist theory, race theory, queer studies, and so forth. Yet, in the scope of the span of centuries that constitute the history of religions as a field, this latest phase covers barely three decades, still a fragile and tenuous exploratory period.

Interpretation of History: Interpretations in Postmodern Comparative Contexts

In what Twiss describes as the current, postmodern phase of religious studies, it is not merely that the subject matter has been opened up to cover groups, issues, and themes largely overlooked in the past. Rather, the very idea that a single narrative framework can encompass the global story of religion is called into question. Not only are there many alternative narratives that mutually contradict one another, but also each has it own logic, its own epistemology, its episteme. Thus, in seeking to represent and interpret different strands of religion, one must probe not only the question of what story to tell but what kind of story, not just what the story is but who is telling it, why they are telling it, and how it is told.

Religious studies emerged within a self-consciously pluralistic context, but it has taken time to begin to recognize just how diverse the context of global religion might be. The demand for recognition, representation, and interpretation of this diversity has in some sense run ahead of the discipline's methodological sophistication in dealing with this diversity. Thus, although individual scholars may recognize the limitation of defining religious studies' subject matter along traditional lines, many departments are still largely organized according to traditional categories of "world religions" such as Judaism, Christianity, Islam, Buddhism, and so forth. Moreover, while specialists representing these religions often comprise the departmental faculty, there is a limited awareness of how to justify the coexistence of these subject religions as constitutive of a coherent department.

As Jonathan Z. Smith noted in his seminal essay published a quarter of a century ago, "In Comparison a Magic Dwells," the justification for the existence of religious studies as an academic field may be said to depend on comparative understanding.[3] What makes "A" and "B" entities both religions and what is the basis for comparison that allows us to simultaneously group them together and differentiate them? In surveying the answers available to him, Smith found them lacking, and the fact that we continue to ask the same questions shows that we have yet to answer them fully.

> We must conclude this exercise in our own academic history in a most unsatisfactory manner. Each of the modes of comparison has been found problematic. Each of the new modes has been found to be a variant of an older mode: Moore, of the encyclopedic [attempt to provide a comprehensive catalog]; Goodenough, of the morphological [attempt to identify common features]; Neusner, of the ethnographic [attempt to define religion by characteristics of local praxis]. We know better how to [critically] evaluate comparisons, but we have gained little over our predecessors in either the method for making comparisons or the reasons for its practice. There is nothing easier than the making of patterns; from planaria to babies, and it is done with little apparent difficulty. But the "how" and the "why" and, above all, the "so what" remain most refractory. . . . It is a problem to be solved by theories and reasons, of which we have had too little. So we are left with the question, "How am I to apply what the one thing shows me to the case of two things?" The possibility of the study of religion depends on its answer.[4]

As so many of the essays in this volume make apparent, and as Smith suggests, there are a plethora of reasons, methods, and findings offered regarding the cross-cultural study of religion, from China to Japan and the West. Yet in the field of religious studies, foundational questions concerning the basic framework of inquiry remain obscure, or "refractory." What makes the work of scholars of, for example, early Confucian ethics, gender and Japanese Buddhism, and Native American religious ritual come together to constitute a coherent field of study? Indeed, whether such topics do belong together under the single rubric of religious studies continues to be debated without a widely agreed upon answer.

Interpretations in Postmodern Globalization

In *Critics Not Caretakers,* Russell McCutcheon expands the scope of critical inquiry framed by Jonathan Z. Smith to include the global social, political, and economic framework within which scholars of religious studies interpret religious history. Rather than questioning merely the objective adequacy of the methods and theories employed by scholars, as Smith does, McCutcheon suggests that scholars must pay closer attention to the intentions and influences that shape their own methods and theories. He criticizes what he perceives to be scholars' tendency to be naive *caretakers* of religion, that is, to too easily affirm the first-person claims of religionists concerning the spiritual or religious value of their own views.[5] Instead, he exhorts scholars to examine the socioeconomic pressures that shape religious discourse about beliefs and practices. "Ultimately," he states, "spirituality, much like humanist talk of universal values, is a commodity that has a specific manufacturing history and is bought and sold daily."[6]

One of the key points in the work of the scholar as *critic* is to call into question "religion" as a universal or sui generis category, subjecting it to the analysis of commodification within the global economy and the flow of social capital along with all other commodities: "Globalized religion, then, turns out to be yet another transnational commodity. There is an economics to the spiritual luxury afforded by the glittering lobby [of the Palmer House Hilton, site of the 1993 World's Parliament of Religions], an economics effectively obscured by the totalizing and inductivist discourse on sui generis religion. Naming and challenging precisely this [false] ideology [of a religion of pure 'spirituality'] comprises" the real task of the critical scholar of religion.[7]

For McCutcheon, scholars who fail to examine the role of globalization and the influence of the global economy on the interpretation of religion are apt to become enmeshed themselves in the legitimation of a romanticized, falsely idealized view of religion.

> The scholar of religion as public intellectual and critic of authorizing practices comes equipped with [and has a duty to exercise] methodologies and theories to identify those homogenizing, ideological strategies so necessary for the manufacture *and* management of human communities— scholarly communities included.[8]

Unlike Smith, then, McCutcheon is interested in examining not only the intellectual history of religious studies but also the social and political history of the discipline in order to uncover the ways in which cultural and institutional influences have shaped the development of the field. In the section that follows, this essay considers several instances in which the examination of the global context of scholarly inquiry may shed some light on East-West historical (mis)interpretations.

Instantiations of Interpretation: Two Cases from India and Tibet

Before going on to a more in-depth examination of cases involving Japanese religion, specifically Buddhism, my own area of specialization, I would like to briefly touch on two cases involving the study of South Asian religions, one concerning India and another concerning Tibet, because they so vividly bring into relief the sociopolitical context of the scholarly interpretation of Asian religious histories. The intent here is not to evaluate the merits of the debaters' arguments but to show what is at stake in the act of interpretation. The first is the case of the interpretation of the religious life of the Indian saint Ramakrishna, and the second is the case of the interpretation of Tibetan Buddhist history.

Kali's Child

In 1995, the scholar Jeffrey Kripal of Rice University published a study of the Hindu saint Ramakrishna entitled, *Kali's Child: The Mystical and the Erotic in the Life and Teachings of Ramakrishna.*[9] It is an interpretation of the life and thought of Ramakrishna influenced by Western psychoanalytic theory, an interpretation that Kripal understood from the very beginning would be controversial. That is because, while traditional Hindu scholarship has interpreted the erotic language and images associated with Ramakrishna in terms of their religious symbolism, Kripal interprets them sexually, in psychoanalytic terms, and makes the provocative claim that Ramakrishna was a latent homosexual. Knowing that his interpretation might not be welcome among a significant portion of Hindus, he anticipated their negative reaction.

> The very first page I ever published in a monograph (page xiii of *Kali's Child*) was addressed directly to my Hindu readers and what I was all too aware would be at least some of their negative responses, [and] that is why the whole motif of "scandal" was central to the book (as it was to the original Bengali texts), and that is why I have spent the last seven years of my professional life doing little else than writing essays about these issues along with literally thousands of letters to Indian readers both powerfully enthused and deeply offended by my writings. After two nationally publicized movements to ban *Kali's Child* in India, the last of which ended in the Lok Sabha [Indian Parliament], and a very thick file of appreciative and angry letters from Hindu friends, colleagues, and correspondents, I would dare say that there are few American Indologists working today who are more aware of their Indian audience.[10]

Despite his foresight, even Kripal might have been surprised at the extent and intensity of the reaction to his work. For our purposes, two responses to the publication of *Kali's Child* are particularly noteworthy, one a scholarly rebuttal and the other an act of political censure.

Swami Tyagananda, minister of the Ramakrishna-Vedanta Society in Boston, composed in 2000 a 173-page rebuttal, "Kali's Child Revisited; or, Didn't Anyone Check the Documentation?" which included, among other things, numerous points of disagreement concerning the purported misleading selection of passages and translations into English of Mahendranath Gupta's *Kathamrita,* a biography of Ramakrishna by one of his foremost disciples. Furthermore, Tyagananda insisted that his rebuttal be included in the next edition of Kripal's book. Kripal agreed that some of his translations were erroneous and corrected them in a later edition, but he refused to include Tyagananda's lengthy rebuttal.

Here, interestingly, we see that there is a shared common ground of interpretation that is open to negotiation, that is, the rendering of a primary text source across linguistic and cultural boundaries through translation. Translation arguably always involves some degree of interpretation; however, translation also implies some degree of objective factual accuracy. On the point of textual interpretation, neither Tyagananda nor Kripal are willing to give significant ground, each remaining largely within his hermeneutical circle. Each has his own scholarly training, and in the representation of their interpretations they remain distinct. Each has a way to influence the larger social reception of the historical Ramakrisha through students, bookstores, and the like. Each has staked out his own territory in the global marketplace of ideas with overlapping but distinct audiences. Kripal offers his account of the history of this contestation of interpretations on his own Web site, an account that seeks to complexify the issues and interactions and relates a story of contestation as well as conciliation. Another account is offered by Arvind Sharma, who sympathetically considers both Kripal's and Tyagananda's views, as well as those of others, and offers constructive criticism to both sides.[11]

Regardless of how this contestation of interpretations is itself interpreted, that this was not a matter confined to the ivory tower becomes quite clear in view of the political fallout. Enough people in India were offended by the publication of *Kali's Child* that it became subject to censure at the national level in the Lok Sabha, the Indian Parliament. For many, the historical interpretation of a saint such as Ramakrishna is by extension a representation of Hinduism and Indian cultural identity. Thus, historical interpretation becomes an index of the global representation of a people and their culture, one that is contested at home and abroad, regardless of whether that home is the Indian academy or the American, religious communities in India or North America, and any cultural or corporate endeavor that is tied to religious representations of Ramakrishna and Hinduism. There is much more to this and other debates involving Hindu studies that is beyond the scope of the present essay, as well as the present author's expertise, but the debates surrounding *Kali's Child* are outlined here because of their vivid illustration of the global consequences of historical scholarship East and West and its perceived misinterpretation, consequences that are tied to such issues as the cross-cultural application of theoretical and methodological paradigms; histories of colonialism, racism, and nationalism; interpretive diversity between and within cultures; and linguistic, textual, and cultural fluency.

Prisoners of Shangri-La

Three years after the publication of *Kali's Child,* the Tibetologist Donald Lopez published a controversial study of Tibetan cultural history, *Prisoners of Shangri-La: Tibetan Buddhism and the West.*[12] In this work he takes to task two figures in particular, the Dalai Lama and Robert Thurman of Columbia University, for promulgating what he regards as false portrayals of the religious history of the Tibetan people.

In assessing the impact of the publication of *Prisoners of Shangri-La,* Thurman challenges Lopez not only on the accuracy of his interpretation of Tibetan history but to be self-reflexive concerning the political fallout of scholarship concerning the Tibetan people's quest for sovereignty.

Lopez's argument is simply another variant on the theme of blame the victim. He argues basically that the Tibetans are victims of their own supporters, not by [sic] their Chinese enemies. He argues that "Tibetophile" scholars and popularizers have created a false Tibet, a romantic Shangri-La paradise, and have imprisoned themselves and the "real" Tibetans in it, making them unreal to the world and hence unworthy of protection from the Chinese genocide . . .

In this way, Lopez joins other scholars, who cater to the currently dominant military-commercial world order and trumpet their invariant syllogism: . . . Tibet is a hopeless lost cause, irretrievably at the mercy of China; . . . therefore the best way to help Tibet is to not to help Tibet as represented by the Dalai Lama—if he loses all support, he will grow quiet, surrender to China's inevitable rule, go home, and help them try to reform his backward, Buddhist romanticizing, Shangrilizing, primitive-minded, idolatrous people.[13]

On Lopez's part, the early reaction was to disavow the political impact of a work of scholarship whose esoteric nature limited its readership. Ultimately, Lopez claims to depict a more complex, realistic view of Tibetan history.

As long as one follows the strategy of attempting to counter the big lie of the Chinese, with many small lies about how wonderful life in old Tibet must have been, then any historical research that complicates this picture . . . can only be read simplistically as saying "bad things about Tibetans," thus generating the kind of extreme hubris which claims that a book like *Prisoners of Shangri-La* helps the Chinese. . . . Of all the adjectives that have been used to describe *Prisoners of Shangri-La*, the one that has saddened me most is "courageous."[14]

According to Erik Davis:

Lopez is not just puncturing myths for the kick of it. He fears that the popular interest in Tibetan religion, which considerably amplifies the Dalai Lama's short-term political pull, may ultimately impede the struggle for Tibetan independence. Instead of affirming Tibet's place in the real world, the West is embracing a lofty simulacrum that unconsciously denies the historical agency of living Tibetans. By reformulating Tibetan Buddhism into a modern and universalizing science of mind, teachers like the Dalai Lama and Robert Thurman may be allowing Tibet to float free from history "in a process of spiritual globalization that knows no national boundaries."[15]

According to this view, the Dalai Lama and Robert Thurman, by presenting a homogenized, romanticized view of the Tibetan people, fail to accurately and effectively represent their diverse identities and thereby the authentic voices of their political agency. Again, the question of historical interpretation is inextricably tied to contemporary questions of globalization, the representation of a people and their religion within the global economy, and the sociopolitical consequences of scholarly interpretation.

Where the fate of a people is at stake, who better represents the real voices of the Tibetan people, the real stories derived from their historical condition? Is it the Dalai Lama and Robert Thurman or Donald Lopez?

Instantiations of Interpretation: Japanese Nationalism, Militarism, Zen, and Pure Land Buddhism: Modern Zen Buddhist Intellectuals

While knowledge of all forms of Buddhism has been increasing in the West, perhaps no other form has gained as wide a currency as Zen Buddhism, such that it has become a global commodity capable of selling everything from desktop Zen gardens to books on the Zen of golf and business and even home-building magazines that criticize kitchen cabinets as "not Zen enough." Perhaps no other term of Asian religion has been so thoroughly packaged and commodified as *Zen*. What sets the history of the interpretation of Zen Buddhism apart from the study of other Asian religions is not just the degree to which it has become a free-floating index of commodification but the particular historical process of globalization. In the case of both Hinduism and Tibetan Buddhism, much of the contestation revolves around the interpretation and misinterpretation of classical sources and premodern practices: Ramakrishna as a classic example of a traditional Hindu saint and Tibet and Tibetan Buddhism before the invasion by Communist China.

In contrast, Zen Buddhism, represented by and associated with such figures as D. T. Suzuki (1870–1966) and the philosopher Nishida Kitarō (1870–1945), emerged on the international stage in concert with Japan's emergence as a modern economic and political force. Rather than a victim of Western imperialism and colonialism, Japan itself became an imperial and colonial power, and in the post-war period, the likes of Suzuki, the Zen philosopher Nishitani Keiji (1900–1990), and the lay Zen master Hisamatsu Shin'ichi have been presented as modern intellectuals in dialogue with and equal or even superior to Western intellectuals such as Rudolf Bultmann (1884–1976), Carl Jung (1875–1961), and Paul Tillich (1886–1965).

In the 1950s and 1960s, the beat and psychedelic movements adopted Zen discourse to express their own visions, and in the ensuing decades not only hippies but also scholars flocked to Japan to imbibe Zen thought and practice. As Eric Cunningham notes:

> Zen became, in stages, universalized as one of the great religions of the world, then re-nativized in the discourse of Japanese cultural nationalism during the early twentieth century. During World War II, Zen became "militarized" as a spiritual component of the "imperial way," before [eventually] being tamed and adopted by postwar middle-class Americans in search of a user-friendly spirituality.[16]

Initially, this postwar adoption of Zen by middle-class Americans often included scholars of Zen Buddhism who were sympathetic to an emic perspective. However, recent scholarship, especially over the last two decades, has increasingly involved critical examination of Zen Buddhism from a more etic stance.

In particular, the complicity of Zen monks and Zen intellectuals in their efforts to support the militaristic efforts of wartime Japan has come under increasing scrutiny and been the subject of considerable debate. Statements made by followers of the so-called Kyoto school of philosophy, such as Nishida Kitarō, his disciple Nishitani Keiji, and his close associate D. T. Suzuki, have been scrutinized closely. Where potentially militarist and imperialist statements have been identified, they have been variously interpreted as temporary deviations made under the pressure of a totalitarian government or as active instruments of aggressive cultural and military expansionism.[17]

Cunningham recounts in some detail the various statements made by Zen Buddhist monks and intellectuals, as well as the findings of various scholars, so I will not rehash them here. What is notable for the purposes of the present are the following. First, Cunningham and others point to the ambiguity of statements made by such figures as Suzuki and Nishida, where often in private they lamented the acts of military aggression carried out by the Japanese government but in public made pronouncements that in varying degrees may be taken to support militant expansionism. Second, the merit of philosophical statements is debated as either demonstrating their abstract, politically ineffectual character or the cosmopolitan, antinationalistic attitudes of the figure in question. Third, actions and statements are analyzed in the totalitarian context in which these figures worked.

From within the subtext of these variant readings, key questions arise. Religions make substantial claims not only concerning what might be possible for the religious destinies of individuals but also for community and global society. What are the claims of Zen-based intellectuals and philosophers? What are the expectations with regard to their actions in the public sphere? What considerations should be given to limitations imposed by the environment in which they worked? How do their social and historical visions match up against their actions and those of the community they influenced?

Modern Shin Buddhist Intellectuals

As Chris Ives has pointed out, there were Zen scholars in Japan, such as Ichikawa Hakugen, who did speak out against their own institutions, although they were the rare exception.[18] Better documented are the cases of priests and scholars of Shin Buddhism, or Jōdo Shinshū, the largest sect of Japanese Pure Land Buddhism. Shin Buddhism emphasizes awakening to human limitations; entrusting oneself to the cosmic Buddha Amida, the buddha of infinite light; and realizing infinite light through the chanting of the name of Amida Buddha, Namu Amida Butsu, also known at the *nembutsu*.

Although Shin intellectuals and institutions were arguably just as complicit as their Zen counterparts in tacitly or overtly supporting Japanese militarism, anticlerical and antiestablishment tendencies existing within the tradition from its beginnings in the thirteenth century also inspired a number of priests and followers to speak out against Japanese imperialism. The founding figure, Shinran (1173–1262), is well known for his statement "I am neither priest nor layman," his refusal to take up residence in a temple, and his alignment with illiterate peasants over and against the established Buddhist sects from which he was banished and to which he refused to return even when granted amnesty.

In the first half of the twentieth century, a number of Shin Buddhists harkened back to Shinran in voicing opposition to Japanese imperial aggression. In effect, here was a case in which a small minority offered their interpretation of a native Buddhist figure, Shinran, to criticize their own institutions and the government. Yet, like their Zen counterparts, their statements and actions were not without ambiguity.

Tanabe Hajime (1885–1962)

One of these intellectuals was Tanabe Hajime, one of Nishida's foremost disciples and a leading member of the Kyoto school who nonetheless eventually opposed the views of his former mentor. Tanabe did not speak out before or during the war, but near the end of it he called for the nation as a whole to repent and move forward as a positive contributor to the global community. Tanabe's most dramatic confession of the tension between his spiritual life and political consciousness comes at the beginning of his *Zangedō to shite no tetsugaku* (Philosophy as Metanoetics, 1944), a work inspired by Shinran's magnum opus, the *Kyōgyōshinshō*.

> On the one hand, I was haunted by the thought that as a student of philosophy I ought . . . to be addressing the government frankly with regard to its policies . . . even if this should incur the displeasure of those currently in power. . . . On the other hand, there seemed something traitorous about expressing in time of war ideas that, while perfectly proper in time of peace might end up causing divisions and conflicts among our people that would only further expose them to their enemies . . .
>
> At that moment, something astonishing happened. In the midst of my distress I let go and surrendered myself humbly to my own inability. . . . My penitent confession—metanoesis (*zange*)—unexpectedly threw me back on my own interiority and away from things external.[19]

According to his reckoning, what he encountered in his own interiority was what he came to call the mediation of absolute nothingness, a term reflecting his appropriation of the cosmic Buddha Amida as Other power. However, as various contributors to the discussion in *Rude Awakenings* suggest, it is unclear as to just how sincere, realistic, and thoroughgoing Tanabe's sociopolitical consciousness was. In the end, Tanabe himself did not take much outward action to embody his political philosophy, and his abstruse, philosophical call for repentance had little effect on either the government or the people of Japan. As James W. Heisig states, these consequences, or the lack thereof, do not by themselves invalidate Tanabe's efforts.[20] Perhaps what we see in Tanabe is just how difficult he found it to reconcile the gap between his inner religious sensibility and outward actions. Whether he took a stance to the left or the right, multiple factions criticized him for being too conservative or not conservative enough, too Marxist or not Marxist enough.

Miki Kiyoshi (1897–1945)

Another disciple of Nishida, Miki Kiyoshi, also left the fold and moved toward the Pure Land thought of Shinran with a decidedly Marxist bent. Although Miki disavowed the Marxist label, much of his life was framed within actions that were closely associated with Marxists, socialists, and communists. In May of 1930, while he was on the faculty of Hōsei University, Miki was arrested and taken to Toyotama Prison, where he was incarcerated for six months for aiding and abetting communists. In a series of informal expositions that he wrote at the time, he explained that he was not a Marxist and in fact saw himself as basically religious. Yet he continued to be associated with communists and Marxists throughout his career, as he found in their statements and actions views that resonated with his own critical historical sense that Japan was heading in an errant, capitalist, and imperialist direction. This critical view of history was heavily informed by his reading of Shinran, and his life came to a close embodying this synthesis of Shin Buddhist thought and Marxist-oriented critique; he died in Toyotama Prison, leaving his final manuscript, *Shinran,* to be published posthumously by his friends and students.

Through his modernist eyes, Miki saw in twentieth-century Japan a significant parallel with Shinran's Kamakura period. For Miki, the time of political and spiritual crisis brought out the true character of a person, in which the contradictions of the material conditions of existence bring into relief the subjective heart of human existence. For him, the Shōwa and Kamakura periods were alike moments of *mappō,* the final, degenerate age in which blind passions and evil karma ruled the day. Miki, however, did not see *mappō* ideology as an excuse to blame one's troubles on the conditions of the age: "The awakening of the self within the historical moment does not lead to the rationalization of the self by conferring responsibility for one's sins on the age in which one lives."[21] Class oppression and imperialism were the outward material manifestations, but their scrutiny helped to reveal the true subjective reality of the self.[22] According to Miki:

> The historical view of the [declining stages of the] Three Ages of the Dharma was not merely a discursive account for Shinran. . . . More than merely [an objective] critique, it became an opening out onto the profound grief [of the self's true existence]. The unsalvageable present overwhelms one as present actuality.[23]

The discursive landscape of *mappō* as relative to other periods in history, then, gave way to the eternal reality of the self as one looked deeper within. There, in the depths of the self, it became apparent that karmic evil was pervasive, an elemental condition rather than a limited historical occurrence. Only in the awareness of this karmic depth could the light of absolute compassion be discerned: "Shinran emphasized the historicity of the teachings. One might ask if such a historicism was not also a kind of relativism. . . . The truth, the true teaching, must be absolute."[24]

> The absolute character of the teaching became known through its eternal character. . . . The teaching of Other power compassionately leads all beings bound by blind passion and evil karma, regardless of whether they live in the age of the True, Semblance, or Final Dharma. . . . On the one hand, this teaching is particularly suited to the final age; on the other, it applies

universally to all ages. . . . Within myself, . . . history is already manifest as the subjectivity of the *nembutsu*.[25]

As Yamamoto Hiroko suggests, Miki strove for a complex synthesis of material history and spiritual myth.[26] The question arises as to why one should act at all in the matrix of such a synthesis. Whether one sees the relative reality of discursive, material conditions as the manifestation of an eternal spiritual myth or vice versa—eternal myth made discernible in the reality of the relative present—it seems hopeless to act within a history in which all ages are fated to be evil.

Yet, paradoxically, Miki may have been moved to action precisely because of this seeming mutual negation of myth and history. Without responding to the historical present, the eternal myth remains hidden, unrealized; without awakening to the subjective depth of eternity, one cannot be moved to manifest the Buddhist way in history. In going into the depths of the self, one might become aware of one's true interconnectedness with all suffering beings, and this could move one to compassionate action.

Not everyone, however, was easily convinced by either Miki's logic or his outward actions. One of his most prominent critics was Hattori Shisō, the son of a Shin Buddhist priest turned Marxist.[27] Hattori also saw in Shinran the forbear of modern Marxism, and he traced a socialist genealogy from the founder of Shin Buddhism through the peasant uprisings of the *ikkō ikki* to postwar Japan. For him, Miki not only failed to realize the materialist promise germinating in Shinran but he ended up reducing the dialectical tension of the twofold truth (mundane/highest, social/religious) to mere idealism.[28] For Hattori, Miki's death in Toyotama Prison was the ignominious end of a failed intellectual, not the courageous self-expression of a true Marxist.

Through his work on Shin Buddhist history, Hattori went on to influence later historians and Buddhologists, but of course *his* dreams of Marxist revolution did not materialize.

It is beyond the scope of the present essay to judge whether Miki's Marxist reading of Shinran was successful or whether Hattori's critique gave the truer picture. Suffice it to say that both Miki and Hattori likely struggled with the constellation of ideology, social reality, and religious life that each confronted within and without. If a common thread can be detected, perhaps it is that their attempts to address issues of classism, imperialism, and other sociopolitical issues with philosophical discourse were simultaneously compelling and disappointing to those around them. Although the ideas they articulated were impressive, as was the impetus to match those ideas to the realities of life, at the same time it is difficult to overlook the apparent gaps between the scale of their rhetoric and the social realities that their discourses affected.

Suekawa Hiroshi (1892–1977)

Suekawa Hiroshi was not a Marxist or a communist. He was a legal scholar, social activist, and chancellor and president of Ritsumeikan University. His worldview was informed by Shin Buddhism religiously and democratic thinking socially and politically. Nevertheless, he has also been called "the leader of the leftists," and the force of socialist ideas have left their indelible mark on his thought and actions.[29]

As a professor of law at Kyoto University during World War II, Suekawa was a leading member of the Society for Social Scientific Research (Shakai kagaku kenkyūkai [SKK]), devoted to the study of Marxism, socialism, and communism. In the very midst of mounting government pressure for all intellectuals to curtail activities related to socialism and communism, Suekawa published some of the results of his research in *Civil and Labor Law in Soviet Russia* (*Sovieto Roshia no minpō to rōdōhō*) and entitled his 1931 doctoral dissertation "Theory of Rights Violations" (Kenri shingai ron).

In 1933, the Department of Education fired Takigawa Kōshin, Suekawa's colleague in the Faculty of Law and a leading member of the SKK, and demanded that the SKK be disbanded. Protesting the violation of academic freedom, Suekawa and other members of the Faculty of Law, as well as graduate students, resigned their posts and left Kyoto University. This has come to be known as the Kyoto University Incident (Kyōdai jiken). It is worth noting that Suekawa's actions differed from those of other intellectuals at Kyoto University, including Nishida, whose statements have at times been described as supporting Japanese militarism, and Tanabe Hajime, who decided to remain silent about his misgivings concerning the Japanese war involvement and stayed in his post at Kyoto University without speaking out until Japan's fate was sealed.

Suekawa's specialization was in civil law with a focus on civil rights. He was also known for his general knowledge of law and was the editor of the seminal *Iwanami roppō zensho* (The Complete Iwanami Edition of the Six Classifications of Law), the first encyclopedia of Japanese law. After the war, he did not return to Kyoto University but went on to become chancellor and president of Ritsumeikan University, an institution known for its evening degree programs for the working class and for its pacifist orientation.[30]

In 1946, labor unions were legalized in Japan for the first time, and Suekawa became the director of the Kyoto Prefectural Labor Board (Kyoto-fu rōdō iinkai kaichō) of the labor union organization. Later, he also became president of the Kyoto Prefectural Korea-Japan Friendship Association, serving as an advocate for Koreans in Japan. In 1948, he became a founding member of the Kyoto Freedom and Human Rights Association (Kyoto jiyū jinken kyōkai) and worked as both a legal advocate and scholar on behalf of the Burakumin, the outcast class of Japanese society.[31]

Although Suekawa's actions and words were not as revolutionary as those of some of his contemporaries, it might be argued that by maintaining a democratic stance informed by social activism he was as or more effective than others who were revolutionary in thought only (armchair Marxists) or who perished in the heat of their struggles. Religiously, Suekawa remained a Shin Buddhist throughout his life, while he worked for and helped to effect what he saw as socially responsible legal and sociopolitical reforms as a scholar, social activist, and administrator.

The influence of Shin Buddhism on Suekawa's understanding of society can be seen in at least three ways. First, he worked on behalf of and in unity with those who had been excluded from various rights and privileges. Second, his religious awareness was inseparable from the courage to stand by his convictions. Third, his Shin Buddhist awareness of his limitations as a human being, as a *bonbu* (foolish being), contributed to a sense of character perceived by those around him as humble and magnanimous.

On the first of these points, Suekawa wrote, "Whether they were farmers or fishermen, Shinran went into their midst; he reflected on and taught about the way [of life and *nembutsu*] with them to the end."[32] Of course, the reflection of this thinking in Suekawa's actions is more significant than the articulation of ideas. One the one hand, one might question whether taking the path of scholarly endeavor and becoming a university administrator really represented a means of becoming one with the people. On the other, he may have been able to do more for various groups—the socioeconomically deprived, Koreans, Burakumin, and the like—precisely by taking the route that he did.

This leads to the second point, the courage to act with conviction. When, as a young man, he went to college, he seriously questioned whether the intellectual pursuits in which he was engaged would lead him to peace of mind, to an authentic life. At eighteen, he quit college and returned to his parents' farm, thinking that, like Shinran, the best way to live would be close to the land and among the people.[33] But he decided that, in his case, this would not be the best way to contribute to society, and he returned to finish his studies.

For Shinran, who lived in the twelfth and thirteenth centuries, to be one with the people meant to live among the farmers and fishermen, even though his exile had been revoked and he could have returned to the urban capital of Kyoto. For Suekawa, living in the urban-centered culture of twentieth-century Japan, to be one with the people meant to leave his birthplace in the countryside, live in the city, and work within its social structures. This determination may have arisen from a religious conviction about what it meant to be faithful to oneself. For this reason, he sometimes took actions that might have led to his exclusion from these structures, as when he resigned his academic post in the Kyoto University Incident.

In his role as administrator, he often found himself at difficult junctures of social, political, and personal conscience. In 1968–69, there were student antiwar protests and demonstrations at Ritsumeikan University, just as there were at other institutions in Japan, the United States, and elsewhere. During this time, the police went to Ritsumeikan to arrest the leaders of these demonstrations. At that time, Suekawa and Saeki Chihiro, a member of the Faculty of Law, had a confrontation with the police. Saeki had been a close colleague of Suekawa ever since the Kyoto University Incident, when both had resigned their posts, and Suekawa had asked Saeki to join him at Ritsumeikan. Saeki spoke out at the time of the confrontation.

> "We will take responsibility for order within this campus. . . . We administrators and faculty will take care of things, so we don't need you police here. We never asked you to come, and we don't want you to come." Then the police chief said that that was not the agreement. I replied, "Who agreed to have you come? No one here made such an agreement." We ended up arguing heatedly, and I said something to the effect, "We can't stop you if you come in by force, but we didn't ask you to come, and we won't cooperate."[34]

The police did force their way onto the campus, and arrests were made. The tension on campus at the time is reflected in the words of Suekawa's secretary, Onuma Yōko.[35] She describes the ways in which people had extreme feelings at the time and how these emotions were expressed in letters sent to Suekawa.

> Sometimes, he received letters that stated, "I'll kill you," or "You're not qualified to be an educator." Even animal carcasses arrived in the mail.
>
> He would read all of these letters and didn't seem to be fazed at all. He soothed my frayed nerves by saying softly, "There are people with all kinds of different ideas in the world."[36]

Suekawa conceived of human beings both as spontaneous expressions of deepest, boundless life and as the creators of their own karmic destiny, as buddha nature and karmic nature, as "created and creator," to use a phrase he cited frequently.[37] He saw in Shinran someone who traversed this difficult intersection of two natures, which he saw in himself as well as others: "I think [Shinran] throughout his life grappled [with these questions]. I don't think he ever reached a point where he felt, 'I'm enlightened, I've found final spiritual repose.'"[38] In his later years, Suekawa is often said to have said, "Bandits in the mountains are easy to defeat, but bandits in the heart are difficult to destroy."[39] He did not have any easy answers to questions concerning the relationship among ideology, society, and action in the life of the Shin Buddhist intellectual, and he apparently did not always achieve the outcomes he sought. What is evident is that not only words on the printed page and statements voiced, but actions also interpret religious texts, figures, and traditions. Questions of interpretation and misinterpretation, then, may depend on actions as much as methods and theories, the actions of figures studied by historians but perhaps also the actions of historians as public intellectuals.

Tanabe, Miki, Hattori, and Suekawa each interpreted Shinran according to his own needs and aspirations. Caught in the churning forces of globalization and commodification, each had to face the circumstances of his life and to make decisions that weighed his religious perspective and social conscience against his professional interests. Whether or not each made the right decisions is not what is significant for this inquiry; rather, it is the fact that each life dramatically illustrates the tension between religious ideology and the forces of society.

Conclusion

This brief foray into questions of (mis)interpretation East and West has explored the increasingly context-sensitive nature of interpretation in the East-West study of religion. Beginning with an overview of the history of interpreting religion within U.S. colleges and universities, and going on to examine methodological issues related to the cultural forces potentially influencing interpretation, this study concluded with an examination of several recent cases of (mis)interpretations contested by scholars of religion. The tensions among religious ideology, the force of sociocultural influences on the delivery of that ideology, and the scholar's own act of interpretation often constellate a single nexus of inquiry. An examination of these constellated factors, then, can tell us as much about the character of a particular interpretation as it does about the subject being interpreted. Each act of interpretation occurs under the pressures of globalization, constituting a creative moment in which the scholar reveals something about his or her own life as the interpreter as well as the subject matter at hand. Insofar as there is never a final interpretation but a series of provisional interpretations in the making—limited, incomplete, and humanly fallible—there is only misinterpretation, wherein not all misinterpretations are equal.

Notes

[1] On this point, see Michael Slater, "Can One Be a Critical Caretaker?" *Method and Theory in the Study of Religion* 19, nos. 3–4 (2007): 332–42.

[2] Frank E. Reynolds, "Reconstructing Liberal Education: A Religious Studies Perspective," in *Beyond the Classics? Essays in Religious Studies and Liberal Education,* ed. Frank E. Reynolds and Sheryl L. Burkhalter (Marietta, GA: Scholars Press, 1990), 3–18; Sumner B. Twiss, "Shaping the Curriculum: The Emergence of Religious Studies," in *Counterpoints-Issues in Teaching Religious Studies,* ed. Mark Hadley and Mark Unno (Providence: Department of Religious Studies, Brown University, 1995), 28–37; Jeffrey Kripal, "The Critical Study of Religion as a Modern Mystical Tradition," in *The Serpent's Gift: Gnostic Reflections on the Study of Religion* (Chicago: University of Chicago Press, 2006).

[3] Jonathan Z. Smith, "In Comparison a Magic Dwells," in *Imagining Religion: From Babylon to Jonestown* (Chicago: University of Chicago Press, 1982).

[4] Ibid., 35.

[5] Russell McCutcheon, *Critics Not Caretakers: Redescribing the Public Study of Religion* (Albany: State University of New York Press, 2001).

[6] Russell McCutcheon, "The Economics of Spiritual Luxury," in *Critics Not Caretakers: Redescribing the Public Study of Religion* (Albany: State University of New York Press, 2001), 97–98.

[7] Ibid., 99.

[8] Russell McCutcheon, "A Default of Critical Intelligence," in *Critics Not Caretakers: Redescribing the Public Study of Religion* (Albany: State University of New York Press, 2001), 142.

[9] Jeffrey Kripal, *Kali's Child: The Mystical and the Erotic in the Life and Teachings of Ramakrishna* (Chicago: University of Chicago Press, 1995).

[10] http://jeffrey-kripal.sulekha.com/blog/post/2002/09/the-tantric-truth-of-the-matter.htm (accessed July 13, 2010).

[11] *Religion in the News* (spring 2004) 7.1., http://www.trincoll.edu/depts/csrpl/RINVol7No1/Hindus%20and%20Scholars.htm (accessed July 13, 2010).

[12] Donald S. Lopez, Jr., *Prisoners of Shangri-La: Tibetan Buddhism and the West* (Chicago: University of Chicago Press, 1998).

[13] Robert Thurman, "Critical Reflections on Donald S. Lopez Jr.'s *Prisoners of Shangri-La: Tibetan Buddhism and the West*," *Journal of the American Academy of Religion* 69, no.1 (2001): 200.

[14] "An Interview with Donald Lopez: On the Resurgence of Interest in Buddhism, His Controversial Book on Tibet, and the Future of Asian Studies at the U-M," *Journal of the International Institute,* University of Michigan, http://www.umich.edu/~iinet/journal/vol8no1/lopez.html (accessed February 14, 2007).

[15] Erik Davis, "Tibet Your Life: A Review of Donald Lopez, Jr.'s *Prisoners of Shangri-La: Tibetan Buddhism and the West* and Robert Thurman's *Inner Revolution: Life, Liberty, and the Pursuit of Real Happiness,*" *Village Voice,* August 25, 1998, 137. See also http://www.techgnosis.com/chunkshow-single.php?chunk=chunkfrom-2005-05-15-1810-0.txt (accessed February 14, 2007).

[16] Eric Cunningham, *Hallucinating the End of History: Nishida, Zen, and the Psychedelic Eschaton* (Bethesda, MD: Academica Press, 2007), 35.

[17] See Michiko Yusa, *Zen and Philosophy: An Intellectual Biography of Nishida Kitaro* (Honolulu: University of Hawai'i Press, 2002); Brian Victoria, *Zen at War,* 2nd ed. (New York: Rowman and Littlefield, 2006); and John Maraldo and James Heisig, eds., *Rude Awakenings: Zen, the Kyoto School, and the Question of Nationalism* (Honolulu: University of Hawai'i Press, 1995).

[18] Christopher Ives, "Ethical Pitfalls in Imperial Zen and Nishida Philosophy: Ichikawa Hakugen's Critique," in *Rude Awakenings: Zen, the Kyoto School, and the Question of Nationalism,* ed. James W. Heisig and John Maraldo (Honolulu: University of Hawai'i Press, 1995), 16–39. The discussion of Shin Buddhism in this section is adapted from Mark Unno, "Shin Buddhist Socialist Thought in Modern Japan," in *Engaged Pure Land Buddhism,* ed. Eishō Nasu and Kenneth Tanaka (Berkeley: WisdomOcean, 1998), 67–87.

[19] Tanabe Hajime, *Philosophy as Metanoetics,* trans. James Heisig (Berkeley: University of California Press, 1986), xlix–l.

[20] James W. Heisig, "Tanabe's Logic of the Specific and the Spirit of Nationalism," in *Rude Awakenings: Zen, the Kyoto School, and the Question of Nationalism,* ed. James W. Heisig and John Maraldo (Honolulu: University of Hawai'i Press, 1995), 288.

[21] Miki Kiyoshi, "Rekishi no Jikaku," in *Shisō dokuhon {Shinran},* ed. Yoshimoto Ryūmei (Kyoto: Hozokan, 1987), 169 (originally published as "Shinran," in *Miki Kiyoshi zenshū* 16 (Tokyo: Iwanami Shoten, 1949).

[22] Of course, in classical Marxism material conditions are the cause of subjective suffering, but Miki was working within a religious appropriation of Marxist ideas.

[23] Miki Kiyoshi, "Rekishi no Jikaku," 172.

[24] Ibid., 173.

[25] Ibid., 174–75.

[26] Yamamoto Hiroko, "Rekishi to chōetsu: Miki Kiyoshi no naka no Shinran," *Bukkyo bessatsu {Shinran}* 1 (November 1980): 206–7.

[27] Yamaori Shisō, "Shinran to kindai Nihon no shisō," in *Kawade jimbutsu dokuhon–Shinran* (Tokyo: Kawade Shuppan, 1985), 195–209. I am particularly indebted to Yamaori for his analysis of Hattori Shisō.

[28] See especially ibid., 205–6.

[29] Kuwabara Takeo, "Saha no chōja," in *Tsuiso: Suekawa Hiroshi,* ed. Suekawa Hiroshi sensei tsuito bunshu henshu iinkai (Tokyo: Yuhikaku, 1979), 247–54.

[30] In 1950, a statue known as the Watazumizō was created as a statement of peace and antiwar sentiment and a symbol of the voice of students who were drafted into the Pacific War. The statue found a home at Ritsumeikan University after other institutions refused to display it because of its antigovernment connotations. It is now housed in Ritsumeikan's World Peace Museum, which opened in 1992.

[31] See Kimura Kyōtarō, "Buraku mondai to Suekawa Sensei," in *Tsuiso–Suekawa Hiroshi,* ed. Suekawa Hiroshi sensei tsuito bunshu henshu iinkai (Tokyo: Yuhikaku, 1979), 283–85.

[32] Suekawa Hiroshi, "Shinran Shonin to watakushi no jinseikan," in *Suekawa Hiroshi: Sono hito to jinseikan,* ed. Asada Sumio (Kyoto: Hyakkaen, 1975), 19.

[33] Ibid.,72.

[34] Saeki Chihiro, "Deai 'Suekawa Sensei no koto,'" in *Suekawa Hiroshi: Sono hito to jinseikan,* ed. Asada Sumio (Kyoto: Hyakkaen, 1975), 110.

[35] Asada Sumio, "Nembutsusha to shite no Suekawa Sensei," in *Suekawa Hiroshi: Sono hito to jinseikan,* ed. Asada Sumio (Kyoto: Hyakkaen, 1975), 78.

[36] Ibid., 78.

[37] Suekawa Hiroshi, "Shinran Shonin to watakushi no jinseikan," 9–10.

[38] Ibid., 19.

[39] Ibid., 51.

Bibliography

Abe, Masao. *Zen and Western Thought.* Honolulu: University of Hawai'i Press, 1989.

Alexander, William. *The Costume of China Illustrated in Forty-eight Coloured Engravings.* London: William Miller, 1805.

Allan, Sarah. *The Shape of the Turtle: Myth, Art, and Cosmos in Early China.* Albany: State University of New York Press, 1991.

Arditi, Jorge. "Geertz, Kuhn, and the Idea of a Cultural Paradigm." *British Journal of Sociology* 45, no. 4 (December 1994): 597–617.

Aristotle. *The Basic Works of Aristotle.* Trans. Richard McKeon. New York: Random House, 1941.

Asada Sumio. "Nembutsusha to shite no Suekawa Sensei." In *Suekawa Hiroshi: Sono hito to jinseikan,* ed. Asada Sumio. Kyoto: Hyakkaen, 1975.

Augustine. *Confessions.* Trans. R. S. Pine-Coffin. New York: Penguin, 1961.

Bacon, John L. "The Yellow Peril." *Newsletter of the CMS Central China Mission,* April 1917.

Badiner, Allan Hunt, and Alex Grey, eds. *Zig Zag Zen.* San Francisco: Chronicle, 2003.

Ballaster, Ros. *Fabulous Orients: Fictions of the East in England, 1662–1785.* Oxford: Oxford University Press, 2005.

Ban Gu. *Han shu.* Beijing: Zhonghua shuju chubanshe, 1997.

Barringer, Tim, and Tom Flynn, eds. *Colonialism and the Object: Empire, Material Culture, and the Museum.* London: Routledge, 1998.

Barrow, John. *An Autobiographical Memoir of Sir John Barrow, Bart.* London: John Murray, 1847.

Bateson, Gregory. *Mind and Nature: A Necessary Unity.* New York: Bantam, 1980.

Bennett, Josephine Waters. *The Rediscovery of Sir John Mandeville.* New York: Modern Language Association of America, 1954.

Berkowitz, Alan. *Patterns of Disengagement: The Practice and Portrayal of Reclusion in Early Medieval China.* Stanford: Stanford University Press, 2000.

Bermingham, Ann. "System, Order, and Abstraction: The Politics of English Landscape Drawing around 1795." In *Landscape and Power,* ed. W. J. T. Mitchell. Chicago and London: University of Chicago Press, 1994,

Berridge, Virginia. *Opium and the People: Opiate Use and Drug Control Policy in Nineteenth and Early Twentieth Century England.* London: Free Association, 1999.

Berry-Hill, Henry, and Sidney Berry-Hill. *George Chinnery, 1774–1852.* Leigh-on-Sea, Essex: F. Lewis, 1963.

Bhabha, Homi K. *The Location of Culture.* London: Routledge, 1994.

Birrell, Anne. *Popular Songs and Ballads of Han China.* Honolulu: University of Hawai'i Press, 1988.

Bloom, Clive, ed. *Cult Fiction: Popular Reading and Pulp Theory.* New York: Macmillan, 1996.

————. *Creepers: British Horror and Fantasy in the Twentieth Century.* London: Pluto, 1993.

Blum, Susan D. "Pearls on the Strings of the Chinese Nation: Pronouns, Plurals, and Prototypes in Talk about Identities." *Michigan Discussions in Anthropology* 13 (1998): 207–37. Special issue: "Linguistic Form and Social Action."

Boreham, F. "Devil Worship among the Chinese Hills." *Church Missionary Gleaner,* September 1919.

Bosshardt, R. A. *The Restraining Hand: Captivity for Christ in China.* London: Hodder and Stoughton, 1936.

Boureau, Alain. *The Lord's First Night: The Myth of the Droite de Cuissage.* Trans. Lydia G. Cochrane. Chicago: University of Chicago Press, 1995.

Brandt, Nat. *Massacre in Shansi.* Syracuse: Syracuse University Press, 1994.

Braque, Georges. *Le Jour et la nuit: Cahiers, 1917–52.* Paris: Gallimard, 1988.

Broomhall, Marshall, ed. *Martyred Missionaries of the China Inland Mission with a Record of the Perils and Sufferings of Some Who Escaped.* London: Morgan and Scott, 1901.

Bunn, David. "'Our Wattled Cot': Mercantile and Domestic Space in Thomas Pringle's African Landscapes." In *Landscape and Power,* ed. W. J. T. Mitchell. Chicago and London: University of Chicago Press, 1994,

Burke, Edmund. *A Philosophical Enquiry into the Origins of Our Ideas of the Sublime and Beautiful with an Introductory Discourse Concerning Taste.* London: R. and J. Dodsley, 1757.

————. "Speech on the Middlesex Election [1771]." In *Selected Writing and Speeches.* Peter J. Stanlis, ed. Reprint. Washington, D.C.: Regnery Publishing, 1997.

Buruma, Ian, and Avishai Margalit. *Occidentalism: The West in the Eyes of Its Enemies.* New York: Penguin, 2004.

Cahoone, Lawrence, ed. *From Modernism to Postmodernism: An Anthology.* Malden, MA: Blackwell, 2003.

Casserly, G. *The Land of the Boxers*. London: Longman, Green, 1903.

Cay, Van Ash. *Master of Villainy: A Biography of Sax Rohmer*. Bowling Green, OH: Bowling Green University Popular Press, 1972.

Chapman, Ian, trans "The Westerner's Ten Laments: Excerpts" by an anonymous author. In *Renditions: Chinese Impressions of the West*. No. 53–54 (spring–autumn 2000): 247–249.

Charbonnier, Jean. *Les 120 martyrs de chine: Cononisés le 1er Octobre 2000*. Paris: Églises d'Asie, 2000.

Chen Taihua. *Alarm Bells*. Trans. Ian Chapman. *Renditions* 53–54 (spring–autumn 2000): 238–46.

Chen Xiaomei. *Occidentalism: A Theory of Counter-discourse in Post-Mao China*. 2nd ed., revised and expanded. Lanham, MD: Rowman and Littlefield, 2003.

Chen Yong, ed. *Jiu zhongguo lüeying, 1868–1945*. Beijing: Zhongguo hua bao chubanshe, 2006.

Chine et ceylan: Letters des missionaries de la compagnie de Jésus. Abbeville: C. Paillart, 1901.

Church Missionary Society, "The Idol's Protection" *Homes of the East*. London: Church Missionary Society, 1910.

Church Missionary Society Archive. Marlborough: Adam Matthew Digital Publications, 1999.

Clark, Anthony. "Early Modern Chinese Reactions to Western Missionary Iconography." *Southeast Review of Asian Studies* 30 (2008): 5–22.

———. "Reflections on the Han View of Truth and Historicity with a Translation of Ban Biao's 'Essay of Historiography'." *Southeast Review of Asian Studies* 28 (2006): 107–19.

Codell, Julie F., ed. *Imperial Co-histories: National Identities and the British and Colonial Press*. Madison and Teaneck, NJ: Fairleigh Dickinson University Press, 2003.

Cohen, Paul A. *China and Christianity: The Missionary Movement and the Growth of Chinese Antiforeignism, 1860–1870*. Cambridge: Harvard University Press, 1963.

———. *History in Three Keys: The Boxers as Event, Experience, and Myth*. New York: Columbia University Press, 1997.

Colebrook, Claire. "Questioning Representation." *SubStance* 29, no. 2, issue 92 (2000): 47–67.

Conger, Sarah. *Letters from China*. Chicago: McClurg, 1909.

Conner, Patrick. "George Chinnery and His Contemporaries on the China Coast." *Arts of Asia* 23, no. 3 (May–June 1993): 66–81.

———. *George Chinnery, 1774–1852: Artist of India and the China Coast.* Woodbridge, Suffolk: Antique Collectors' Club, 1993.

Criveller, Gianni. *The Martyrdom of Alberico Crescitelli: Its Context and Controversy.* Hong Kong: Holy Spirit Study Centre, 2004.

———. *Preaching Christ in Late Ming China: The Jesuits' Presentations of Christ from Matteo Ricci to Guilio Aleni.* Taipei: Taipei Ricci Institute, 1997.

Cronin, Vincent. *Li Madou zhuan.* Trans. Si Guo. Taizhong: Guangqi chubanshe, 1982.

Crossman, Carl L. *The Decorative Arts of the China Trade: Paintings, Furnishings, and Exotic Curiosities.* Woodbridge, Suffolk: Antique Collectors' Club, 1991.

Crouch, Archie. *Rising through the Dust: The Story of the Christian Church in China.* New York: Friendship, 1948.

Cunningham, Eric. *Hallucinating the End of History: Nishida, Zen, and the Psychedelic Eschaton.* Bethesda, MD: Academica Press, 2007.

Dai Xuanzhi. *Yihetuan yanjiu.* Taipei: Wenhua chubanshe, 1963.

Damascene, Hiermonk. *Christ the Eternal Dao.* Platina, CA: Valaam, 1999.

Darley, Mary. "Kien-Ning Prefecture and Its Needs." *India's Women and China's Daughters.* London: Church Missionary Society, 1905.

Davis, A. R. *Tao Yuan-ming, AD 365–427, His Works and Their Meaning.* 2 vols. New York: Cambridge University Press, 1983.

Davis, Erik. "Tibet Your Life: A Review of Donald Lopez, Jr.'s *Prisoners of Shangri-La: Tibetan Buddhism and the West* and Robert Thurman's *Inner Revolution: Life, Liberty, and the Pursuit of Real Happiness.*" *Village Voice* August 25, 1998.

De Blarer, M. T. *La bienheureuse Marie Hermine de Jésus et ses compagnes.* Vanves: Franciscaines Missionaires de Marie, 1947.

De Malpière, D. Bazin. *La Chine, Moeurs, Usages, Costumes, Arts et Metiers, Peines Civiles et Militaires, Cérémonies Religieuses, Monuments et Paysages.* Paris: Fermin Didot, 1825.

De Montaigne, Michel. *Les Essais de Montaigne.* Paris: Nouveaux classiques illustres Larousse, 1976.

De Montgesty, G. *Two Vincentian Martyrs.* Trans. Florence Gilmore. New York: Catholic Foreign Missionary Society of America, 1925.

De Quincey, Thomas. *Confessions of an Opium Eater,* in *English Prose and Poetry (1137–1892),* selected and annotated by John Matthews Manly. Boston: Ginn, 1916.

Denker, Ellen Paul. *After the Chinese Taste: China's Influence in America, 1730–1930.* Salem, MA: Peabody Museum of Salem, 1985.

Derrida, Jacques. *Writing and Difference*. Chicago: University of Chicago Press, 1978.

Diocese of Hong Kong Theological Center, ed. *Yihetuan yundong yu Zhongguo jiduzongjiao*. Taipei: Furen daxue chubanshe, 2004.

Dinneen, Alice Maud Dalton. "The Worship of Gang Niang." *Newsletter of the CMS Central China Mission*, no. 21 (1917).

Dower, John. *War without Mercy: Race and Power in the Pacific War*. New York: Pantheon, 1986.

Dudink, Ad. "Opposition to the Introduction of Western Science and the Nanjing Persecution (1616–1617)." In *Statecraft and Intellectual Renewal in Late Ming China: The Cross-Cultural Synthesis of Xu Guangqi (1562–1633)*, ed. Catherine Jami, Peter Engelfriet, and Gregory Blue. Leiden: Brill, 2001.

Dunch, Ryan. *Fuzhou Protestants and the Making of a Modern China, 1857–1927,* New Haven: Yale University Press, 2001.

Dunne, George H. *Generation of Giants: The Story of the Jesuits in China in the Last Decades of the Ming Dynasty*. London: Burns and Oats, 1962.

Eberly, Peter, and Andrew Morton, eds. *When East Meets West: International Sinology and Sinologists*. Taipei: Sinorama, 1991.

Eby, Cecil Degrotte. *The Road to Armageddon: The Martial Spirit in English Popular Literature, 1870–1914*. Durham: Duke University Press, 1987.

Eggers, Dave. *A Heartbreaking Work of Staggering Genius, Based on a True Story*. New York: Vintage, 2001.

Entenmann, Robert E. "Christian Virgins in Eighteenth-Century Sichuan." In *Christianity in China: From the Eighteenth Century to the Present*, ed. Daniel H. Hayes. Stanford: Stanford University Press, 1996.

The Epic of Gilgamesh. Trans. N. K. Sandars. London: Penguin, 1972.

Esherick, Joseph. *The Origins of the Boxer Uprising*. Berkeley: University of California Press, 1987.

Fairbank, John K. "Patterns behind the Tientsin Massacre." *Harvard Journal of Asiatic Studies* 20, no. 3–4 (1957): 480–511.

Fang Xuanling et al. *Jin shu*. 10 vols. Beijing: Zhonghua shuju, 1998.

Feyerabend, Paul. *Against Method: Outline of an Anarchistic Theory of Knowledge*. London: Verso and New Left Books, 1978.

Fields, Rick. *How the Swans Came to the Lake: A Narrative History of Buddhism in America*. Boston: Shambala, 1992.

Fortune, Robert. *Three Years' Wanderings in the Northern Provinces of China, Including a Visit to the Tea, Silk, and Cotton Countries, with an Account of the Agriculture and Horticulture of the Chinese, New Plants, Etc.* London: John Murray, 1847.

Foucault, Michel. *The Archeology of Knowledge and the Discourse of Language.* Trans. A. M. Sheridan Smith. New York: Pantheon, 1972.

———. *Discipline and Punish.* Trans. Alan Sheridan. New York: Vintage, 1977.

———. *The Order of Things.* London: Tavistock, 1970.

Four Jesuits Martyred in China in the 20th Century. Taipei: Commission for Canonization of Saints and Martyrs of China, 2000.

Frank, André Gunder. *Re-ORIENT: Global Economy in the Asian Age.* Berkeley: University of California Press, 1998.

Freedberg, David. *The Power of Images: Studies in the History and Theory of Response.* Chicago: University of Chicago Press, 1989.

Freud, Sigmund. *Civilization and Its Discontents.* Trans. James Strachey. New York: Norton, 1961.

Friedman, Thomas L. *The World Is Flat 3.0: A Brief History of the Twenty-first Century.* New York: Picador, 2007.

Gasperetti, Elio. *In God's Hands: The Life of Blessed Ableric Crescitelli of the Missionaries of Saints Peter and Paul, P.I.M.E.* Detroit: The Missionaries of Saints Peter and Paul, PIME, 1955.

Geertz, Clifford. *The Interpretation of Cultures.* New York: Basic Books, 1973.

Gell, Alfred. *Art and Agency: An Anthropological Theory.* Oxford: Clarendon, 1998.

Gernet, Jacques. *China and the Christian Impact: A Conflict of Cultures.* Trans. Janet Lloyd. Cambridge: Cambridge University Press, 1985.

———. *Chine et christianisme.* Paris: Editions Gallimard, 1982.

Ghazoul, Ferial J. "Orientalism: Clearing the Way for Cultural Dialogue." *Religion* 34, no. 2 (April 2004): 123–27.

Gilpin, William. *An Essay on Prints.* 5th ed. London: Cadel and Davies, 1802.

———. *Three Essays: On Picturesque Beauty, On Picturesque Travel, and on Sketching Landscape to Which Is Added a Poem, On Landscape Painting.* London: R. Blamire, 1792.

Girardot, Norman J. *The Victorian Translation of China: James Legge's Oriental Pilgrimage.* Berkeley: University of California Press, 2002.

Goodwin, James. *Autobiography: The Self Made Text.* New York: Twayne, 1993.

Goody, Jack. *Capitalism and Modernity: The Great Debate.* Malden, MA: Polity, 2004.

————. *The East in the West*. Cambridge: Cambridge University Press, 1996.

Gu Weimin. *Jidujiao yishu zai hua fazhan shi*. Shanghai: Shanghai shudian chubanshe, 2005.

————. *Zhongguo tianzhujiao biannian shi*. Shanghai: Shanghai shudian chubanshe, 2003.

Gunn, Geoffrey C. *First Globalization: The Eurasian Exchange, 1500–1800*. Lanham, MD: Rowman and Littlefield, 2003.

Guo Dengfeng. *Lidai zixu zhuan wenchao*. Taipei: Taiwan shangwu, 1965.

Haight, G. S, ed. *The George Eliot Letters*. Vol. 2. New Haven: Yale University Press, 1954.

Harrison, Charles, Paul Wood, and Jason Gaiger, eds. *Art in Theory, 1648–1815*. Oxford: Blackwell, 2000.

Harte, Bret. *The Best of Bret Harte*. Boston: Houghton Mifflin, 1947.

Heidegger, Martin. *The Metaphysical Foundations of Logic*. Trans. Michael Heim. Bloomington: Indiana University Press, 1992.

————. *What Is a Thing?* Trans. W. B. Barton Jr. and Vera Deutch. Lanham, MD: University Press of America, 1967.

Heisig, James W. "Tanabe's Logic of the Specific and the Spirit of Nationalism." In *Rude Awakenings: Zen, the Kyoto School, and the Question of Nationalism*, ed. James W. Heisig and John Maraldo. Honolulu: University of Hawai'i Press, 1995.

Helsinger, Elizabeth. "Turner and the Representation of Britain." In *Landscape and Power*, ed. W. J. T. Mitchell. Chicago and London: University of Chicago Press, 1994.

Herd, H. *The March of Journalism: The Story of the British Press from 1622 to the Present Day*. London: Allen and Unwin, 1952.

Herodotus. *The Histories*. Trans. Aubrey de Sélincourt. Harmondsworth: Penguin, 1983.

Hevia, James, L. *English Lessons: The Pedagogy of Imperialism in Nineteenth-Century China*. Durham: Duke University Press, 2003.

Hipwell, W. E. "Union in Face of the Foe; or, Co-operation in Evangelistic Effort in China." *Church Missionary Gleaner*, December 1907.

Howe, Nicholas. *Visions of Community in the Pre-modern World*. South Bend: University of Notre Dame Press, 2002.

Huang Zichen. "Pixie jie." In *Shengchao poxie ji*, ed. Xu Changzhi. Rpt., Hong Kong: Jiandao Shenxueyuan, 1996.

Hughes, Robert. *The Shock of the New.* New York: Knopf, 1981.

Humphreys, Christmas. *Zen Buddhism.* London: Diamond, 1996.

Hung, Eva and Tam Pak Sahn, trans. "Anti-Christian Propoganda" by anonymous authors. In *Renditions: Chinese Impressions of the West.* No. 53–54. (Spring and Autumn 2000): 250–255.

Hunter, Jane. *The Gospel of Gentility: American Women Missionaries in Turn-of-the-Century China.* New Haven: Yale University Press, 1984.

Huntington, Samuel P.. *The Clash of Civilizations and the Remaking of World Order.* New York: Free Press, 2002.

Hutcheon, Robin. *Chinnery.* Hong Kong: Form Asia, 1989.

Ives, Christopher. "Ethical Pitfalls in Imperial Zen and Nishida Philosophy: Ichikawa Hakugen's Critique." In *Rude Awakenings: Zen, the Kyoto School, and the Question of Nationalism,* ed. James W. Heisig and John Maraldo. Honolulu: University of Hawai'i Press, 1995.

Jami, Catherine, Peter Engelfriet, and Gregory Blue, eds. *Statecraft and Intellectual Renewal in Late Ming China: The Cross-Cultural Synthesis of Xu Guangqi (1562–1633).* Leiden: Brill, 2001.

Jarry, Madeleine. *Chinoiserie: Chinese Influence on European Decorative Art, 17th and 18th Centuries.* New York: Vendome, 1981.

Jay, Gregory S. "Knowledge, Power, and the Struggle for Representation." *College English* 56, no. 1 (January 1994): 9–29.

Jensen, Lionel M. *Manufacturing Confucianism: Chinese Traditions and Universal Civilization.* Durham: Duke University Press, 1997.

Johnson, Frances. "Powers of Darkness." *Fukien Diocesan Magazine,* July 1917.

Johnson, Samuel and John Walker. *Dictionary of the English Language.* London: William Pickering, 1828.

Kasulis, Thomas P. *Zen Action, Zen Person.* Honolulu: University of Hawai'i Press, 1981.

Kawai Kouzô. *Chūgoku no jiden bungaku.* Tokyo: Soubunsha, 1996.

Keightley, David N. *The Ancestral Landscape: Time, Space, and Community in Late Shang China.* Berkeley: Institute for East Asian Studies, University of California, 2000.

Keown-Boyd, Henry. *The Boxer Rebellion.* New York: Dorset, 1991.

Kern, Stephen. *The Culture of Time and Space, 1880–1918.* Cambridge: Harvard University Press, 1983.

Kimura Kyōtarō. "Buraku mondai to Suekawa Sensei." In *Tsuiso–Suekawa Hiroshi,* ed. Suekawa Hiroshi sensei tsuito bunshu henshu iinkai. Tokyo: Yuhikaku, 1979.

Kipling, Rudyard. "The Ballad of East and West." In *A Victorian Anthology, 1837– 1895,* ed. Edmund Clarence Stedman. Cambridge: Riverside, 1895.

Knechtges, David. *The Han shu biography of Yang Xiong (53 B.C.–A.D. 18).* Tempe: Center for Asian Studies, Arizona State University, 1982.

Knoblock, John, and Jeffrey Riegel. *The Annals of Lü Buwei.* Stanford: Stanford University Press, 2000.

Kohn, Livia, and Harold Roth, eds. *Daoist Identity: History, Lineage, and Ritual.* Honolulu: University of Hawai'i Press, 2002.

Kripal, Jeffrey. "The Critical Study of Religion as a Modern Mystical Tradition." In *The Serpent's Gift: Gnostic Reflections on the Study of Religion.* Chicago: University of Chicago Press, 2006.

―――. *Kali's Child: The Mystical and the Erotic in the Life and Teachings of Ramakrishna.* Chicago: University of Chicago Press, 1995.

―――. *The Serpent's Gift: Gnostic Reflections on the Study of Religion.* Chicago: University of Chicago Press, 2006.

Kuwabara Takeo. "Saha no chōja." In *Tsuiso–Suekawa Hiroshi.* Edited by Suekawa Hiroshi sensei tsuito bunshu henshu iinkai. Tokyo: Yuhikaku, 1979.

Lancashire, Douglass. "Anti-Christian Polemics in Seventeenth-Century China." *Church History* 38, no. 2 (1969): 218–41.

Lanciotti, Lionello, ed. *Venezia e l'Oriente.* Florence: Leo S. Olschki, 1987.

Landes, David S. *The Wealth and Poverty of Nations: Why Some Are So Rich and Some So Poor.* New York: Norton, 1999.

Larson, Wendy. *Literary Authority and the Modern Chinese Writer: Ambivalence and Autobiography.* Raleigh: Duke University Press, 1991.

Lenin, Vladimir. "The War in China." In Vladimir Lenin, *Collected Works.* Vol. 4. Moscow: Progress Publishers, [1960] 1972.

Les 120 Martyrs de Chine: Canonisés le 1er octobre 2000. Études et Documents, no. 12. Paris: Églises d'Asia, 2000.

Levine, Noah. *Dharma Punx: A Memoir.* San Francisco: HarperCollins, 2004.

Lewis, C. S. "Transposition." In *The Weight of Glory and Other Addresses.* San Francisco: Harper, 2001.

Lewis, Mark Edward. *The Construction of Space in Early China.* Albany: State University New York Press, 2006.

Lewis, Martin W., and Kären E. Wigen. *The Myth of Continents: A Critique of Metageography.* Berkeley: University of California Press, 1997.

Li Jingde, ed. *Zhuzi yulei.* Chuanjing tang edition. N.p., n.d.

Li Jiubiao. *Kouduo richao: Li Jiubiao's Diary of Oral Admonitions: A Late Ming Christian Journal.* Ed. Erik Zürcher. Vol. 56 of Monumenta Serica Monograph Series. Institut Monumenta Serica, 2007.

Liu Dajie. *Wei-Jin sixiang lun.* Shanghai: Shanghai guji chubanshe, 2000.

Liu Yiqing. *Shishuo xinyu jiaojian.* Beijing: Zhonghua shuju chubanshe, 1999.

Liu Yu. *Xishi ji.* N.p., 1263. Liu Zhiji. *Shi tong.* Taipei: Wenhai chubanshe, 1953.

Lopez, Jr., Donald S. *Prisoners of Shangri-La: Tibetan Buddhism and the West.* Chicago: University of Chicago Press, 1998.

Lothrop, Francis B. *George Chinnery, 1774–1852, and Other Artists of the China Scene.* Salem, MA: Peabody Museum of Salem, 1967.

Lovecraft, H. P. *Tales of H. P. Lovecraft, Selected by Joyce Carol Oates.* Hopewell, NJ: Ecco, 1997.

Lowie, Robert. *The History of Ethnological Theory.* New York: Rinehart, 1937.

Luo Weihong. *Christianity in China.* Trans. Zhu Chengming. Beijing: China Intercontinental Press, 2004.

Lutz, Jessie Gregory. *Chinese Politics and Christian Missions: The Anti-Christian Movements of 1920–28.* Notre Dame: Cross Cultural Publications, 1988.

Ly, André. *Journal d'André Ly, prêtre chinoise, missionaire et notaire apostolique, 1747–1763.* Ed. Adrien Launey. Paris: Picard, 1906.

Ma Sheng-mei. *The Deathly Embrace: Orientalism and Asian American Identity.* Minneapolis: University of Minnesota Press, 2000.

Macartney, George. *An Embassy to China: Being the Journal Kept by Lord Macartney during his Embassy to the Emperor Ch'ien-lung, 1793–1794.* Ed. J. L. Cranmer-Byng. London: Longmans, 1962.

MacKenzie, John. *Orientalism: History, Theory, and the Arts.* Manchester and New York: Manchester University Press, 1995.

MacPhilib, Séamus. "Jus Primae Noctis and the Sexual Image of Irish Landlords in Folk Tradition and in Contemporary Accounts." *Bealoideas: The Journal of the Folklore of Ireland Society* 56 (1988): 97–140.

Madsen, Richard. *China's Catholics: Tragedy and Hope in an Emerging Society.* Berkeley: University of California Press, 1998.

Mandeville, John. *The Travels of Sir John Mandeville.* London: Penguin, 1983.

Maraldo, John, and James Heisig, eds. *Rude Awakenings: Zen, the Kyoto School, and the Question of Nationalism.* Honolulu: University of Hawai'i Press, 1995.

Martyred Missionaries of the China Inland Mission with a Record of the Perils and Sufferings of Some Who Escaped. Ed. Marshall Broomhall. London: Morgan and Scott, 1901.

Marx, Karl. *The Eighteenth Brumaire of Louis Bonaparte.* Trans. Daniel de Leon. Chicago: Charles H. Kerr, 1913.

Mather, Richard. *A New Account of Tales of the World.* Ann Arbor: Center for Chinese Studies, University of Michigan, 2002.

McClellan, Robert F. "Missionary Influence on American Attitudes toward China at the Turn of This Century." *Church History* 38, no. 4 (December 1969): 475–85.

McCutcheon, Russell. *Critics Not Caretakers: Redescribing the Public Study of Religion.* Albany: State University of New York Press, 2001.

———. "A Default of Critical Intelligence." In *Critics Not Caretakers: Redescribing the Public Study of Religion.* Albany: State University of New York Press, 2001.

———. "The Economics of Spiritual Luxury." In *Critics Not Caretakers: Redescribing the Public Study of Religion.* Albany: State University of New York Press, 2001.

McMahon, Keith. *The Fall of the God of Money.* New York: Rowman and Littlefield, 2002.

Medhurst, Walter. *A Dissertation on the Theology of the Chinese with a View to the Elucidation of the Most Appropriate Term for Expressing the Deity, in the Chinese Language.* Shanghai: Mission Press, 1847.

———. *An Inquiry into the Proper Mode of Rendering the Word God in Translating the Sacred Scriptures into the Chinese Language.* Shanghai: Mission Press, 1848.

———. *Of the Word Shin, as Exhibited in the Quotations Adduced under That Word, in the Chinese Imperial Thesaurus, Called the Pei-Wan-Yun-Foo.* Shanghai: Mission Press, 1849.

Mellor, Philip A. "Orientalism, Representation, and Religion: The Reality behind the Myth." *Religion* 34, no. 2 (April 2004): 99–112.

Mengzi yizhu. Annotated Yang Bojun. Taipei: Wu nan tushu chuban, 1981.

Mertens, Pierre-Xavier. *La légende dorée en chine: Scènes de la vie de mission au Tchely Sud-Est.* Paris: Editions Spes, 1926.

———. *The Yellow River Runs Red: A Story of Modern Chinese Martyrs.* Trans. Beryl Pearson. London: B. Herder, 1939.

Michiko Yusa. *Zen and Philosophy: An Intellectual Biography of Nishida Kitaro.* Honolulu: University of Hawai'i Press, 2002.

Miki Kiyoshi. "Rekishi no Jikaku." In *Shisō dokuhon {Shinran}*. Edited by Yoshimoto Ryūmei. Kyoto: Hozokan, 1987. Originally published as "Shinran," in *Miki Kiyoshi zenshū* 16. Tokyo: Iwanami Shoten, 1949.

Milligan, Barry. *Pleasures and Pains: Opium and the Orient in Nineteenth-Century British Culture.* Charlottesville: University Press of Virginia, 1995.

Miner, Luella. *China's Book of Martyrs: A Record of Heroic Martyrdoms and Marvelous Deliverances of Chinese Christians during the Summer of 1900.* Cincinnati: Jennings and Pye, 1903.

Misch, George. *A History of Autobiography in Antiquity.* 2 vols. Cambridge: Harvard University Press, 1951.

Mitchell, Sally. *Daily Life in Victorian England.* Westport, CT, and London: Greenwood, 1996.

Mitchell, W. J. T. "Imperial landscape." In *Landscape and Power*, ed. W. J. T. Mitchell. Chicago and London: University of Chicago Press, 1994,

———. "Introduction." In *Landscape and Power*, ed. W. J. T. Mitchell. Chicago and London: University of Chicago Press, 1994.

Mitchell, W. J. T., ed. *Landscape and Power.* Chicago and London: University of Chicago Press, 1994.

Montaigne, Michel de. *The Complete Essays.* Michael Andrew Screech, trans. and ed. Penguin Classics Series. Reprint. New York: Penguin Classics, 1993.

Moule, Arthur E. "The Use of Opium and Its Bearing on the Spread of Christianity in China" *Church Missionary Society.* London, 1877,

Moy, James. *Marginal Sights: Staging the Chinese in America.* Iowa City: University of Iowa Press, 1994.

Mungello, David E. *Curious Land: Jesuit Accommodation and the Origins of Sinology.* Honolulu: University of Hawai'i Press, 1989.

———. *The Forgotten Christians of Hangzhou.* Honolulu: University of Hawai'i Press, 1994.

Munro, Donald. *The Concept of Man in Early China.* Ann Arbor: Center for Chinese Studies, University of Michigan, 2001.

The Newly Canonized Martyr-Saints of China. Taipei: Commission for Canonization of Saints and Martyrs of China, 2000.

Nissim-Sabat, Charles. "On Clifford Geertz and His 'Anti Anti-Relativism'." *American Anthropologist,* n.s., 89, no. 4 (December 1987): 935–39.

Ng, Janet. *The Experience of Modernity: Chinese Autobiography of the Early Twentieth Century.* Ann Arbor: University of Michigan Press, 2003.

Olney, James, ed. *Autobiography: Essays Theoretical and Critical.* Princeton: Princeton University Press, 1980.

Orange, James. "George Chinnery: Pictures of Macao and Canton." *Studio* 94, no. 415 (October 1927): 231–39.

Ormond, Richard. "George Chinnery's Image of Himself." *Connoisseur*, part 1, 176, no. 672 (February 1968): 89–93; part 2, 167, no. 673 (March 1968): 160–64.

Our Wonder World: A Library of Knowledge in Ten Volumes. Vol. 1. Chicago: Geo. L. Shuman, 1918.

Oxford English Dictionary. Prepared by J. A. Simpson and E. S. C. Weiner. Oxford: Clarendon, 1989.

Pascal, Roy. *Truth and Design in Autobiography.* Cambridge, MA: Harvard University Press, 1960.

Pasquin, Anthony [John Williams]. *A Critical Guide to the Exhibition of the Royal Academy, for 1796, in Which All the Works of Merit Are Examined, the Portraits Correctly Named, and the Places of the Various Landscapes: Being an Attempt to Ascertain Truth and Improve the Taste of the Realm.* London: H. D. Symonds, 1796.

————. *A Critical Guide to the Present Exhibition at the Royal Academy for 1797: Containing Admonitions to the Artists on the Misconception of Theological Subjects and a Complete Development of the Venetian Art of Colouring, as Is Now So Much the Rage of Imitation.* London: H. D. Symonds, 1797.

————. *A Liberal Critique on the Present Exhibition of the Royal Academy: Being an Attempt to Correct the National Taste, to Ascertain the State of the Polite Arts at this Period, and to Rescue Merit from Oppression.* London: H. D. Symonds, 1794.

Pomeranz, Kenneth. *The Great Divergence: China, Europe, and the Making of the World Economy.* Princeton: Princeton University Press, 2000.

Preston, Diana. *The Boxer Rebellion: The Dramatic Story of China's War on Foreigners That Shook the World in the Summer of 1900.* New York: Walker, 1999.

Price, Nancy Thompson. "The Pivot: Comparative Perspectives from the Four Quarters." *Early China* 20 (1995): 93–120. Pritchard, Earl H. "Letters from Missionaries at Peking Relating to the Macartney Embassy (1793–1803)." *T'oung Pao* 31 (1935): 1–57. Pu Youjun. *Zhongguo wenxue piping shi lun.* Chengdu: Ba-Shu shu she, 2001.

Qu Zhi-ren. "George Chinnery, Painter." *Arts of Asia,* March–April 1971, 34–41.

Quilley, Geoff, and Kay Dian Kriz, eds. *An Economy of Colour: Visual Culture and the Atlantic World, 1660–1830.* Manchester and New York: Manchester University Press, 2003.

Ramsey, William M. *Representation Reconsidered*. New York: Cambridge University Press, 2007.

Redner, Harry. "Representation and the Crisis of Post-Modernism." *PS: Political Science and Politics* 20, no. 3 (summer 1987): 673–79.

Reed, John Shelton. *Glorious Battle: The Cultural Politics of Victorian Anglo-Catholicism*. Nashville: Vanderbilt University Press, 1996.

Reinders, Eric. *Borrowed Gods and Foreign Bodies: Christian Missionaries Imagine Chinese Religion*. Berkeley: University of California Press, 2004.

Remnick, David. "Struggle for His Soul." *Observer,* November 2, 2003.

Reynolds, Frank E. "Reconstructing Liberal Education: A Religious Studies Perspective." In *Beyond the Classics? Essays in Religious Studies and Liberal Education*, ed. Frank E. Reynolds and Sheryl L. Burkhalter. Atlanta: Scholars Press, 1990.

Reynolds, Graham. "Alexander and Chinnery in China." *Geographical Magazine* 20 (September 1947): 203–11.

Ricci, Matteo [Li Madou]. *Tianzhu shiyi*. In *Tianxue chuhan*, vol. 1, ed. Li Zhizao. Taipei: Xuesheng shuju, 1965.

Richard, Timothy. *Forty-Five Years in China*. London: Fisher Unwin, 1916.

Richards, James A., ed. *Outline of Knowledge*. Vol. 15. New York: J. A. Richards, 1924.

Rienstra M. Howard, ed. *Jesuit Letters from China, 1583–84*. Minneapolis: University of Minnesota Press, 1986.

Robel, Ronald A. "The Life and Thought of T'an Ssu-t'ung." PhD diss., University of Michigan, 1972.

Rodd, Miss, and Miss Bryer. "In Chinese Villages." *India's Women: The Magazine of the Church of England Zenana Missionary Society*. London, 1893.

Rohmer, Sax. *The Book of Fu-Manchu*. New York: R. M. McBride, 1929.

———. *The Insidious Dr. Fu Manchu*. New York: Dover, 1997.

———. *The Mystery of Dr Fu-Manchu*. London: Methuen, 1913.

———. *Tales of Chinatown*. New York: Doubleday, 1922.

———. *The Yellow Claw*. New York: A. L. Burt, 1915.

Rorty, Richard. *Philosophy and the Mirror of Nature*. Oxford: Blackwell, 1980.

———. "Relativism and Pragmatism." Tanner Lectures. University of California, Berkeley, January 31, 1983.

———. "Solidarity or Objectivity." In *From Modernism to Postmodernism: An Anthology*, ed. Lawrence Cahoone. Malden, MA: Blackwell, 2003.

Rosaldo, Renato. "Response to Geertz." *New Literary History* 21, no. 2 (winter 1990): 337–41.

Ross, Andrew C. *A Vision Betrayed: The Jesuits in Japan and China, 1542–1742*. Edinburgh: Edinburgh University Press, 1994.

Ross, Stephanie. "The Picturesque: An Eighteenth-Century Debate." *Journal of Aesthetics and Art Criticism* 46, no. 2 (winter 1987): 271–79.

Rüsen, Jörn, ed. *Meaning and Representation in History*. New York: Berghahn, 2006.

Rushdie, Salman. *East, West*. New York: Vintage International, 2006.

Ryan, Thomas F. *Jesuhui shi zai zhongguo*. Trans. Tao Weiyi. Taizhong: Guangqi chubanshe, 1965.

Saeki Chihiro. "Deai 'Suekawa Sensei no koto.'" In *Suekawa Hiroshi: Sono hito to jinseikan,* ed. Asada Sumio. Kyoto: Hyakkaen, 1975.

Sage, Victor. "Empire Gothic: Explanation and Epiphany in Conan Doyle, Kipling, and Chesterton." In *Creepers: British Horror and Fantasy in the Twentieth Century,* ed. Clive Bloom. London: Pluto, 1993.

Sahn, Seung. *Only Don't Know: The Teaching Letters of Zen Master Seung Sahn*. San Francisco: Four Seasons Foundation, 1982.

Said, Edward. *Orientalism*. New York: Vintage, 1979.

Sailey, Jay. *The Master Who Embraces Simplicity: A Study of the Philosopher Ko Hung*. San Francisco: Chinese Materials Center, 1978.

Saint-Exupéry, Antoine de. *Airman's Odyssey*. Orlando: Harcourt Brace, [1939] 1984.

Sardar, Ziauddin. *Orientalism*. Buckingham: Open University Press, 1999.

Sawara Tokusuke and Zhexi'ouyin. *Quanfei jishi*. 6 vols. N.p., 1901.

Sha Baili, *Zhongguo jidutu shi*. Taipei: Guangqi wenhua shiye, 2005.

Shaku Sōen. "The Law of Cause and Effect, as Taught by Buddha." In *The World Congress of Religions: The Addresses and Papers Delivered before the Parliament and the Abstract of the Congress*, ed. J. W. Hanson. Chicago: W. B. Conkey, 1894.

Sharf, Frederic A., and Peter Harrington. *China 1900: The Eyewitnesses Speak*. London: Greenhill, 2000.

Sharf, Robert H. "Whose Zen? Zen Nationalism Revisited." In *Rude Awakenings: Zen, the Kyoto School, and the Question of Nationalism,* ed. James W. Heisig and John Maraldo. Honolulu: University of Hawai'i Press, 1995.

Sima Qian. *Records of the Grand Historian: Han Dynasty II*. Rev. ed. Trans. Burton Watson. New York: Columbia University Press, 1993.

———. *Shiji*. Beijing: Zhonghua shuju, 1999.

Slater, Michael. "Can One Be a Critical Caretaker?" *Method and Theory in the Study of Religion* 19, nos. 3–4 (2007): 332–42.

Smith, Arthur. *The Uplift of China*. New York: Educational Department of the Board of Foreign Missions of the Presbyterian Church in the U.S.A., 1907.

Smith, Jonathan Z. "In Comparison a Magic Dwells." In *Imagining Religion: From Babylon to Jonestown*. Chicago: University of Chicago Press, 1982.

———. *Imagining Religion: From Babylon to Jonestown*. Chicago: University of Chicago Press, 1982.

———. *Map Is Not Territory: Studies in the History of Religion*. Leiden: Brill, 1978.

Spelman, Douglas G. "Christianity in Chinese: The Protestant Term Question." Papers on China, no. 22A. Cambridge: Harvard University Press, 1969.

Spence, Jonathan. *The Search for Modern China*. 2nd ed. New York: Norton, 1999.

Stanislaus, Jen. *The History of Our Lady of Consolation Yang Kia Ping*. Hong Kong: Caritas Printing Centre, 1978.

Stock, Eugene. *The History of the Church Missionary Society*. London: Church Missionary Society, 1916.

———. "The Opium Question." *Church Missionary Gleaner*. July 1906.

The Story of the Greatest Nations from the Dawn of History to the Twentieth Century. Vol. 8. New York: Niglutsch, 1906.

Suekawa Hiroshi. "Shinran Shonin to watakushi no jinseikan." In *Suekawa Hiroshi: Sono hito to jinseikan*, ed. Asada Sumio. Kyoto: Hyakkaen, 1975.

Suleri, Sara. *The Rhetoric of English India*. Chicago: University of Chicago Press, 1992.

Suzuki, D. T. "History of Zen Buddhism from Boddhidharma to Hui Nêng (Yen)." In *Essays in Zen Buddhism, First Series*. New York: Grove, 1961.

———. "On Satori: The Revelation of a New Truth in Zen Buddhism." In *The Essentials of Zen Buddhism*, ed. Bernard Phillips. New York: Dutton, 1962.

———. "Zen in the Modern World." In *The Essentials of Zen Buddhism*, ed. Bernard Phillips. New York: Dutton, 1962.

Suzuki, D. T., Erich Fromm, and Richard De Martino. *Zen Buddhism and Psychoanalysis*. New York: Grove, 1963.

Suzuki, D. T., Alan Watts, Ray Jordan, Robert Aitken, and Richard Leavitt. "Drugs and Buddhism: A Symposium." *Eastern Buddhist* 4, no. 2 (October 1971): 38–40.

Tan, Chester C. *The Boxer Catastrophe*. New York: Norton, 1971.

Tan Sitong. *An Exposition of Benevolence: The* Jen-hsüeh *of T'an Ssu-t'ung*. Trans. Chan Sin-wai. Hong Kong: Chinese University Press, 1984.

———. "Renxue." In *Tan Sitong chuanji*. Beijing, 1954. Tanabe Hajime. *Philosophy as Metanoetics*. Trans. James Heisig. Berkeley: University of California Press, 1986.

Tao Juyin. *Xin yulin*. Shanghai: Zhonghua shuju, 1930.

Taylor, Charles. *Sources of the Self: The Making of Modern Identity*. Cambridge: Harvard University Press, 1989.

Thompson, Richard Austin. "The Yellow Peril, 1890–1924." Ph.D. diss., University of Wisconsin, 1957.

Thurman, Robert. "Critical Reflections on Donald S. Lopez Jr.'s *Prisoners of Shangri-La: Tibetan Buddhism and the West*." *Journal of the American Academy of Religion* 69, no. 1 (2001): 191–202.

Tillotson, Giles. *The Artificial Empire: The Indian Landscapes of William Hodges*. Richmond UK: Curzon, 2000.

Tobin, Beth Fowkes. *Picturing Imperial Power*. Durham and London: Duke University Press, 1999.

Tolkien, J. R. R. "On Fairy-Stories." In *Poems and Stories*. Boston: Houghton Mifflin, 1994.

Tong Xun. *Beijing zongjiao wenhua yanjiu*. Beijing: Zongjiao wenhua chubanshe, 2007.

Toulmin, Stephen. *Cosmopolis: The Hidden Agenda of Modernity*. Chicago: University of Chicago Press, 1990.

The Travels of Marco Polo. Trans. Ronald Latham. London: Penguin, 1958.

Tsuchiya Masaaki. "Confession of Sins and Awareness of Self in the *Taiping jing*. In *Daoist Identity: History, Lineage, and Ritual*. Ed. Livia Kohn and Harold Roth. Honolulu: Univerity of Hawai'i Press, 2002.

Tu Wei-ming, ed. *Confucian Traditions and East Asian Modernity: Moral Education and Economic Culture in Japan and the Four Mini-Dragons*. Cambridge: Harvard University Press, 1996.

———. *The Living Tree: The Changing Meaning of Being Chinese Today*. Stanford: Stanford University Press, 1995.

Turner, Victor. "Symbols in Ndembu Ritual." In *Sociological Theory and Philosophical Analysis*, ed. Dorothy Emmet and Alasdair Macintyre. New York: Macmillan, 1970.

Twiss, Sumner B. "Shaping the Curriculum: The Emergence of Religious Studies." In *Counterpoints-Issues in Teaching Religious Studies,* ed. Mark Hadley and Mark Unno. Providence: Department of Religious Studies, Brown University, 1995.

Unno, Mark. "Shin Buddhist Socialist Thought in Modern Japan." In *Engaged Pure Land Buddhism,* ed. Eishō Nasu and Kenneth Tanaka. Berkeley: Wisdom Ocean,1998.

———. *Shingon Refractions: Myōe and the Mantra of Light*. Somerville, MA: Wisdom, 2004.

Victoria, Brian. *Zen at War.* 2nd ed. New York: Rowan and Littlefield, 2006.

Wakeman, Frederic E., Jr. *The Great Enterprise: The Manchu Reconstruction of Order in Seventeenth-Century China*. Vol. 1. Berkeley: University of California Press, 1985.

Wang Chong. *Lunheng jiao shi*. 4 vols. Beijing: Zhonghua shuju, 1996.

Wang Minglun, ed. *Fan yangjiao shuwen jietie xuan.* Jinan: Qi lu shushe, 1984.

Wang Xue. *Jidujiao yu Shaanxi*. Beijing: Zhongguo shehui kexue chubanshe, 2007.

Wang Yunxi. *Wei-Jin nan bei chao wenxue piping shi*. Shanghai: Shanghai guji chubanshe, 1989.

Warner, Brad. *Hardcore Zen: Punk Rock, Monster Movies, and the Truth about Reality.* Boston: Wisdom, 2003.

———. *Sit Down and Shut Up.* Novato, CA: New World Library, 2007.

Watts, Alan. "Beat Zen, Square Zen, and Zen." In *This Is It and Other Essays on Zen and Spiritual Experience.* New York: Pantheon, 1958.

———. "The New Alchemy." In *This Is It and Other Essays on Zen and Spiritual Experience.* New York: Pantheon, 1958.

———. *This Is It and Other Essays on Zen and Spiritual Experience.* New York: Vintage, 1973.

Weber, Max. *The Protestant Ethic and the Spirit of Capitalism.* Trans. Talcott Parsons. New York: Scribners, 1958.

White, Hayden. *Tropics of Discourse: Essays in Cultural Criticism.* Baltimore: Johns Hopkins University Press, 1978.

White, W. C. "Three Weeks with 'Opium Fiends'." *Church Missionary Gleaner.* January 1907.

William Alexander: An English Artist in Imperial China. Brighton: Brighton Borough Council, 1981.

Wilson, Rob. "Theory's Imaginal Other: American Encounters with South Korea and Japan." *Boundary 2* 18, no. 3 (autumn 1991): 220–41.

Witchard, Anne. "Aspects of Literary Limehouse: Thomas Burke and the 'Glamorous Shame of Chinatown'." In *Literary London: Interdisciplinary Studies in the Representation of London* 2, no. 2. (September 2004), n.p.

Wolferstan, Bertram. *The Catholic Church in China from 1860 to 1907*. London: Sands, 1909.

Wong, R. Bin. *China Transformed: Historical Change and the Limits of European Experience*. Ithaca: Cornell University Press, 2000.

Woodbridge, Samuel. *Fifty Years in China*. Richmond, VA: Presbyterian Committee of Publication, 1919.

Wu Chengen. *Xiyou ji*. Taipei: Sanmin shuju, 2003.

Wu Pei-yi. *The Confucian's Progress: Autobiographical Writings in Traditional China*. Princeton: Princeton University Press, 1990.

Xiaojing baihua zhuyi. Taipei: Guanzhong yan xie he, 1959.

Xu Guangqi. "Bianxue shugao." In *Tianzhu jiao dongchuang wenxian xubian*. Taipei, 1965.

Xu Shen. *Shuowen jiezi*. N.p., n.d.

Xu Zongze. *Ming Qing jian Jesuhui yi zhe tiyao*. Shanghai: Shanghai shudian chubanshe, 2006.

Yamamoto Hiroko. "Rekishi to chōetsu—Miki Kiyoshi no naka no Shinran." *Bukkyo bessatsu {Shinran}* 1 (November 1980): 206–7.

Yamaori Shisō. "Shinran to kindai Nihon no shisō." In *Kawade jimbutsu dokuhon: Shinran*. Tokyo: Kawade Shuppan, 1985.

Yan Kejia. *Catholic Church in China*. Trans. Chen Shujie. Beijing: China Interconti-nental, 2004.

Yang Bojun, ed. *Chunqiu zuozhuan zhu*. 4 vols. Beijing: Zhonghua shuju, 2000.

Yang Mingzhao, ed. *Baopuzi waipianjiaojian*. 2 vols. Beijing: Zhonghua shuju, 1997.

The Yi Ho Tuan Movement of 1900. Beijing: Foreign Languages Press, 1976.

Yihetuan. 4 vols. Ed zhongguo shi xue hui. Shanghai: Shanghai renmin chubanshe, 1957.

Zambon, Mariagrazia. *Crimson Seeds: Eighteen PIME Martyrs*. Trans. Steve Baumbusch. Detroit: PIME World Press, 1997.

Zhang Fengzhen. *Tang Ruowang yu zhongguo*. Tainan: Wen dao chubanshe, 1992.

Zhang Li and Liu Jiantang. *Zhongguo jiao an shi*. Chengdu: Sichuan sheng shehui kexueyuan chubanshe, 1989.

Zhang Yuanji, ed. *Tan Sitong quanji*. N.p., n.d.

Zhao Guoxi. "Sima Qian xie 'Shiji Taishigong zixu' wei ziji shubei lizhuan." *Jilin shifan xueyuan xuebao* 9 (1996): 6–9.

Zhao Rugua. *Zhufan zhi*. N.p., 1225.

Zhao Youwen. *Cao Zhi ji jiao zhu*. Beijing: Renmin wenxue chubanshe, 1998.

Zhou Qufei. *Lingwai daida*. N.p., 1178.

Zhouyi shizhu. Ed. Zhou Zhenfu. Beijing: Zhonghua shuju, 1999.

Zhu Xi. "Shishi lun xia." In *Hui'an xiansheng Zhu Wengong wenji xuji*. Sibu congkan chubian jibu edition. Vol. 10. Shanghai: Shangwu chubanshe, n.d.

———. *Zhuzi yülei*. 8 vols. Taipei: Zhongwen chubanshe, 1970.

Zhuangzi jinzhu jinyi. Ed. Chen Guying. Beijing: Zhonghua shuju, 1994.

Zou Rong. *Geming jun*. N.p., 1902.

Zürcher, Erik. "Giulio Aleni et ses relations avec le milieu des lettres chinois au XVIIe siècle." In *Venezia e l'Oriente*, ed. Lionello Lanciotti. Florence: Leo S. Olschki, 1987.

Index

Lightning Source UK Ltd.
Milton Keynes UK
UKHW012037270521
384493UK00004B/135